POLICE UNION POWER, POLITICS, AND CONFRONTATION IN THE 21ST CENTURY

ABOUT THE AUTHORS

Ron DeLord served as the President of the Combined Law Enforcement Associations of Texas (CLEAT) for 30 years and is currently the Executive Director of CLEAT. He is an internationally recognized police unionist who is known for his leadership style and visionary ideas. Mr. DeLord lectures to law enforcement groups in the United States and abroad, and writes extensively about the police labor movement. He writes a frequent column in *The American Police Beat* and is one of the co-authors of the highly regarded textbook – *Police Association Power, Politics, and Confrontation: A Guide for the Successful Police Labor Leader* (Charles C Thomas, 1997). Mr. DeLord is a graduate of Lamar University, Sam Houston State University (MA), and the South Texas School of Law; and is licensed to practice law in Texas. He can be contacted at Ron.Delord@cleat.org.

John Burpo is a nationally-recognized police union leader who worked for many years with CLEAT and now serves as Director of the law enforcement division of the Communications Workers of America He wrote the seminal publication in the field, *The Police Labor Movement: Problems and Perspectives* (Charles C Thomas, 1971); and he was one of the co-authors of the 1997 *Power, Politics and Confrontation* book that preceded this book. He frequently lectures to law enforcement organizations throughout the country. Mr. Burpo is a graduate of the University of Tennessee and Tennessee School of Law; and is licensed in Arizona. He can be contacted at johnburpo@yahoo.com.

Michael R. Shannon is an award-winning political consultant from Washington, D.C. who assists both candidates and police unions. He has assisted police unions from across the country on issues such as candidate support or opposition, staffing campaigns, and pay increase campaigns. He is a frequent contributor and program lecturer for *Campaigns and Elections* magazine and *Governing* magazine. Mr. Shannon is also one of the co-authors of the book *Police Association Power, Politics, and Confrontation*. He can be contacted at mandate@comcast.net.

Jim Spearing is a Florida-based political and media consultant who works on behalf of police and firefighter unions throughout the United States. He does extensive work on behalf of the Florida Police Benevolent Association both in public campaigns and candidate support/opposition. He also provides media training to police and fire labor organizations. He can be contacted at jim_spearing@yahoo.com.

Second Edition

POLICE UNION POWER, POLITICS, AND CONFRONTATION IN THE 21ST CENTURY

New Challenges, New Issues

By

RON DeLORD

JOHN BURPO

MICHAEL SHANNON

JIM SPEARING

CHARLES C THOMAS • PUBLISHER, LTD.
Springfield • Illinois • U.S.A.

Published and Distributed Throughout the World by

CHARLES C THOMAS • PUBLISHER, LTD.
2600 South First Street
Springfield, Illinois 62704

© 2008 by CHARLES C THOMAS • PUBLISHER, LTD.

ISBN 978-0-398-07820-1 (hard)
ISBN 978-0-398-07821-8 (paper)

Library of Congress Catalog Card Number: 2008013264

With THOMAS BOOKS *careful attention is given to all details of manufacturing
and design. It is the Publisher's desire to present books that are satisfactory as to their
physical qualities and artistic possibilities and appropriate for their particular use.*
THOMAS BOOKS *will be true to those laws of quality that assure a good name
and good will.*

Printed in the United States of America
LAH-R-3

Library of Congress Cataloging-in-Publication Data

Police union power, politics, and confrontation in the 21st century : new challenges, new issues / by Ron DeLord... [et al.]. -- 2nd ed.
   p. cm.
  Revised ed. of: Police association power, politics, and confrontation : a guide
for the successful police labor leader / by John Burpo, Ron DeLord, Michael
Shanon.
  ISBN 978-0-398-07820-1 (hard) -- ISBN 978-0-398-07821-8 (pbk.)
  1. Police--Labor unions--United States. I. DeLord, Ron. II. Burpo, John H.
Police association power, politics, and confrontation. III. Title.

HV8143.B87 2008
331.88'1136320973--dc22

                                      2008013264

CONTRIBUTORS

Mark Burgess joined the New South Wales (NSW) Australia Police Force in 1988, graduating from the Police Academy in January 1989 and served in various postings over the next 10 years. In May of 1998 he was elected President of the NSW Police Association, the largest police association in Australia and was re-elected to that position unopposed in May 2000. In December 2000 Burgess took up his current role as Chief Executive Officer of the 47,000-member-strong Police Federation of Australia (PFA). Mr. Burgess has attained the qualifications of a Bachelor of Social Science (Justice Studies) in 1995 from Newcastle University as well as a Master of Public Policy and Administration in 1998 from Charles Sturt University.

Jenny Fleming joined the Tasmanian Institute of Law Enforcement Studies within the School of Government in July 2006. Formerly she was a Fellow with Security 21 at the Australian National University. Professor Fleming has been working with police organizations both in Australia and the UK/US for over 15 years. Her research expertise covers a variety of police policy issues; and has published widely both nationally and internationally in these areas. Her recent book (with Jen Wood), *Fighting Crime Together: The Challenge of Policing and Security Networks* was published in 2006.

Ted Hunt was a Los Angeles Police Officer from 1975 until his retirement in 2007. In 1995 he was seated as secretary and later as president of the Los Angeles Police Protective League, the largest police union in California. He was a member and Chair of the California Commission for Peace Officer Standards and Training; Chair of the California Alcohol Beverage Control Appeals Board, and served on numerous boards of directors of non-profit organizations and professional associations. Mr. Hunt earned his Doctorate in Public Administration from the University of La Verne in 1996.

Monique Marks holds a Ph.D. in Sociology from the University of Natal, South Africa. She is currently a Senior Lecturer at the University of Kwa-

Zulu-Natal and a visiting fellow of the Australian National University. Her research work has focused on youth social movements, ethnographic research methods, police labor relations, police organizational change and policing governance. She has published three books. Over the past ten years, Doctor Marks has worked with police organizations in both South Africa and Australia in finding new ways of forging policing partnerships and police innovations.

Greg O'Connor a 31-year veteran member of the New Zealand Police and is currently in his sixth term as full-time president of the New Zealand Police Association (NZPA). The NZPA represents 8,000 sworn police officers, as well as over 2000 non-sworn or civilian employees. Mr. O'Connor has raised the profile of the NZPA with members, lawmakers, and the voting public; and is a frequent commentator on law and order issues in the media and politically. He currently chairs the International Council of Police Representative Associations (ICPRA), a group of national police associations and federations who have come together to advance the cause of police unionism internationally.

For Shevy Wright and all the other officers who have dedicated their lives to the profession and the police labor movement.

PREFACE

The four co-authors meet once a year in Las Vegas to train police labor leaders on the principles of building and using power, becoming politically active, and when and how to engage in confrontations. On a recent gathering, one of our band of merry wordsmiths suggested that we write a sequel to our 1997 publication *Police Association Power, Politics, and Confrontation*, also published by Charles C Thomas.

The response from the others was, to say as judiciously as possible, underwhelming. Did we really want to again endure the agony of such a draining project? Could we find enough new material so that the end product would not be a rehash of the first book? Had we not said pretty much everything that a police labor leader needed to know about building a strong organization?

The first two questions were ultimately answered in the affirmative. We all agreed to complete the project, notwithstanding the time imposition that goes along with writing a book. Also, there was an abundance of new material that could be used because of our collective new experiences and major changes in the labor movement over the past decade. For example, the reader will find an entire section devoted to the state of police unionism and policing in the United States, and will hopefully come away rethinking many of the assumptions that many police union leaders make that it is just about the money. There is a new chapter on message, a subject of considerable importance that we gave little attention to in the first book. The sections on political action and news media have been reworked and expanded. The section on building power has been completely revamped. While some of the chapters on confrontation have been retained, there have been significant additions as well. Updated case studies have been added to illustrate the principles discussed in the book. In fact, the only resemblance to the first book is Chapter 3 about the principles of Saul Alinsky, Chapter 29 on initiatives and referendums, Chapter 30 on political consultants, and Chapter 31 concerning what happens when a police union loses in a confrontation.

The third question became the greatest hurdle for us. We wanted to believe that the first book was the ultimate word on the subject; and that nothing more needed to be said – the vanity of four large egos hard at work! In the end, however, we recognized that the police labor landscape had changed dramatically since 1997; and that new strategies and tactics have become necessary to deal with challenges that did not exist ten years ago.

The First Challenge: Police Officers Are Well-Paid Compared to Others In Their Community

Two of the co-authors began their law enforcement careers around the time that Richard Nixon began his first term as President. The economic benefits of police officers at the time were, in a word, pitiful. Salaries were meager; overtime was sporadically granted; pensions often given only after 30 years of service; equipment was substandard; and many police administrators practiced coercive policies to keep officers in line.

Leaping ahead almost forty years, the scene has changed dramatically. As a result of collective bargaining rights in all but a few states and increased political activism among police unions, officers are for the most part well-compensated. Salaries in many urban areas exceed $100,000, where the central department and suburbs must keep up with each other in order to recruit the most qualified candidates.

The wages are only part of the story – officers can look forward to all forms of overtime benefits, quality health care at a relatively low cost, twenty-year and out pensions, longevity pay, specialty pay, education and training incentive pay, out-of-classification pay, and on and on. The majority of officers are now protected from the overzealousness of police administrators through civil service systems, arbitration, and capable union attorneys who protect officer rights at every step of the disciplinary process.

No one should begrudge law enforcement officers these benefits and job protections – it is a tough job and the compensations should be commensurate with the work. The problem is that police officers are well-entrenched in the middle class, outdistancing many other workers in the community who don't receive the array of benefits and protections that officers do.

Police unions must depend on public support for their pursuit of better wages and benefits; and support becomes more difficult when other workers in the community make considerably less in wages; pay high monthly premiums for substandard health insurance; and are struggling for economic survival. As one police labor leader told a co-author recently when discussing the possibility of a public fight with the city over a contract, "I can't do it – we don't want the public to know how much we make."

So the first challenge is: how do police unions keep asking for more, when others in their community are doing with less?

The Second Challenge: Holding on to Active and Retiree Health Care and Pension Benefits

The escalating cost of active and retiree health care and underfunded pensions in the public sector is the five-hundred pound gorilla in the room. The private sector has been wrestling with this issue for years, as labor unions spend much of their time at the bargaining table trying to preserve decent health care for members, and save retiree health care and pension plans. As one national private sector union leader stated at a recent seminar on health care, "All we ever talk about now in bargaining is health care, and we wind up putting more and more money into health care that should be going into wages."

If any police union leader reading this book believes that this development is only a problem in the private sector and that it will never happen to the cops, then you're just not paying attention. Every day, somewhere in the country, some public official is talking about how employee health care benefits cost are too generous, premiums are too low, retiree health care is out of control, or the pension plan is underfunded. Public administrators have begun to realize that the costs of employee health care and pensions are no longer sustainable at current levels, and that other options must be explored.

Police officers are not exempt from this move toward cost control. San Diego police retirees lost their health care plan in 2005. The City of San Antonio has made active and retiree health care cost sharing by officers the number one priority in the last two contract negotiations; and caused serious friction not only between the police union and the City, but internally among union members as well. The State of California and some of its cities and counties have been pushing in recent years for pension benefit reductions, including the elimination of defined benefit plans. Police unions and their members have come into the cross-hairs of the national health care crisis and pension underfunding.

The second challenge is: how can police unions tiptoe through the minefield of health care and pension issues without losing great benefits that have been achieved through successful contract negotiations and lobbying over the past forty years?

The Third Challenge: The Police Profession is Rapidly Changing, and Police Unions Are All Too Often Sitting on the Sidelines

The world of policing is fluid, with new issues always coming to the forefront. Some of the issues in recent years have included civilianization of previously sworn positions, staffing, recruitment, new technologies, and career ladders that will retain officers who would otherwise be peaked out at the top of their salary range. These issues baffle and paralyze some police union leaders. They often sit idly by or mindlessly obstruct management initiatives by police administrators without thinking about how to effectively respond to the rapid changes that are taking place in the police profession.

Staffing levels are an excellent example of how police union leaders often tend to be reactive when more creative solutions should be considered. There is no question that many law enforcement agencies are understaffed, often to the point that even authorized levels can't be maintained; and that these shortages create stress for officers on the street and a risk to public safety.

However, the typical "We need more officers" demand of some union leaders overlooks the more complex reasons why staffing continues to be a problem: too many Generation Y potential applicants disinterested in the police profession; too many police departments competing for a shrinking pool of qualified applicants; and too many competing interests for public resources that would be required to increase the police department's staffing levels, even assuming enough qualified applicants could be found to fill the positions.

The third challenge is: how do police union leaders become an active participant in dealing with professional issues that affect members rather than be an observer on the sidelines?

The Fourth Challenge: You Are Not the Only One Reading This Book!

Our first book and this one have been written as a guide for leaders that will make their police union powerful so they can achieve the goals that will benefit their members. Just remember though that the public officials sitting across the bargaining table have probably read the book too, because they want to be prepared for whatever the union will pull out of its bag of tricks next.

After the publication of our first book, several police contract disputes that the co-authors were involved in became heated to the point that public officials called press conferences and pointed to parts of the book to demonstrate the tactics that the police union was employing. These media events involved considerable condemnation of the co-authors as a bunch of bomb-throwers and rabble-rousers. We were all greatly appreciative of these calls of attention to our book because every time it happened, book sales spiked!

The fourth and final challenge is: in the rough and tumble game of police labor-management relations, how do union leaders stay creative and always one step ahead of management so that their goals can be achieved?

This book is not for every police union leader. Some leaders will be more comfortable with the legalistic approach where you bargain, and then mediate and/or arbitrate – it is a safe, non-confrontational way to do business. Or they might be comfortable with a more recent type of approach where you dazzle management with numbers that show economic comparability relationships between agencies, avoid any type of confrontational tactic, and magically persuade the other side that you are right.

Both of these styles have fatal flaws. In the bargain-mediate-arbitrate system, the police union will never break through with a new benefit or an extra percent or two in wages above the pack – it's all about how your union stacks up comparable cities and the employer's ability to pay. In the "dazzle-them-with-numbers" method, any experienced negotiator knows that management will argue a different set of numbers and then what do you do? As Benjamin Disraeli once said, "There are three kinds of lies: lies, damned lies, and statistics." The "dazzle them with numbers" system is nothing more than the same economic comparability arguments that are made in the legalistic bargain-mediate-arbitrate system.

The co-authors have a completely different view of the world. It is a view grounded in the reality that public officials will only do what they are forced to do. We believe in good faith bargaining, and up to a point, the notion of "getting to yes."

The ultimate question becomes: what happens when good faith bargaining and getting to yes fail to achieve the goals that your police union has set? Do you wilt up and call it a day, or do you take steps that will earn the attention and respect of the public officials you are dealing with? Are you willing to go to the Court of Public Opinion and demand that the mayor, council, and/or city manager do the right thing? These questions will be answered in the pages that follow.

One of the observations that each author occasionally hears is that this book only applies to large, urban police unions and not to smaller groups that have significantly less resources. Nothing could be further from the truth. There is plenty of solid advice for every police union – large, medium, or small. In fact, the principles in this book can be often more readily used in smaller communities because it is much easier to reach out and touch elected officials and citizens than in larger ones. You just have to configure the ideas in this book to suit the culture and dynamics in your own community.

Three final points are in order. First, on the matter of word usage, the term "union" will be used exclusively in this book. We believe the day has come when police union leaders and members are comfortable with the word; and that the term "association" can be finally and gladly discarded from common usage. Any references to the government employer and employees in this book will normally use the word "city" and "police officers," even though the principles apply to counties and employees such as deputies and probation officers; and to states and employees such as troopers and correctional officers. We intend no disrespect to county or state law enforcement officers – it is just easier to use one employer and employee designation for matters of writing simplicity.

Second, Jim Spearing is our fourth co-author this time in addition to Mssrs. DeLord, Burpo, and Shannon from the first book. Jim is an experienced Florida political and media consultant who assists police and fire associations; and he is a welcome addition to our group.

Third, we wish to acknowledge the gracious and excellent guidance provided to us by Susan Collins, Senior Director of Administrative Services for the Combined Law Enforcement Associations of Texas on the chapter about money; and Melissa Burpo, scientific and technical writing wizard on the communications chapter.

We hope that every police union leader who reads this book will take something away that benefits the organization and most important, the members. If these goals are achieved, then the pains of authorship will have been well worth it.

Ron DeLord
John Burpo
Michael R. Shannon
Jim Spearing

CONTENTS

PART VII – UNITED STATES CASE STUDIES

PART VIII – INTERNATIONAL CASE STUDIES

POLICE UNION POWER, POLITICS, AND CONFRONTATION IN THE 21ST CENTURY

Part I

ABOUT POWERFUL UNIONS, MESSAGE, AND SAUL ALINSKY

Chapter 1

ABOUT POWERFUL POLICE UNIONS

This first part of the book will look at three important foundations of a powerful police union. This chapter will identify some general reasons why some police unions become powerful, and others do not. Then the crucial principles of message will be explored – the concept of message underlies just about everything that leaders do and say. Finally, the timeless ideas of Saul Alinsky will be discussed as they were in the first book.

Wha' Hopp'ned?"

Fred Willard's great line in the movie *A Mighty Wind* is fitting for the first important point: *Unions are divided into three groups: Those who make things happen; Those who watch things happen; and Those who ask "what happened?"*

If you ask a room full of police union leaders to pick which of the three groups they believe their unions are in, 20 percent would believe they make things happen, 80 percent would believe they watch things happen, and 20 percent would believe they are always asking "what happened?" Those percentages are probably accurate. What they fail to recognize is that unions can move between the three groups at any time.

Even unions who are making things happen can get lazy or start believing that they can live on past accomplishments. This is particularly true when a powerful president has led the union to several victories and then retires. The new president may not have the leadership skills needed or simply does not understand the principles of creating a powerful union and staying on top. Living in the shadows of a former successful union leader can cause the union to drift from making things happen to watching things happen, or even worse, asking what happened.

Will Rogers was quoted as saying, "Even if you are on the right track, you will get run over if you just sit there." Successful police union leaders need to wake up every day worried about what might happen. If you are the top of your game, you only have one way to go if you lighten up. Powerful forces are at work every day to take the union and its president down a peg or two on the ladder. Those forces are both external and internal. You might easily recognize the external forces such as the mayor, city manager, chief or sheriff, but the internal forces can be just as deadly since they will stab you in the back. There is always a small faction inside the union that wants the union to stumble so they can get control and oust the leaders.

Since 80 percent of unions linger periodically in the "watching things happen" category, it is important to recognize when you are drifting and make efforts to refocus the union to rebuilding its power. Generally the union has the resources available in money, members and talent, but they are either missing opportunities to engage management or elected officials, or they do not understand why they should be more active. Remember, good things do not just happen to good people. If that were true, we would not need the union as all employers would pay fair and equitable wages and benefits and provide the necessary officers and equipment to do the job.

If you believe your union is in the third category, and you are always asking "what happened," you have serious work to do to get the union back on its path to power. It is not easy and apathy by the officers is probably the biggest reason the union is ineffective. Rome was not built in a day. Start with baby steps and gain some small victories. Perhaps this will motivate the members to get involved and support the union's efforts. If you lie down and let elected officials and management kick you, then you deserve what you get. If you decide to fight back and demand respect, you may be surprised how quickly things will change.

Principles of a Powerful Union

Too many union leaders believe that all of their efforts should be directed toward preparing for collective bargaining. They focus on reading the contracts of other unions and pulling provisions out of these contracts without any understanding of how these provisions even got into those contracts. It is amazing how many times union leaders will create the "perfect cut-and-paste contract" and circulate it to the members only to have the air taken out of their magic balloon when the city's negotiators start laughing at them. If your union is more concerned about the four corners of the contract than on the organizational theory behind how to get a great contract, you are doomed from the start.

Understanding organizational theory is more important than the mechanics of bargaining. Building a powerful union is more than a table game every few years when the contract comes up for renewal. When should you start preparing for the next contract – the day you sign the current contract! Why? Because you already know every issue that was left hanging or unresolved and you know exactly what the employer will want the next round of negotiations. Unions have to be in the power game every day and not just during bargaining negotiations.

Getting to "Yes" without conflict is always the best solution. Fortunately 99 percent of police unions reach an accord with very little turmoil. While many public employers, chiefs and sheriffs have publicly attacked the authors as advocating and even encouraging unions to seek conflict or confrontation just for the hell of it, that is far from the truth. The truth is that most police unions do not know what to do when confronted with **NO** at the bargaining table.

The key is to understand that you cannot get to **YES** without a **RESPECT** for **POWER**. The respect for power required by unions does not come without a price and that price is the willingness to engage in conflict and confrontation in order to get the respect needed to get to **YES**. It seems so simple, yet most police union leaders are not prepared to do what it takes to get off dead center and fight back effectively.

The Four Pillars of a Powerful Union

Organizational Power. The mission statement of every union should be, "the sole purpose of the union is the accumulation and use of power to achieve the goals of the union." All other functions of the union are secondary and pale in comparison to the importance of this mission statement. If you doubt this statement, evaluate your union by giving a percentage value to each function of the union – power building, retirement dinners, social functions, fund-raising events, conferences, seminars, etc. If the majority of your time and energy is spent on things other than accumulating and using power to advance the goals of the union, the best bet is that you have a weak union that is not respected by management or elected officials.

This mission statement has generated much media controversy and is often quoted by reporters upset with the authors. Journalists like to quote Lord Acton, "power corrupts, and absolute power corrupts absolutely" in condemning unions for seeking power. One humorous de-motivational poster stated it better by adding the tag line, "but it rocks absolutely, too." Unions did not invent the power game. It has existed since the beginning of time and will continue to exist to the end of time. The union can be a player or observer, but the game will be played with or without the union.

Political Action. It is the **ONLY** power game in town. Twenty years ago it was difficult to find a police union with a political action committee or even one that was regularly endorsing candidates for political office. The police were viewed as paramilitary and required to be above politics. Many states and cities had laws against political activity by its unions or officers. Today, virtually all unions are in the political game at some level even if it is just endorsements.

It is still common to hear officers bad-mouthing the union's political involvement and pining for the good old days of no political involvement. Somehow they believe that if they remain apolitical, the power brokers will give them better wages, benefits, staffing and equipment. We all know that left to their own devices, and with no pressure from the union, these power brokers will do no such thing. Name one major police agency in the United States where the union is not involved in the political process that is paid top wages and benefits? It does not exist. We cannot go back to the good old days, and why should we?

Politics is all about numbers. Every police agency is governed by a political body whether elected or appointed by elected officials. Every one of these political bodies will vote on wages, benefits, staffing and equipment. If you have the votes to get what you need, then your union is probably doing all of the right things. If you do not have the votes, you will have to listen to **NO** again or seek arbitration. Count your votes and determine who is not voting with you. Now you understand who you have to politically engage to get the votes you need.

Media Involvement. Remember, the media requires you use it or it will use you. There is no middle ground. The newspaper will be printed every day, the television news will be broadcast all day, and the radio news will run every hour. You will have influenced the media story or the media will run the story using other sources. But it will run every hour-on-the hour with or without you.

Second to political involvement, dealing with the media is the next most distasteful activity for almost all union officials. Powerful unions understand the media and how it works. They make an effort to keep track of what is happening every day and insert the union into stories that impact the union or its members. Successful unions do not allow management or elected officials to speak for the rank and file members. That is the job of the union and not management or elected officials. It takes a lot of energy and time to watch the media and get your message out, but the alternative is to allow someone else to tell your story. The battle is always in the Court of Public Opinion, and if you forget that, your union will get into trouble.

Confrontation. All confrontations are a tool to maintain respect between the union and management and elected officials. Confrontation for the sake of confrontation is self-defeating and wears out the members, media and public. Screaming wolf too many times will cause the union to lose respect and when a real crisis arises no one will take the union seriously.

Confrontations are stressful, time-consuming and come with high risks that include possible failure. However, you cannot gain or retain respect without a willingness to engage in a confrontation. It is far worse when a union official allows management or elected officials to disrespect the union without a fight. Power brokers have no respect for the weak. The union is better off to fight and lose than to allow management or elected officials to disrespect the union. Even if power brokers prevail, they may not want to engage in another fight and will prefer to negotiate in a more fair and balanced manner.

The four pillars are the fundamentals for a powerful union. Unions that ignore one or more of the pillars do so at their own risk. First, concentrate on accumulating and using power to achieve the goals of the union. Second, get involved in the political activities of the community and not just during the political season. Third, use the media to get your message out and never ever allow management or elected officials to determine your message. And finally, reserve confrontations as a means to gaining and maintaining respect. Not every slight warrants a confrontation, but some do and the power brokers will be watching to see if you have the willingness to fight.

Three Reasons Union Leaders Fail

Union leaders fail to understand that without power there can be no professionalism. First comes power, and then professionalism can follow. Not vice versa. Organizations representing doctors, lawyers, airline pilots, architects, and so forth accumulated power and used it to create professional standards that included strict educational and licensing requirements, which have resulted in higher wages and benefits. Unions representing firefighters, nurses, teachers and police officers who have understood this principle have used their power to improve the living and working conditions of their members and developed professional standards that have resulted in higher wages and benefits.

Where union leaders fail is that they assume professionalism comes first and they ignore accumulating power. They assume because they say they are professionals, the resulting standards, wages and benefits will just occur on their own. Look at states where unions representing these employees are weak and lack political power. Standards are low, requirements to obtain these jobs are minimal, turnover is high, and wages and benefits are below comparable jobs in states where the unions are powerful.

Then look at the states where unions are strong and use their power to improve the living and working conditions of their members and to demand professional standards. Almost all have high standards for entry into the profession, low turnover, and high wages and benefits. It is not magic that these things happen in those states. Elected officials and management cannot, and will not, seek to regulate themselves without a powerful force demanding changes.

They fail to understand how to move the union toward achieving the power needed to accomplish their goals. Some union leaders are paralyzed with fear at having to ask the members to do what it takes to accumulate power. In order to avoid asking members to be involved, the leadership depends upon the same five members who do all the work in every union. Why upset the masses anyway? Well, the members set goals that can only be accomplished by using the power of the union. Failure to engage the membership in these tasks generally means a high probability of failure and at the least some finger-pointing at the leadership when the goals are not met.

Setting goals is great, but getting the goals accomplished means that the leadership has to engage the members and motivate them to do things they simply wish to avoid. That is the leadership challenge. When members set a goal, let's say they want to improve their health insurance plan, the union's leadership must explain that to accomplish that goal the union has to have three votes on the five-member city council. The union has two votes and needs to sway one of the remaining three undecided or no votes. Ask that a "war chest" be created by having each member contribute $50 to the union political action committee. Define what the members must do to give the leadership the ability to get it done.

Union leaders fail when they do not have a plan to move the members to achieve the power needed to achieve the goal, or they are afraid to tell the members the truth about what they will have to do to achieve the goal. There is nothing wrong with having a poor health insurance plan if the majority of the members are not willing to join in the fight.

They are distracted from achieving power by failing to avoid the individual interest and misdirection of some members. Even when union leaders know what the members need to do to build power and achieve their goals, they are often distracted by nay-sayers and whiners who have their own agenda. These members try to derail the union leadership with misdirection or with their own individual interests. One example is a member who opposes the union endorsing an incumbent because the member is related to the opposing candidate. The opposition has nothing to do with the best interests of the union, but is simply opposition to advance their own interests. Another example is the member opposing the endorsement of a candidate because of political party affiliation. The union should endorse based solely upon the candidate's support of the stated goals of the union, not the member's personal political beliefs.

The best way to defeat individual interests and misdirection is to clearly articulate the goals of the union to the members prior to the endorsement process. Make sure all questionnaires, surveys and forums ask only questions directly related to the stated goals. For example, do you support the police union's efforts to retain health insurance for retired officers? If Candidate A supports the goal and Candidate B does not, then there should be no question as to who gets the endorsement. Candidate A may support liberal causes and Candidate B supports conservative causes, but only Candidate A supports the stated goal of the union.

Chapter 2

MESSAGE DEVELOPMENT

Police unions are continually frustrated by their inability to generate enough public support to achieve their goals. Unions that have collective bargaining agreements are forced to put the fate of their members in the hands of an arbitration hearing that often results in unsatisfactory results, because they could not produce enough pressure on elected officials to win through the negotiation process.

Unions without bargaining agreements don't even have that option. These luckless unions with collective begging depend, like Blanche Dubois, on the kindness of strangers to generate raises, pension benefits and other forms of improved compensation for their members.

So if the police labor movement has learned by painful experience that life without collective bargaining is hell, but life with collective bargaining isn't always heaven; what is the missing ingredient needed to successfully advocate on behalf of your members?

The answer is simple: a compelling message that generates enough support among the public to pressure elected officials to do what you want them to do.

Ready, Fire, Aim

Unfortunately, police unions are collections of extremely sensitive individuals who often get their feelings hurt. As a result these police union leaders have a tendency to lash out emotionally, without considering the big picture. As a result they only generate negative news coverage that heats up a controversy without shedding any light on matters of concern to the public.

At first glance you'd think this description applies more to social workers than cops, but how else do you explain the startling number of news stories where the president of the union is complaining that the mayor or city council is being unfair to the police?

What does unfairness have to do with anything? The media and public do not care if the city is fair or not to the police union. Life is unfair for most of the world. Lashing out in anger about unfairness isn't a message the public cares about, it's a tantrum.

I call it **Ready, Fire, Aim**. This is usually characterized by frenzied activity. It's the *Sherwin-Williams* – cover the world – approach to communication where haste to respond and showing the members you won't stand for this unfair treatment becomes the message that causes a backlash from the media and public.

As a practical matter, this works to the detriment of the union. Production without planning is a short–term activity that ignores your long–term needs and can damage the organization's reputation and electoral chances, while wasting time and money.

Goals + Message = Successful Communication

The first step in developing a successful message is asking questions and formulating your goals. Without a goal you cannot devise a successful message. So regardless of whether you want more pay, a better pension, parity with comparable agencies or improved health insurance; you must first answer these three questions:

1. What do your members want?
2. What outcome is the maximum possible given your political situation?
3. What is the minimum your members will accept and still allow you to plausibly claim victory?

Once you determine your goal, then and only then you can begin work on the message that will help you achieve your goal. Not surprisingly, the initial work on message development also involves the use of questions. There are six key questions that must be answered to everyone's satisfaction if you want to maximize your chances for success in any communication campaign. These questions are:

1. What is your organization's current public image? Does it help your cause or harm it?

2. What individual or group is the primary target for your message and campaign?
3. Does this group have the power to grant your wishes or will they have to influence or pressure the group that does have the power?
4. What is your issue positioning? Are you attacking, defending or educating?
5. Can you devise a message that will appeal to other groups or individuals who will join your campaign?
6. Do you have members of the board and general membership who will volunteer to work on their own time in the campaign; or do you have enough money in the treasury to pay for a public information campaign?

There are no shortcuts to success. These questions must be answered as part of the planning process before you go public. The planning process takes time and effort but the results have proven to be worth the wait.

The Message Pyramid

The Message Pyramid is a visual representation of how information is distributed and diluted within any system or campaign. To illustrate, imagine Old MacDonald's Farm as a pyramid: Mac's at the top, the family's just below, the cows are at the mid–point and the corn is at the bottom. Each step down the slope introduces a larger population with less information.

Why do you care about this? Because your message trickles down through the public in the same manner, and if you don't apply the lessons of the Message Pyramid to your campaign, you can't succeed.

In your pyramid it's experts at the top – entropy at the bottom. You function at the apex and the people you're most comfortable with – board members, opinion leaders, command staff and political staffers – are up at the summit with you.

The problem is they are not the people who are going to influence public policy. Public safety and law enforcement are important to them, but your campaign is not the top priority of the vast majority of taxpayers. In fact, you can devise a message that meets with universal approval among your peers, and still fail to influence the public.

Here's another example: remember the last time you were at a computer store? Assuming you could tackle a salesperson and ask a question, do you remember the sinking feeling you had as a torrent of industry jargon and technical terms engulfed you? You may have only wanted to buy a new monitor, but instead you were soon adrift in a sea of graphics cards, processor RAM, refresh rates, LCDs and the like.

Hold that thought, because that's how the vast majority of America feels when we start talking politics or public policy to them. They aren't at the bottom of the pyramid because they are stupid, any more than you are stupid because you are not a computer monitor expert. They are at the bottom because city, county or state politics is not a priority.

If you want to win, you must tailor your message to reach a broad audience that is not actively seeking to receive communication from you, mostly because in many instances, they either don't know you exist or they don't pay much attention.

In the political message pyramid the population breaks down this way:

   1 percent: Elected officials, staff members, you and other experts on the issue

  10 percent: Your board members and opinion leaders in the community, including activists, political donors, political volunteers, reporters, consultants and other experts

  15 percent: The informed public – newspaper readers and avid followers of political and municipal issues

  75 percent: Politically passive voters. They have the power but they don't necessarily have the interest in your issue.

So you can see how it's possible to reach everyone in the know with your issue and still fail because the vast majority of the public was not involved. There is also another complicating factor in message development and that's audience orientation. At the top of the pyramid it's an intellectual issue exercise. These people are interested in facts and data. But at the bottom of the pyramid, it's emotional and the question is: how does the issue affect me personally and why should I care?

Therefore, as your message penetrates into the general public it must undergo a transformation from a data–based message into a motivating emotional message if you want to reach a critical mass of support.

In fact, communications experts Tucker and Nufer have found that during a communication campaign "most people have difficulty transferring information to behavior without help. Focusing only on sharing information leaves the action up to the receiver. The risks are great that an individual will pass up information, not because it isn't useful, but because you haven't helped create a mental picture of how to use it." A complete message will not only lay out the problem or the issue; it will also tell the public exactly what they need to do to solve the problem.

Internal and External Message Pyramids

Police union leaders have an additional audience they must reach and this group often requires a different message from that of the general public. This exclusive group is your own membership and it is, as you know, a tough audience. The knowledge breakdown within this group is remarkably similar to the public message pyramid.

1 percent: You, particularly involved board members and other experts

10 percent: Board members

15 percent: Informed membership – those that attend meetings and read the newsletter

75 percent: Apathetic, donut-eating loudmouths. They never volunteer, rarely attend meetings, but are always ready to complain about your incompetence.

What's more, the message that motivates your members will often be different from a message that moves the public, meaning you have to devise two messages instead of one. The classic example of this is a campaign for a pay raise. Telling your members that you need their help in a campaign to increase police pay is an easy sell. Taking the same message public is a recipe for failure. When you tell the average man-on-the-street the cops want a raise the usual response is he wants a raise, too. So what?

This message violates the rule of the Message Pyramid because it does not apply to the general public and it certainly does not reach them in an emotionally positive manner. Going statistical and telling the public that your department ranks tenth in pay while the city is third in population in the state is an intellectual argument that appeals to the top of the pyramid, not the bottom where the votes are.

So what do you do? Look at the overall big picture and see how it affects public safety, which in turn affects family safety. You can talk about retention rates: we are losing our experienced, highly trained officers to other jurisdictions and that costs the city money and you protection. You can talk about the quality of the department: our starting pay is so low that the city cannot attract the best and brightest of the recruit pool, which means our department may be less effective and your family less safe. Or you can talk about overall manpower: our salaries are so low that we can't hire enough new officers to replace the cops we lose to attrition; fewer cops means less protection for your family.

It should be emphasized here that the way to message success among the general public does not mean that you have to mislead them. Instead, you need to take a comprehensive look at all the elements that compose your issue and highlight the elements that are most important to the general public; and do the same with your membership.

The 7–Step Message Test

Another way to evaluate a potential message is to apply the 7–step message test before you go before your members or the public. The steps are:

1. **SIMPLE**: The overall message or theme should be short. People are busy and they are not going to devote a lot of time to absorbing all the subtle nuances of your issue. If you can't make your point penetrate the audience in less than 15 seconds, you need to sharpen your point.

2. **REPETITIVE**: As the politicians say you need to "stay on message." You use the same message from the day you announce the campaign until the day you win. Yes, you will get tired of saying the same thing, but you must remember that the public has to be exposed to a message approximately six times before they understand and retain it. If you have different messages or different ways of expressing the message you run the risk of confusing the public.

3. **BELIEVABLE**: Being true does not mean it's believable. One Midwestern police union was in a battle with the mayor over manpower. During the fight a database publisher released crime

rankings for cities. The union leadership was surprised to find that their city was listed as being more dangerous than Los Angeles, CA. The union produced a radio spot using this new information, hoping to put more pressure on the mayor. The results were disappointing because people didn't believe it. Los Angeles is the home of the Crips and the Bloods – they saw this kind of Hollywood crime on TV, but the public didn't feel like their town was *that* dangerous, so they rejected the message.

4. **INCLUSIVE**: Your message must include the target audience. This is why the police need a pay raise doesn't work with the general public. There is no money in this issue for them. On the other hand, a lack of safety or potential for more crime does include the target audience, which is why this message is more effective.

5. **RELEVANT**: There is a great deal of overlap between inclusive and relevant. Relevant can also mean immediate. A threat ten years from now is not a motivating factor, while one ten days from now can get action.

6. **EMOTIONAL**: This is not directed toward the target audience. If your message is inclusive and relevant it will strike an emotional chord with the audience. This test is for you. When you discuss the message you have to care, and you have to communicate that concern to all the target audiences.

7. **EFFECTIVE**: Once the message is in the field you must have some evidence it's working. Public opinion polls are one method. If you can't afford that, then listen to talk radio. Are the hosts discussing the issue? Are you appearing on talk radio and do the calls support you? Are there letters to the editor? Do you have any support on the city council or county commission? Does anyone show up at your rallies? Is the media covering the issue? Are you getting pushback from elected officials? Have they surrendered? If you don't have some positive feedback, then the message is not working.

Message Enemies

Obviously there will be opposition to what you are trying to do – because if you were getting your way you wouldn't need a message in the first place. The chief's office may try to undermine you and your statistics. Many times the chief is more a political creature than a police officer, and if he has an adversarial relationship with the union anyway, he may view this as an opportunity to put those labor upstarts in their place.

Some elected officials will almost always be in the forefront of the opposition. Going public usually embarrasses them and their ego requires retaliation. Of course if they had agreed or negotiated with you when you first approached them, none of this public effort would have been necessary.

Since law enforcement occupies a special place in government, there will also be accusations of abusing your power. These charges will usually come from the media, members of the establishment and community activists. The criticism here will be on the order of why do the cops think they are special? Why can't they work within the system like the grief counselors? If we give the cops a raise we have to give everyone a raise, and so on.

So far, no surprises – and if you are not prepared to deal with the heat generated from these sources then you have no business going public in the first place. What many labor leaders do find surprising is the heat generated from within their own organization. Think back to our discussion of the two message pyramids you must develop: the external and the internal messages. Two message targets double the sources of potential opposition.

From within the union you have dissidents who don't like the way you run the organization and certainly don't agree with anything you do in public. You will also be confronted with grumbling from members who are uncomfortable with going public in the first place. They view politics as dirty and not something with which the union should be involved. But law enforcement forces its members to interact with all sorts of unsavory characters, so why avoid politicians? These members will whine and complain about all this unwanted attention. Finally, you may have members that undermine your message because they are too eager and talk out of turn or they are sunk too deeply into the Dirty Harry mindset and say something offensive.

You may also find a message enemy when you look in the mirror. Messengers often get tired of their own message. This is message fatigue and it comes from saying the same thing over and over again. You are tired of hearing the same old song and you assume the audience does, too.

But that is not the case. The composition of your audience changes on a daily or hourly basis. You can never be certain who is hearing you at what time and even those who have heard the message in the past may not have been paying attention or grasped all the message points. Studies show that the average television viewer needs to see a commercial six times before they retain the entire selling message. Your public message is no different. The effectiveness of your message communication relies in large part on the commitment and energy you put into communicating it.

Think of an actor on the stage. If he's performing the part of Hamlet the language is going to be the same night after night. But the audience does not think poorly of the actor because he doesn't change his lines or freshen them towards the end of the play's run. He's judged on the interpretation and emotion he puts into the lines and his ability to make a connection with his audience.

Message Example

Think of your message like it's a diamond and in the course of your campaign you will highlight different facets of the diamond depending on the audience that you are attempting to reach. Here's an example from a mayor's race where the police union was trying to defeat an incumbent mayor. The union-backed candidate was well–funded, had been elected to other offices and was considered a credible opponent. Crime rates had been on an upswing in the city and the newspaper was filled with reports of violent crime.

It was a perfect setting for an effective public safety message and fit in with the union's goal of hiring more cops and defeating the incumbent mayor. Unfortunately the challenger just did not understand the message. He kept arguing that you cannot run a citywide campaign on crime and public safety. He said not all areas of the city suffer the same crime rates and people want to hear about other issues. He saw himself as an encyclopedia of issues, brimming with public policy prescriptions and solutions.

This global view is fine if your goal is to be elected chairman of the Political Science Department at your local community college, but it's deadly in real politics. The union-backed challenger was told that he could indeed run a winning campaign on crime and public safety and the message would resonate throughout the city. His contention was the Southeast part of the city is a rich area with little crime and the Southwest portion of the city was a Republican area with even lower crime. Both examples were completely true and completely beside the point. He could not see the forest for all those pesky trees.

Crime and public safety is a message that would work regardless of geography or size of bank account. The issue in the Southeast part of the city is crime and education: we owe the children of our great city a great education and they cannot get an education if gangs are taking over the schools. Children all over the city deserve to feel safe in school and that's why we need more officers on the street to keep them safe going to school and more school resource officers to keep kids safe in school. Sure, the schools in our part of town don't have these problems now, but they could have them in the future if we don't do something right now.

In the Southwest the issue is crime and property values: crime in the central business district is out of control and ruining neighborhoods in many areas of the North. If businesses pull out of the city and head for the suburbs because of crime; and if people abandon their homes in other areas, property values in the city will begin to plummet. When that happens the mayor will look to our area to take up the slack and that means your property taxes will skyrocket because of crime. You may be safe from criminals where you live, but your wallet won't be safe from the tax increases that crime will cause if it's not brought under control. That's why we need more officers on the street right now and our candidate is the man to do it. Finally, in the areas of the city that are suffering from crime you talk about police and public safety.

It's the same diamond and the same message – the candidate simply shines a light on the facet that makes the most sense to the audience he's addressing. Your job is to mine the right diamond for your situation. Then cut and polish that diamond and show it to your members and the public in a manner designed to get what you want from those with the power to give it to you.

Chapter 3

SAUL ALINSKY – STILL THE MAN
WITH THE PLAN

Our first book devoted considerable space to the writings and philosophies of Saul Alinsky. If you did not read the first book, then this chapter is a must because the origins of just about every strategy and tactic in this book can be traced back to Alinsky. If this read is your second go-around with our work, then a review of this chapter wouldn't hurt since there are some updates from the original text.

Alinsky's writings include many memorable quotes, but his key adage is: "Change comes from power; and power comes from organization." We have tried to follow this advice in both books by starting with the basics of how you become organized in order to build power, and then how to effectively use this power to force a change in your relationship with the bureaucrats and elected officials who make the decisions that affect your workplace. While many police union leaders know little or nothing about Saul Alinsky, every time they set up a PAC, endorse a candidate, call for a demonstration or picket line, run a radio ad attacking the City Manager, or otherwise take on the Powers-That-Be, they're doing things that would have brought a smile to Alinsky's face.

Who Was Saul Alinsky and Why Are His Ideas So Important?

Saul Alinsky was a Chicago native who left a promising career in criminology at the University of Chicago in the 1930s to become a social activist. His initial interest was in organizing poor people in the Chicago slums to fight for their rights as citizens so that their lives would be better. He ultimately received international acclamation for his success in forming urban community organizations that made a difference in the lives of the underprivileged.

The central theme in all of Alinsky's work is that people on the lower end of the social and economic scale who have nothing (people he calls "the Have-Nots") must organize for the purpose of accumulating and using **POWER** to make their lives better. The heart of Alinsky's teaching is that if the "Have-Nots" are to get out of their impoverished conditions, then **CONFLICT** must be brought to bear on people who have the money and power ("the Haves").

Some of Alinsky's sayings about what a group should do when it doesn't have power and want it are real classics:

- The only thing you get is what you're strong enough to get, so you better organize.
- No issue can be negotiated unless you first have the clout to compel negotiations.

I'm Not a Poor Person, So This Chapter Doesn't Apply To Me

We made it very clear in the Preface that police officers are not exactly standing in bread lines these days to feed their families. Wages and benefits are generally in pretty good shape compared to other middle-class workers. So you might be thinking: "I've got better things to do than listen to this nonsense!" Before you dismiss the wisdom of Saul Alinsky so quickly however, you might want to read on.

Late in his career, Alinsky saw that poor people weren't the only folks in America having the screws turned to them. He became equally concerned about the middle-class, people he referred to as the "Have-Some-and-Want-Mores" – by the way, except for any of your members with trust funds, that category would be you and your co-workers. Alinsky saw that people in the middle class had been lulled into a false sense of security with their suburban homes and two-car garages – what he referred to as the "Gilded Ghettoes." The people with the **REAL** power – the politicians and money people behind the politicos who make the decisions that affect every citizen, continue to act in their own self-interest, and only every now and then throw a few little crumbs to middle-class folks.

If you don't think that this description of your relationship with the Powers-That-Be is accurate, take a good look at the world around you.

Politicians at all levels of government continue to be protected by the power of incumbency, in large part due to the money provided by wealthy contributors. Political choices are made first for the benefit of the contributors and other people with money. On the other hand, you and your co-workers have to scratch and claw to maintain the buying power of your paychecks, and to hold on to precious health care and pension benefits that have been so under assault in recent years.

Saul Alinsky won't have a whole lot of relevance to your world if you are from a community where wages and benefits for police officers are at the top of the scale, where every call for service is answered immediately because cops are falling all over each other, and the community thinks that the local police are the greatest thing since the invention of the Internet. But there are many cities and counties which only throw an economic bone to the cops every now and then, but only after all the swimming pools have been built, the Friends of the Library get every book they asked for in the budget, and the Arts Council pushed through that big pay raise for the ballerinas in your local dance company. These are the same communities where Widow Jones has to wait 30 minutes for a cop to show up to find out whether that creep hanging around in the back yard is the milkman, a Peeping Tom, or a rapist; and the community do-gooders start screaming for civilian review every time one of the bad guys gets a torn thumbnail during a resisting arrest encounter. If your police union falls into the latter category, then keep reading.

Every issue faced by a police union leader can be addressed in the teachings of Saul Alinsky. You can be assured that there's always an answer somewhere in Alinsky's collection of works about how to make that hard-headed council member move off of a position, or how to make the big-shot Chamber of Commerce guys and gals pay attention to the law enforcement needs of the community rather than which of the downtown business crowd is going to get the next sweet tax abatement from the City Council.

Don't be fooled into thinking that just because your union is in a state with the Best Collective Bargaining Law in the Universe, that you can stop reading this chapter. Even in states like Wisconsin, Washington, or Oregon, which have model binding arbitration laws, unions have found that if they are going to get that extra percent or two beyond what every comparable city is receiving in a given year, they must use Alinsky's rough-and-tumble tactics in order to get the City

Council's attention, because the rarified, legalistic atmosphere of an arbitration hearing won't get the job done.

If You're Gonna Make the Power Structure Squirm, You've Got To Leave All of Mama's Childhood Preachins' Outside the Front Door of the Union Hall

Think about the last time that as a union leader, you thought about a confrontation with your employer. For example, you've been given a low-ball offer at the bargaining table, so in order to move the City off of its position and toward your goal of an 8 percent pay raise, you think about putting pressure on City Hall: your union will get the City's attention by opposing the $400+ million bond issue being pushed by the City Manager, Council, and Chamber of Commerce because its loaded with such non-essential goodies like building an art museum, a covered parking lot for city employees, and construction of a minor league baseball park in a prime real estate area around which local developers will likely build shopping malls and amusement park. There is nothing in the bond proposal for essential public safety services. You plan to run radio ads and do member block walks in opposition to the bonds.

You get all excited about this plan, and then all of a sudden, you're overcome with guilt because your mama told you many times long ago that nice folks don't speak of or do ill to others. Or maybe you outline the plan at a membership meeting, and one hand-wringing member says, "I agree that we should get the pay raise but it's not right to oppose the City bonds."

Alinsky warns us about this "means versus ends" argument; that is, the agreement over the goals but disagreement over how to get there. Another of his famous maxims is "If you're too delicate to exert the necessary pressure on the power structure, then you might as well get out of the ballpark." The point here is that so long as it's legal, you do what has to be done; otherwise you will never achieve your goals.

A union leader must throw out all those traditional notions of right and wrong; and always beware of "means-versus-ends" arguments made by members of the union. When you start talking about the bond opposition idea at your membership meeting, be prepared to overcome some of these responses:

- That's unprofessional! [or, Police officers shouldn't do that!]
- This isn't the time. [or, Let's not rush into anything too quickly.]
- And here is the absolute biggest cop-out to worm out of a confrontation: "Let the lawyers take care of it." Sorry, labor lawyers, but if there's anything that will get in the way of making city officials do the right thing, it's attorneys who want to file complaints with the labor board or lawsuits in court, slowing down the issue into a morass of motions, oral arguments, and long delays, all operating to the benefit of the employer.

Whenever your union is faced with an issue that requires a heavy-handed response, Alinsky tells us that there are only three questions that the leadership needs to ask; and if there's a reasonable probability that these questions can be answered **YES**, then you need to move forward with your plan:

1. Is the end **achievable**? [Can we get the 8% pay raise we are seeking?]
2. Is the end **worth the cost**? [Will the $20,000 we spend on a public campaign against the City Council, and the heartburn it's going to cause even some of our close political and community allies, be worth the 8%?]
3. Will the means **work**? [Are those radio ads and block walks against the bonds enough to make the Council move off of its low-ball position and give us the 8%?]

When You Become a Union President, You Need to Rethink Some of Those Words You've Always Thought of as "Bad"

There are certain words common to the world of Saul Alinsky that we all think of in a negative way: words like "power," "self-interest," "conflict," and "compromise." We have come to view these terms as evil; whereas, Alinsky gets us to see them a more positive way.

Alinsky asks a very simple question about the word "power": "If power is such a bad thing, why are so many people and organizations seeking it?" Every organization, he says, should exist for only one reason – the accumulation of power in order to have the ability to act, or to produce a result. If your union does not exist for this purpose, it probably has very little reason to exist at all.

"Self-interest" is another word that gets a bum rap according to Saul Alinsky. We all have self-interest, he says, and it's important to recognize the constant conflict between professed moral principles and self-interest. Police union leaders are constantly attacked by members who believe that the leader is gaining something from his or her tenure as an officer in the union. Hopefully, the leader sought the office at least in part to improve the living and working conditions in the department. But any union leader would be less than truthful if he or she denied that they had some self-interest at heart (e.g.; attraction to the pursuit of power, being the head of a union).

"Conflict" is seen as a good thing by Alinsky. Without it, he says, the *status quo* would never be changed. For example, without conflict, many police unions would never have gotten bargaining laws passed, negotiated the attendant agreements with excellent wages and benefits, or achieved civil service rights. While most police officers see themselves as preservers of the *status quo* and therefore dislike conflict, it is conflict forced on the power structure that brings change to the system.

Finally, many people, and in particular union members, view the notion of "compromise" with considerable suspicion. It is seen as weakness or betrayal. But Alinsky says that while conflict is important to move toward a better result, compromise is the only way you ultimately get there.

When You've Got to Go to the Mat With Your Employer, There's No Better Guide For Action Than Saul Alinsky

If your union gets in a fight with the city over wages, benefits, manpower, or the latest Big and Hot Topic such as civilian review, and if you're looking for ideas on what's going to make the employer move closer to your position, the answer can be found in the teachings of Saul Alinsky. Here's an overview of some of Alinsky's more well-used power tactics that have worked time-and-again for police unions around the country:

1. Power is not only what you have, but what your enemy thinks you have. Power is an illusion. If it was something other than illusion, the Communists would still be in power in Eastern Europe, and there would still be a USSR today! So when your union's "war chest" is in a healthy state for a looming fight with the City, or the PAC account has enough money to take on that mayor who has been a thorn in your side (and everyone in town knows about your financial condition), the less likely it will be that the city council will think twice about taking too firm a position against the union.

2. Always go outside the experience of the enemy. One of the authors was negotiating a contract a few years ago for some municipal police officers in a small New Mexico city where management was known for its hardball bargaining positions. Negotiations reached a stalemate, so the union ran an ad in the *Buffalo Nickel* – that would be one of those dishrag advertising papers where the print runs off on your fingers. You would have thought that the world had come to an end! The city accused the union of unprofessional tactics and threatened to file a bar complaint against the negotiator. On a scale of one to ten, with ten being the highest rating, this tactic would have ranked less than a one on the Scare-O-Meter; it would have been laughable in a major urban market where even hard-hitting television ads have trouble penetrating a jaded, unconnected community. In this city, however, it was far beyond the employer's experience and caught public officials off guard, ultimately paving the way to a settlement.

3. Never go outside the experience of your own people. This concept is pretty clear. You never – well almost never – engage in a tactic that will make your members question the union's actions. The Bull Head City, Arizona case study in Chapter 42 is a good example of this principle. The union took a tough stance in negotiations against a City Manager who liked to play hard ball and dared the union to do something about it. The union attacked the City Manager's questionable purchase of property from a real estate developer who was also on the City Planning and Zoning Commission, which turned the dispute into an ugly community conflict. This union had never had so much as a ripple of a conflict, so the members had trouble seeing the relationship between the bargaining dispute and the attack on the City Manager, creating some disunity within the union.

4. Ridicule is man's most potent weapon. There's a great deal of enjoyment to be had in poking fun at your enemy, particularly in these days and times where public officials are not on the list of 10 Most Respected People in America. Many of your adversaries simply take themselves entirely too seriously. For example, any Police Chief who wears more stars on his hat than General George Patton does not take kindly to being made the object of scorn. Any Mayor who is a wealthy businessman and lives in a gated community by the premier local golf course will not be pleased when you poke fun at his lack of insensitivity to the plight of people in the community of lesser status. Many police unions that become embroiled in a conflict use a broadsword to beat City Hall over the head when instead, rapier-like wit will do much better in getting the job done. There will be specific examples of this principle in the section on confrontations.

5. A good tactic is one that your people enjoy. This example of a deputy union in the western part of the country was used in the first book and we have yet to find a better illustration than this one. This union was in contract negotiations when there was considerable confusion over the Fair Labor Standards Act and overtime benefits. At the bargaining table, the Sheriff contended that correctional officers were completely off the clock during their lunch hour and could leave the jail; in actual practice, officers were ordered to stay in the jail, go back to work before the lunch hour was up, and not be compensated for it. So during one bargaining session, the deputies' union held a free barbecue lunch underneath the window where the negotiations were taking place; corrections officers told their supervisors that the sheriff had said it was okay in negotiations to take a half-hour outside for lunch; and they walked outside to eat! Supervisors knew they couldn't stop the exodus because all parties to the contract were at the site; the tactic caused a serious manpower problem in the jail; and it forced everyone involved to find a solution to the lunch versus overtime issue. The converse of this tactic is that "any tactic that drags on for too long becomes a drag." If the union had kept the free lunch idea up day-after-day, the members would have quickly become bored and stopped coming outside.

6. The threat is usually more terrifying than the thing itself. Any man can recall the elementary school bully who told you that at the end of the day, he was going to whip your ass in front of the entire school over some real or imagined grievance. You worried about this confrontation over the course of the entire school day; and the worry was as bad, or almost as bad, as the beating that might take place. The same principle applies in any conflict with your employer. In a 2007 confrontation between a Southwestern police union and City, the City had an inviolate policy that all employees received the same compensation package in negotiations – a practice called "internal equity" by the City. The union could make adjustments to benefits, but only within limitations of what every other union had negotiated. This particular union decided that "internal equity" needed to go and after the City made its final offer – the same as all the other unions had settled for, the union took an entirely different path. The City was in the middle of pushing a $450 million bond issue that had drawn some community opposition. The union started all the elements of a bond opposition campaign: filing a political action committee with the City Clerk opposing the bonds; producing radio ads and block walk flyers that conveniently got into the hands of every public official in the City; and calling an emergency meeting of the membership to get approval of this campaign. Word quickly got back to City officials that the union was pulling out all the stops to oppose the bond; and the correlation between the bonds and the contract negotiations was not lost on the City Hall. The union had painted a dire picture of what would happen if negotiations did not have a different outcome and *presto*, the principle of "internal equity" was quickly abandoned, the contract settled for considerably more than the imposed city standard, and the union magically withdrew its opposition to the bonds (which subsequently passed). The moral of this story: paint the picture to the other side that bad things will happen if a better outcome can't be found. But here's an important admonition: when you make a threat, be prepared to carry it out or your credibility will be shot – in the case of this particular union, the leaders had every intention of waging a campaign against the bonds if the City has not changed its position.

7. Keep the pressure on. This principle is sometimes called the "cockroach theory." When you have trapped a cockroach under your shoe, you never, ever under any circumstances let the bug up to come back another day. Any time that the police union is in a fight with the employer, the group must keep coming up with a new tactic that will keep the other side reeling until the union's goal is achieved. One tactic in and of itself will not do the trick; if you stop to let the other side take a breath, it will only prolong your ability to prevail.

If You Want to Know More about Saul Alinsky

Saul Alinsky wrote two books in his life: *Reveille for Radicals* and *Rules for Radicals.* The books are published by Vintage Press (Random

House) and can be purchased or ordered at your local bookstore or one of the many on-line book services. The second book – *Rules*, is much easier to read and more relevant to contemporary issues and conflict.

Part II

THE BUILDING BLOCKS OF INTERNAL AND EXTERNAL POWER

Chapter 4

SOME PRELIMINARY OBSERVATIONS ABOUT POWER

The core premise of this book is that the accumulation and effective use of power can achieve the goals of the police union. This premise raises some troubling questions that were never really addressed in our first book: What is power? How can it be measured? When do you know that your union has acquired power; or, when it does not have it?

Let's start with a basic definition of power that will serve the reader well throughout the book. Power is the **PERCEPTION** that people and organizations in the community have about the police union's ability to achieve its goals. Given this definition, several observations about power are in order.

Power is an Illusion

Unless your organization has achieved power by getting your opponent to concede while looking down the barrel of a gun (not a recommended tactic in this book by the way!), then the police union's power is really nothing more than an illusion. To paraphrase one of Alinsky's famous observations from Chapter 3: "Power is not only what you have, but what the other side thinks you have."

There is no objective formulation of power whereby you can use one of the five senses to determine its existence. It is simply the accumulation of people's subjective observations about the police union that it has taken certain actions to make it a force to be reckoned with.

Or conversely, it has done nothing to merit the designation as a powerful organization.

The conclusion is therefore obvious. The more the police union does to create the perception that it is powerful, the more people will believe it.

All Power is Transitory

Think about some public official in your community who is considered "powerful;" for example, the City Manager who rules his domain with an iron fist, always convincing the City Council to do his or her bidding and keeping the employees and labor organizations on a short leash. This state of affairs can go on for years and then suddenly, some event occurs that topples the City Manager – financial or sexual improprieties, a drunk driving or drug possession arrest, or intervening to cover up the criminality of a family member or friend. One day the City Manager is King of the Hill, the next day, looking for another job.

The same principle applies to police unions. In 1988, a western police union was riding high – through excellent leadership and a high-powered political action program, the union negotiated a monster contract that gave police officers tremendous pay and benefits competitive with any police department in the nation. In subsequent years, there was a strong public backlash against the contract; the City Charter was changed to provide term limits for council members (making for the frequent turnover of political friends); and the union leadership and membership began a period of in-fighting. Contract negotiations became more difficult; and the public perception became that the union had become less of a player in the public arena. Only in recent years has this union restored some of the luster it had in the late eighties.

The point is that the dynamics of power in any community are fluid, never static. Just remember that when your police union makes it to the top of the mountain, and then sits back with smug satisfaction believing that there is nothing else left to do, there is only one place to go . . . and it ain't up.

The Elbow Grease Principle

Wouldn't life be grand if every police union leader could just rub a magic genie bottle and make these three wishes that come true: the union will be the most powerful interest group in the community forever; the local newspaper will only write complimentary articles about the police; and all union members will talk only about what a great job you and the rest of the leadership are doing . . . as if any of these results are really going to happen.

As the building blocks for internal and external power are discussed in this section, you will quickly observe that the development of power is no easy task. It takes commitment, and an investment of time, energy, and emotions. There are no "quick fixes" to bring your union up to speed.

Whether the union leader is developing a political action program, building community coalitions, working on image building, or doing one of the other activities discussed in this section, it takes hard work – elbow grease, to get the job done. If you are not willing to expend some elbow grease, then the prospects for success are at best slim.

Whomever is Holding the Cards of Power on Any Issue Normally Wins

Any reader who has watched ESPN's Texas Hold 'Em card tournaments in Las Vegas understands that the goal is for a player to build the best hand as the cards are drawn, and then convince other opponents that the hand is too good to bet against. This game has considerable application to police labor-management relationships because the union is building power – building the best hand, and then convincing public officials that the union's position can't be beat.

At the point that any issue, disagreement or conflict arises between the police union and the employer, the side holding the best hand of power cards will normally win. If the power dynamic is such that the employer has the upper hand, then the police labor leader must be careful about overplaying a weak hand. If the union has worked hard to develop power, then it is in a stronger position to prevail and can push out to what the authors will frequently describe in this book as "the edge of the envelope" to achieve whatever goal has been set.

Power Can Be Derived Internally and Externally

Police union power comes from two sources – internal and external. Internal power means the organizational strength that comes from the membership. A membership that is mobilized and willing to support and work for a particular issue will go a long way toward success. On the other hand, a divided, contentious membership spells trouble for any leader.

External power arises from the police union's political position, coalitions with key community leaders and organizations, image in the community, and relationship with the media. A police labor leader who expends the energy developing external power (see "The Elbow Grease Principle," above) will see a return on this investment.

Sometimes a police union will be externally strong and internally weak, or vice-versa. When faced with any difficult issue, a shrewd police labor leader will analyze the union's internal and external power before charting a course of action. If you are upside down on either the external or internal side of the power analysis, then caution is well-advised.

When Your Union Tries to Get a Seat at the Table, the Powers-That-Be Will Not Be Pleased

A small core of people and organizations normally control the ebb and flow of community priorities and how tax money will be spent. This group includes not only City administrative and political officials, but also powerful business interests. Whenever a police union leader makes the decision to become a player in this game and grab a seat at the table where the Big Boys convene, there will be a horrified reaction.

The first time that the police union endorses a candidate or backs an issue that runs contrary to the approval of the community elite, or embarrasses a public official who has the support of this same select in-crowd, expect some serious unpleasantness. The local newspaper – often the pimp for the downtown business establishment and City agenda, will editorialize about the "power hungry" police union "demanding its own narrow agenda" and "seeking to divert tax dollars away from crucial public interests." This theme will be reinforced by some combination of the City Manager, Mayor and Council members, who will repeat the same themes at downtown civic club meetings and other settings.

The message is clear: *they* have the right to seek and have power – you don't; *they* have the right to push their agendas – you don't; and *they* can promote the use of tax dollars for matters they deem in the public interest – you can't. When this kind of pushing and shoving goes on, understand that you have hit Pay Dirt and gotten the attention of the community leaders that matter. Disregard their reactions and keep moving ahead.

This section will explore the many ways that a police union can develop power. Without these building blocks, no police union will have the capacity to achieve its goals. The specific areas that will be discussed include:

- Strong leadership
- Proficiency in technical skills
- Strategic planning
- Acquiring and using money
- Effective communications
- Mobilizing the membership
- Coalition building
- Image building

The building block of a good message has already been discussed, and political action and news media are so important and complex that these subjects will be discussed in two later, separate parts of the book.

Chapter 5

STRONG LEADERSHIP

A multitude of books have been written on the principles, theories, and styles of leadership. Instead of exploring the general concepts of leadership, this chapter will examine leadership issues specific to the police labor leader.

The Pressures of Leadership and the Principle of
Non Illigitimi Carborundum

Do any of the following statements sound familiar? At a meeting where a controversial contract settlement is being presented to a packed room, members (some of whom are your good friends) scream, "We want more!". . . or, "We need another union to represent us.". . . or, the absolute worst condemnation: "Sell out!" Your spouse complains, "Why do you spend so much time down at the union hall and not enough time with the children and me?" The police chief or city manager reprimands, "The union's tactics are unprofessional and hurt the city's image." The newspaper editorial column denounces, "The police union leaders are just a bunch of whiny, greedy officers."

These kinds of pressures brought to bear day-in and day-out are demoralizing and will wear down even the strongest of leaders. That's why the tenures of most police union leaders in the United States are short-lived – most simply can't, or won't, put up with the aggravation and stress.

Any police union leader who wants to survive with a small measure of sanity must apply the principle of *non illigitimi carborundum*. Since most readers were undoubtedly Latin scholars in their high school or college days, the following loose translation is only for the few that never had the good fortune to learn the "Dead Language." The term means "Don't let the bastards grind you down," and it offers sound advice, although it would be well-advised that your spouse doesn't read this part of the book! Otherwise your spouse might think that *he* is the product of illegitimacy, or *she* is viewed by you as a . . . well, you know.

Successful police labor leaders understand that they must keep their eyes **only** on the goals of the union, and figuratively tune out all of the bothersome background noise that distracts from the accomplishment of these goals. If you take to heart every complaint about your conduct or your choices, there will be no energy left to accomplish the work.

This advice is sound in the abstract, but the reality is of course much different. Any leader who has been the object of membership condemnation over a controversial contract, has seen a once solid marriage become shaky since taking over as president, or has endured denunciation from public officials, community power brokers and the media over some union tactic, understands that the reality is much different than the theory.

Still, it is imperative to keep emotions and resentment in check, understand that membership interests always come first, and that at some point down the road, you will be turning over the mantle of leadership to someone else. You can then return to the simpler task of doing real police work and spending quality time with the family. As all of the constant finger-pointing, carping, whining, and other signs of people's displeasure swirls around you, just remember: this too shall pass.

The First Day in Office, Pull Out Your Compass

Upon assuming leadership of the police union, you will likely feel confused and lost. The task ahead appears overwhelming. What does a hiker do when lost on a trek through the woods? Pull out a compass and get a quick read on the right direction.

The immediate first step is to take a brief snapshot – an inventory, of where the union stacks up on the power grid. Unless you know where you are, you will have no idea where to go.

You should conduct a "union power rating" right away that will provide a brief sketch of your organization's ability **today** to achieve its goals. A union power rating appears in Appendix 1. It offers a statistical analysis of the union's present position with respect to leadership, membership, finances, political action, communications, public image, community coalitions, and a strategic plan.

Once this rating is completed, there will at least be a notion, however obscure, of the best direction to follow. From this exercise, the first steps can be taken toward moving the union in the right direction. The power rating should not be confused with developing a strategic plan, which is a complex exercise explored more fully in Chapter 7.

Overcoming a Basic Human Need

In the 1998 movie *A Bronx Tale*, a young teenager asks his Mafia mentor whether it is better to be loved or feared. The Mafioso unhesitatingly responds that he can do without the love, and that it is fear that maintains gang loyalty and neighborhood support. We can hear it now – our critics will take this example out of context and say that we're not only a bunch of bomb throwers and rabble rousers, but that we're mobbed up to boot!

Think about this analogy. Everyone has a basic human need to be liked – even the authors of this book. When people like us, then there is no ill will and tension when we walk into the room.

Unfortunately, the police union business is about making hard choices that inevitably will draw fury from someone – members, the media, public officials, and/or community leaders. If you can't overcome the desire to be liked, you will be more apt to make spineless choices that adversely affect the membership. Here are a few examples of when a police union leader can expect the Wrath of Khan:

- Members have paid no health insurance premiums for thirty years and you make what seems like a reasonable concession at the bargaining table for a $20 per month premium for families and modest changes in health care benefits;
- The Mayor runs on a campaign of improving the police department retention rate and then after the election offers a meager pay raise. The union runs a week-long radio spot asking the public whether the Mayor is just another typical politician who will say anything to get elected.
- The police union complains about gang and crime problems in the community and the City's lack of respect for officers at the bargaining table; and the police union makes noises about op-

posing a bond election to build a new art museum and other improvements to create a "world class city."

The authors are not the Stephen Kings of the police labor world – we can't invent fictional stories like these in our only moderately creative brains. The three examples above all occurred in cities in three different states in 2006–07; and there were unpleasant consequences for the police union leaders in each case. In the first example, the members became so enraged that they turned on the president and voted the contract proposal down. In the second, the Mayor and city's negotiator complained bitterly that the union wasn't "playing fair" and threatened to make an even worse offer. In the third case, the President of the Chamber of the Commerce, the Mayor, several city council members, the City Manager, and the Police Chief all contacted the union president – now that's a lot of management firepower, and told him to stop messing with the bonds, "or else."

Fortunately, each of these leaders understood that in spite of the condemnation and pressure aimed at them, they had to overcome their desire to be liked and do what was right for the membership. In all three instances, there was a positive outcome for the union – the parties went back to the bargaining table in the first example and negotiated a new agreement with no health care premium; the Mayor made a much better offer in the second round of negotiations that was accepted by the union; and in the last example, the City made a respectable proposal at the bargaining table and the bond opposition was quickly forgotten.

Let's end where we began this section with the reference to *A Bronx Tale.* Some police union leaders might be uncomfortable with the term "fear." If that word bothers you, here is an easier term for you to accept and one that is central to this book: **respect**. If your police union does not have the respect of the public officials who make all the decisions affecting your members, then it will be difficult to do business in a way that results in an outcome favorable to the union. Whether you call it fear or respect, in the end it is indeed better than being loved.

You are Not the CEO of a Fortune 500 Company

Unless you are the president of a major city police union, your organization might be fortunate enough to function with a small full or part-time staff, and hopefully on a good day, a few membership volunteers. The hard-charging, delegating style of leadership style that might be found in a Fortune 500 company will not succeed in the typical police union environment. If you want to sit in the corner window office overlooking the river, preside over meetings in the mahogany-paneled board room, and dictate memos all day to your executive assistant, then apply for the CEO position at Exxon, but don't run for president of the Salt Lake County Deputies Federation (our good friends at the Federation hopefully won't take offense at their comparison to Exxon).

In the typical police union, the president and other board members must roll up their sleeves and do the same work as the other members who have volunteered to assist on a particular project, whether it is putting up yard signs or block-walking for an endorsed candidate, circulating petitions for a staffing initiative, or showing up at a press conference in protest over the employer's latest contract proposal. This small and medium-sized police union world is one where a large part of leadership is setting an example. If you are not willing to show your commitment to a particular cause, why should any other member bother to care?

Create the Vision, Communicate the Vision

Many police union leaders become wrapped up in the day-to-day mechanical aspects of the work: handling a grievance, representing a member in an internal affairs interview, setting the agenda for the next membership meeting, writing checks to union vendors and so forth. This kind of leader becomes so preoccupied with these routine tasks that the broader consideration of where the union is headed never comes up for discussion.

What are some of the broader questions? Based on our current relationship with the employer, are we going to be a cooperative union, a confrontational one, or something in between? What is our strategic plan for the next three years; and based on this plan, what are our priorities and how do we go about achieving them? What is the union's relationship with our members; and if it's not a good one, how can we make things right? What major bargaining table issues can we foresee which might cause a conflict with the employer, or which might create a membership backlash if we make a concession? If we see a concession as inevitable, how do we prepare our members for it? These and other kinds of broad questions that move beyond the mundane daily work – those kinds of questions that the first President George Bush disparagingly called "that vision thing," must be asked.

If you don't ask them, your police union will never move beyond what Teddy Roosevelt once called "the grey twilight that knows neither victory nor defeat." Your union might be adequate, but it will never be exemplary, never a force to be reckoned with.

Once the leader has created a vision – the road map of where the union is headed, then the vision must be communicated. Your vision is not a national security secret: the members should understand what their union has in store for them. The employer should also know as well so that there are no surprises when the union takes a hard position against some decision that the employer has made.

No "Middle of the Road"

Jim Hightower was a colorful, liberal Texas politician in the 1970s and '80s. When liberalism went the way of the Tyrannosaurus Rex in the Lone Star State, he was voted out of office and became a successful political commentator and writer.

One of Hightower's famous observations was that "The only two things in the middle of the road are yellow stripes and dead armadillos." If you live anywhere outside the Southwest, then substitute your own local road kill for armadillos.

Hightower could have been talking to every police labor leader in the country when he coined this phrase. You must inevitably make tough choices. If you waffle, hedge your bets, or otherwise always take the path of least resistance because you don't want to make waves, then expect minimal return from your choices. On the other hand, if you quit straddling the fence – that is, you get over on one side of the road or the other and do what is best for your members, you will find more often than not that your decisions pay huge dividends for your organization.

Make the History of the Union Come Alive

One of the authors attended a police union meeting in 2007 where the City's controversial contract proposal was discussed. A retired officer who had been president when the union negotiated its first contract back in the mid-seventies came to the meeting and handed out that very first agreement and talked about how far the union had come in 30 plus years, and how much officers had to be thankful for where they stood today in terms of wages and benefits. The disinterest among the members was apparent and sad – they had no appreciation that this gentleman had been in the forefront of achieving bargaining rights for their union in the first place, negotiated the first and subsequent agreements, and served several terms as president over a twenty-year period.

This state of affairs should never be allowed to occur. Police officers who enter the service today have no idea about the pains, struggles, and sacrifices that the union leaders who came before them endured on behalf of the membership. The union must memorialize the history of the union; otherwise, your members today have no appreciation or context for the considerable benefits that they enjoy.

This observance can be done in many ways. "Myths" and "legends" should be created – a written and oral tradition of talking about those leaders who were larger than life. One police union created an annual membership award in recognition of the officer who drew the organization's logo and was shortly thereafter killed in the line of duty. Another union named an annual membership award in the name of a revered leader who died unexpectedly at an early age. The "old-timers" should be pulled out of mothballs from time-to-time to speak at union meetings, banquets or other events about famous controversies or confrontations that they were involved in.

Your website and/or publication should contain pieces about the union's past and leaders. Some unions have published excellent historical books about their organization. Others have used DVDs for highly sophisticated histories in movie or power point formats.

Developing the Next Generation of Leaders

There is a police union president who, for reasons immediately apparent will remain unnamed, has rigged his by-laws so that no one can run for president unless they have been a member of the union for 25 years. Now this fellow really wants to be president for a long time!

Since you undoubtedly have no intention of being President for Life, your tour of duty will be for a finite duration, somewhere on average in this business between two and six years. It should therefore be abundantly clear to you and the other leaders around you that the mantle of leadership must be handed off at some point. If you do not prepare now for this leadership transition, there will be a power vacuum when you, or maybe your successor, decides to call it a day.

As you work with members on campaigns or projects, always be looking for the next generation of officers who will lead the membership after you and others in the current generation of leaders have moved on. You should begin grooming these future leaders by giving them gradually increasing responsibilities so that they have an understanding of what the union is about.

You should in no way feel threatened by the younger generation – if they are eager to help, you should be eager to accept their help. Show them the way so that they will be able to lead as well as you have!

Some Concluding Observations About Leadership

Leadership of a police union is not for the faint of heart. There are hard choices that must be made every day; and there will be consequences for every one of those choices that affect you, your organization, your members, and relationships with elected officials and community leaders.

On those days when the pressure and stress seems to overwhelm you and members are nit-picking over every decision you have or have not made, take a step back and think about these two very important points. First, remember why you ran for union office in the first place – there were very good reasons that drove you to seek a leadership role. These same reasons should still motivate you today.

Second, no matter what you do, it will never be enough to satisfy every member. There will always be some whiner, naysayer or cynic who will attack your every move. Just remember that you still have a lot of friends among the membership who support you, and those who do not will still benefit from the right choices that you make.

Chapter 6

PROFICIENCY IN TECHNICAL SKILLS

Your management counterparts are normally well-versed in their various roles. City managers, mayors, and/or their aides have had training in how to deal with labor organizations. Human resources directors have spent time learning about personnel matters. Government attorneys know about labor and other personnel laws. Finance directors are skilled in public budgeting and accounting practices.

Unlike their management counterparts, leaders of many police unions don't have the luxury of specialization. You must be, to coin the old adage, "A jack of all trades and master of none." At a minimum, you should have a basic understanding of the following issues: fundamental local, state, and federal laws that affect your union and your members; building and effectively using power; negotiating and administering collective bargaining agreements; managing a labor organization; and internal organizing. This chapter will cover each of these issues.

Know the Law

There is a baseline of legal knowledge that every police labor leader must possess. Often, some of the items listed below might in some states be found in a local ordinance or charter provision; whereas in other jurisdictions found in a state law.

1. Local ordinances, including structure of the government, powers of government officials, budgetary authority, any provisions relevant to negotiations, and taxing authority.

2. Local charter provisions, particularly civil service requirements and how the charter may be amended.

3. State laws, including the collective bargaining statute, other labor law provisions (e.g., right to work law), minimum wage and benefit standards, open records and open meeting requirements, police officers bill of rights, occupational safety statutes, whistleblower laws, fair employment practices; and in a few instances, local initiatives and referendums.

4. Federal laws such as the Fair Labor Standards Act, the Family Medical Leave Act, the Equal Employment Opportunity Act, and if you are a federal law enforcement officers, then the Federal Labor-Management Relations Act.

5. Laws and court decisions related to officers' rights in disciplinary matters.

6. The law and court decisions related to the duty of fair representation.

While it is not essential that you know every word and nuance of every law, there must at the very least be an understanding of what these laws represent and where to find a relevant law and when the time comes, use it. The availability of competent counsel will allow any police union leader to consult on the fine points of any labor law question that might arise.

Understand How to Negotiate and Enforce a Contract

Many police labor leaders believe that the central purpose of the union is to negotiate and enforce the collective bargaining agreement. Sadly, this same view is perpetuated by many of the high profile trainers in our field. The authors disagree with this view – we believe that the sole purpose of the union is to build and use power to achieve organizational goals; and that the negotiations process will thereafter see a result more favorable to the union.

Having gotten that point off of our collective chests, the importance of having the technical skills to do the basic mechanical work of bargaining the contract and then insuring its proper administration must be given its proper due. You must understand the dynamics of how to get from the beginning to the end of the collective bargaining process without becoming lost along the way. You must also know what to do when a member comes to you with a potential violation of the contract; otherwise the substance and integrity of the agreement will be lost and even worse, there are potential liabilities to the union for failure to observe the duty of fair representation.

There are many organizations that conduct excellent negotiation and contract enforcement seminars. When you assume office, attendance at this kind of training should be on your to-do list.

Learn How to Move Your Union in the Right Direction by Building Power

Many police union leaders are under the impression that collective bargaining begins the day that the parties sit down on the first day of negotiations. Any leader who follows this course is doomed to failure.

The fact is that bargaining starts the same day as the ink dries on the last contract! If you don't begin preparations *immediately* by building power on behalf of your union, the organization will find itself standing on the figurative edge of the cliff. If you are a forward-thinking leader who plans well in advance for negotiations, your preparedness on this issue will pay off no matter what other problems face the union.

So how do you go about learning to build organizational power? Now we offer a crass and commercial plug: the first and most obvious place is to read this book! The authors would like to think their ideas are pretty unique and will be helpful in advising police union leaders on how to succeed.

If you want the Great Broadway Production of the ideas contained herein, you can also attend their annual seminar, normally in Las Vegas in September. Information about this program can be found at the following website: www.policeandfirelabor.com. You can also contact any one of the co-authors for advice, assistance, or training possibilities for your union leadership.

Learn How to Manage Your Organization

The police union leader's first day on the job can be a very overwhelming experience. You need to know, and most likely don't know, much about how to manage the organization. This knowledge requires a complex set of skills, such as tracking negotiations, contract grievances, and membership; interpersonal skills required to deal with elected officials, community leaders, and members; management of a non-profit organization, in particular financial management; writing and speaking skills to effectively communicate goals; and something so basic as how to conduct a board and membership meeting.

Many police union leaders have gotten tripped up by not understanding one or more of these essential elements of the job. There are many resources available that can teach a new labor leader about these skills: software tracking programs; and all sorts of training courses on organizational writing, speaking, non-profit management, and how to conduct a union meeting.

By far the best form of training though is mentorship. Assuming that you didn't beat the former union president in a knock-down, drag-out election, a great source of instruction is your predecessor. The former leader will have learned through some combination of the instructional methods cited above and from the School of Hard Knocks. This source of knowledge and experience will prove invaluable to the new leader, so don't be too proud to ask for help! And if you are the former president, be gracious with your time and information so that your successor has a better chance to succeed.

Don't Forget to Organize!

One of the themes that runs throughout this book is the importance of members and money, because when you have an abundance of both, the greater potential your union has to become powerful. While police and fire union membership tends to run at higher percentages than other public sector labor organizations, there are always the holdouts that absolutely refuse for any number of reasons – principle, financial, fear, or concern over future promotion opportunities, to join the union.

If your union is located in a right-to-work state, there will always be the obstinate officers who haven't joined for one reason or another; and in an agency shop state, the officers who will pay a fair share fee but not join the union. It is the leader's duty to constantly strive for one-hundred percent membership. The higher the percentage of members, the greater the perception will be of organizational unity.

There is a famous story of a police labor leader who was president of a large urban union in the Southwest in the eighties. As a part of building a powerful organization, he decided that his union would have one-hundred percent membership. He went to the non-union holdouts and asked them to join; all but a handful agreed to become members. He then went back to the handful that still had not joined and told them that if they didn't join, he was going to put their names on the front page of the magazine under the title "Freeloaders." This threat whittled the list down even further but one of the continuing holdouts told the president that he didn't have the guts (that wasn't the exact word the officer used, but this book does have a G rating so we must show some decency) to print his name on the cover. The next publication did have the few remaining non-union officers on the cover under the title "Freeloaders." The Freeloader list only appeared one time because by the time the next publication came out, the membership was at 100 percent!

The authors do not recommend that you try this tactic – it is a bit far past the edge of the envelope; and most leaders would be uncomfortable employing it. There is a much less threatening method of membership recruitment that is used in most national union organizing programs – the one-on-one internal campaign. Internal leaders are identified on each shift or in each work unit. These leaders are then given a list of the non-members, and also given a simple set of messages to use in talking to non-members about the importance of belonging to the union. The internal leaders then rate the non-members according to their likelihood of responding positively to a request to join. The internal leaders talk to each non-member one-on-one, starting with the easiest "sells" and moving later to the harder ones. This system works well and should be a part of any police union leader's game plan.

Chapter 7

MAP OUT WHERE THE UNION IS HEADED WITH A STRATEGIC PLAN

Our first book included a chapter on strategic planning inspired by Boston University professor David Weil. Doctor Weil developed an excellent template of questions that every union leadership should periodically ask if it wants to stay ahead of the game. These questions focus on the environment – the union's political and community strength; organizational priorities; the union's resources, in particular finances that become especially significant if there is a contract fight brewing; and organizational structures such as governance and communications. A template of strategic planning questions appears in Appendix 2.

Strategic Planning Really Does Work

When we wrote our first book, the chapter on strategic planning was thrown in as an afterthought because "strategic plans" were a trendy thing ten years ago. Today, we can say with conviction that the template of questions really does work and has been used by police unions as a tremendous form of self-analysis and pathway to improved business methods. Some of the groups that the authors have worked with in recent years include the San Antonio Police Officers Associations, El Paso Municipal Police Officers Association, West Virginia Troopers Association, Tucson Police Officers Association, Henderson (NV) Police Officers Association, and Rio Rancho (NM) Department of Public Safety Association.

There was a commonality to the initial analyses that these unions made in their respective strategic planning sessions. Relationships with community organizations and leaders were generally seen as limited and weak, a problem that faces most police unions (see Chapter 11 for more on this subject). That universal bane of the police labor movement – membership participation, was seen as a big issue among the leaders of these groups as well (see Chapter 10). In all of these organizations, the leadership took some steps to correct identified problems, some with more success than others.

Do's and Don'ts of a Strategic Planning Session

When your union leaderships agrees to establish a strategic plan, some initial thought and preparation can make the final outcome more beneficial than if a meeting is simply slapped together at the last minute. Here are some suggestions that will make for a more productive strategic planning session:

- Depending on the structure of your union, the size of the group should be small, either the Executive Board in a larger organization or Board of Directors in a smaller one.
- Make the meeting a special event and not a part of some other regularly called meeting (or backed up to another meeting); otherwise, the importance of the exercise will be lost.
- Depending on the amount of participation and serious dialogue, the exercise can take as little as 3 hours and as long as 8 hours. Arrange a location that will provide a comfortable setting that is away from the hustle and bustle of the union office so that participants can reflect without interference.
- Insist that all electronic gadgetry – cell phones, Blackberries, e-mail usage, and other similar toys, are checked at the door and not used during the session.
- Designate a good notetaker who will compile a record of the session and complete a written synopsis that will be used to track the future progress of the plan.
- Assign specific tasks and responsibility as each point is discussed. For example, if the participants agree that the union's two messages for the next year will be that crime has become a serious threat to the community and staffing levels are dangerously low, then someone should be assigned to gather back-up

statistical data on crime rates, response times, population growth, national and local area agency staffing comparisons, and other relevant information that can be used in support of those messages. A timeline should be set for completion of the assignment.

There's No Point to a Strategic Plan If There's No Follow-Through

When union board members meet to establish a strategic plan, there is a great deal of creativity that can come out of such a meeting. For example, the leadership can decide that each Board member is going to join a key community civic organization; the Political Action Committee contributions are going to be doubled; and this year's priorities are going to be improvement of the legal representation plan, the purchase of property on which to start construction of a building; and hiring an editor for the newsletter.

These priorities are all commendable, but just remember the old adage that "the road to hell is paved with good intentions." It is very easy for the leadership to talk about all the great things they are going to do; but talk is cheap. It is altogether a different story when leaders have to go out and actually try to accomplish these goals.

Once a plan is set out by the leadership, it is vital that there is follow-through – periodic meetings where leaders discuss what specifically has been done to achieve the strategic planning goals. It will be clear very quickly after a few of these meetings whether the leadership is truly committed to the goals, or instead, has just been engaged in all talk and no action.

Chapter 8

MONEY: THE ROOT OF ALL POWER AND A LOT OF BAD STUFF THAT CAN HAPPEN, TOO

The need for money in the union coffers should at this point be self-evident to even the most novice police labor leader. The people sitting across the bargaining table include hired gun management negotiators, insurance and pension consultants, people skilled in the art of financial misdirection, and so on, all being supported by your tax dollars hard at work. So if you don't have some comparable fire-power on your side of the table, you are at the very least at a perceived, if not actual, disadvantage.

That is why your union needs the money to hire sharp labor and administrative law attorneys, occasionally a criminal attorney for job-related criminal matters, insurance/pension consultants, and financial actuaries. For example, when management tells you during negotiations that health insurance costs are way out of control, it is helpful to have an expert who can delve into the budget and point to how the employer overestimates health insurance costs every year by more than $2 million and uses the overage as a kind of mini-contingency fund.

Setting the Right Dues Structure

So many times over the years the authors have heard labor leaders complain that police officers are just a bunch of "cheap bastards." This perception of stingy cops is aggravated by the highly competitive nature of the police labor world, where so many organizations are boasting about how they can do so much more for members for a whole lot less.

The fact is that police union members will pay reasonable dues if they have confidence that the leadership is going to do what is in the best interests of the membership; that is, that they are being well represented in contract negotiations and enforcement matters, and whenever they are in a jam that might result in termination or worse, a job-related criminal indictment. Stop worrying about whether your members are a bunch of penny pinchers and whether the "Brand X" union is going to raid you because dues have been raised five bucks a month. If you are doing your job well – hopefully following the principles in this book, then your members should feel comfortable paying the going rate.

So what is the going rate, you ask? That is a tough question to answer and is relative to many factors such as local area costs, what "Brand X" is charging (we said not worry, but it is still a factor), the last time dues were raised, and the amount of money left over for contingencies (no union should budget to the penny and spend every dime budgeted).

More police unions are moving away from the flat rate (e.g., $30 per month), and using a percentage dues structure tied to a classification pay grade. For example, dues could be set at one percent (or higher) of a top step police officer's base wage rate. The advantage to this system is that union dues will increase every time wages increase, and hopefully members will see the correlation between their wage increases and the union's efforts in contract negotiations.

The Worse, Worser, and Worst Persons in the World

MSNBC commentator Keith Olberman's nightly *Countdown* show has a segment called the "Worst Person in the World." He starts out with the worse person, then goes to the worser person (that word gets flagged by Spell Check every time!), and then the worst person in the world – all three are public figures who have done some heinous thing or failed to do what they should have done.

We have our own examples of these "worse, worser, and worst" people in the police labor world – those leaders who steal union funds and achieve immediate induction into the Police Union Hall of Shame. Thankfully these crimes don't come along very often, but still more often than they should; and when they occur, a dark shadow falls over the organization.

The type of union leadership criminality varies. It can be an authorized check signer writing a union check to himself or herself, to a family member, a friend or a vendor for a personal purchase. Abuse of the union credit card sometimes occurs. Fraudulent expense reimbursement requests are sometimes made as well. A more insidious and difficult to trace crime is a kickback arrangement between a union official and vendor such as an attorney or fund raiser. If no one is paying attention, any of these schemes might continue for long periods of time.

When these types of misdeeds are exposed, the consequences to the union can be devastating. Members lose faith in the leadership; the union's public image becomes tarnished; it becomes more difficult to achieve the union's goals; and sadly, a close friend and co-worker faces possible incarceration.

Putting Accountability Into the Union's Financial Procedures

The best way to insure that someone is always paying attention is to establish a system of accountability. Accountability is important because union members have entrusted the leadership to spend their dues money prudently and for their interests. So long as there are strong checks and balances in place, the temptation for those few bad apples that might be susceptible to mismanagement of funds, fraudulent expense reporting or stealing is reduced.

Here are some suggestions for police union financial accountability procedures:

- An annual budget should be established, with a monthly tracking system that analyzes year-to-date expenditures with what has been budgeted. The status of the budget should be discussed at every Executive Board meeting. This function can be delegated to a committee or sub-group of the board, especially if this group is actively involved in the administration of the union's financial affairs.
- It is important to segregate the financial duties of the union as much as possible. In a large police union, the financial duties of the union should be segregated due to the high volume of business, significant money flow, and staff involved. One person

should make deposits of dues money; another person should authorize payments; another person should issue checks based on that authorization; and then an independent party such as a CPA or union Finance Committee should monthly reconcile the bank and financial statements to confirm deposits and dues that should have been paid, and also to review checks that have been written.

- In a medium-size or small police union, this kind of segregation can still be achieved. For example, the union Secretary could make deposits, the President could authorize payments, and the Treasurer could issue checks based on that authorization. The Finance Committee could then conduct a monthly audit of all transactions.

- Ideally, the union would have an annual audit by an independent Certified Public Accountant (CPA) or accounting firm. Since an annual audit is only as good as the information provided to the auditor, the monthly reviews of all transactions are still the best control over the financial system. Audited financial statement can be used by the union to negotiate better lending rates with financial institutions. The interaction between the auditors and union officials can be used to help the union identify and implement changes in the organization to strengthen its checks and balances and improve internal accountability. These professionals will also help the union anticipate and address tax compliance issues.

- Union credit cards should be carefully monitored every month. The union should establish a written policy for credit card usage that covers travel usage and purchase of consumer goods. The union policies should outline and define the essential elements of reporting that meets IRS guidelines. Careful attention must be paid to whether purchases on the credit card were authorized and consistent with the written policy. As a part of the monthly review, the CPA or Finance Committee should examine all credit card usage. For example, if three cases of beer were authorized for the annual union picnic, six cases were purchased, and only three showed up at the picnic, someone has a lot of explaining to do.

Shining a Light on Vendor Transactions

As mentioned previously, collusive arrangements between vendors and union officials are the most difficult to uncover. For example, a union president might suggest to his Executive Board that the monthly newsletter be printed by the XYZ Printing Company at a cost of $1,000 per monthly issue. The president and owner of XYZ are good friends and also agree, without knowledge of the Executive Board, that after each month's newsletter job, the printer will give the president a "consultant fee" or other euphemistic rationalization of $250 for the right to do business. This arrangement is clearly unethical; under certain circumstances is illegal; and it should not be condoned in any fashion.

Even when someone is paying attention, these kinds of schemes are difficult to unmask. Here are some suggestions for dealing with this issue:

- On general vendor relationships such as printers, office supplies, vehicle sales, and website maintenance, the union should request bids for the work. The Finance Committee or other independent group should review the bids and make a decision based on cost and reputation for efficient service. If there are specific requirements or preferences for doing business with the union, those criteria should be outlined and agreed upon by the group prior to contacting vendors or taking bids. For example, the union or board might want to give preference to union or minority providers. If the prevailing criterion is price alone, then it is important to agree to that priority from the start. It is burdensome to evaluate each business relationship annually, but a rotation system should be established for evaluating vendor, banking and supplier relationships. In this way, every year some relationships are evaluated or reviewed, and over the course of time, the major business relationships would be reviewed.
- More specialized vendor relationships such as attorneys are trickier. There are usually only a few attorneys in most communities who specialize in police and/or labor relations matters. Bids are hardly relevant here; only an attorney's results matter, whether real or perceived. Some things to look for in this situation are whether the cost of doing business is in line with what other attorneys in the area are charging; and whether someone

on the Board seems overeager to maintain the relationship with the attorney. If there are red flags, the choices are difficult – turning the matter over to authorities or the state bar association can give the union a black eye among members and the community. Sometimes though, leaders have to do the right thing to insure the union's financial integrity.

• For all vendor relationships, the Executive Board or any other Board member involved in contractual approvals should be required to reveal any family or friends that are vendors; and should also be required to submit an affidavit to the union stating that he or she has no financial interests with any union vendors. While a person who is inclined to take a kickback is also likely to lie on an affidavit, it might make the person think twice about the improper behavior. It is not necessarily bad business to bring a personal vendor relationship to the organization if the vendor provides a good, reasonably priced service. However, all parties – board member and vendor, need to publicly acknowledge and define the relationship that exists.

One Final Word on Money: Get Out of the Solicitation Business

In our last book, telephone solicitations used to raise money for the police union were described as "the crack cocaine of the police labor movement." This admonition is even more compelling today than ten years ago.

State and local officials carefully scrutinize police union fund-raising practices. High-pressure sales tactics, fraudulent pitches by solicitors, and meager returns to the union (i.e.; the solicitor gets most of the money) are frequently exposed and bring adverse publicity and a black eye to the police union.

Other than solicitations for a very limited, specific purpose – such as a Shop-With-A-Cop program (see Chapter 12 on image building), police unions would be well served to get out of the solicitation addiction. The only winner in this set-up is the solicitor.

Police union operations should be supported by dues only, because dues are a guaranteed, certain amount of money. The loss of solicitation money should be replaced by a dues increase; and if explained correctly to members, they will normally understand.

Chapter 9

EFFECTIVE POLICE UNION COMMUNICATIONS

In the subsequent chapter on membership, we discuss the high degree of member apathy and disinterest at length. Members don't come to meetings, they don't volunteer for union projects, and they just don't want to get involved. Even on a good day, police officers are a tough crowd to communicate with. That is why it is so important to understand what you should say to members (and as discussed below, politicians and the community) and how to deliver the information. If members aren't getting the information, disconnect between union and member becomes even worse.

When our first book was completed in 1996 and published in 1997, the Internet was just coming into its own as a driving force in American business. Our focus was solely on hard-copy publications, because, except for membership meetings where three members would show up, that was the best means of communications at the time. Today, member-to-leader and member-to-member communication can be achieved in much more sophisticated systems such as e-mails, web sites, and blogs.

Even though the methods of communication have been radically transformed, the principles of communication remain unchanged. We will first review these important principles before looking at the new processes for transmitting the police union's messages. When the term "communication" is used hereafter in this chapter, it refers to every form of contact between police union leadership and members, and to some extent with management officials and the public. These forms of communication include meetings, letters, periodic publications, e-mails, list serve mail, websites, blogs, and forums, which are on-line discussion groups where participants with common interests can exchange open messages.

Overcoming the Union's Communications Culture

There are many suggestions in this chapter that are contrary to how many police unions communicate internally and externally. Picture this scenario: the new editor of the police union newspaper has just read this chapter, thinks the authors are the Shakespeares of the police labor movements (if that were only true) and decides to make whole-sale changes in the publication's format. So the editor axes many of the columns that have appeared in the union newspaper for the last 25 years: the retirees' column; the spouses' club column; the annual bowling, fishing, hunting, and football tournaments; the committee reports; and so on. In fact, the deletions are so great that there is no longer any need for a 50-page paper, but instead, an 8-page newsletter that contains just the points recommended in this chapter.

Can you picture the outcome? The Tar and Feather Committee will be out in full force, ready to run the editor out of town on the first rail: the retirees, spouses, bowlers, fishermen, football players, and every other member who has seen his or her ox gored will be a part of the lynching party.

The point is that police unions are relatively conservative institutions where change often occurs at a snail's pace. When the union has a communications culture that has operated in the same way for a long period of time, change must occur incrementally, through leadership and membership consensus. Any effort to make communications changes swiftly and radically will likely result in no change at all.

The Three Purposes of Police Union Communications

The first and foremost purpose of your communications system is to "sell" the union internally among your members. The union is in the business of providing labor, legal, and in some instances legislative services, and its "customers" are its members. As in any customer-service business, in particular one as competitive as the police union world, there should be frequent reminders to the members that the union is protecting their interests and that their choice to pay dues to the union is a wise investment.

The second purpose of your communications is to discuss the messages and priorities that your union is focusing on; and to get this word out not only to your members, but to the outside world as well. For example, let's say that your primary message for the next year is that the City must make public safety its main concern due to population and crime increases; and in an effort to deal with these problems, the union's priorities are to work on increased staffing and increased wages for better recruitment and retention of officers. All of your communications should refer to this message and priorities in one form or another.

When this message is communicated, you are talking not only to members – you also want for the public officials, community leaders, and organizations to "eavesdrop" on this conversation. When you allow the outside world to listen in on your message, it is an excellent way to educate people not familiar with the law enforcement world. It is an effective way to make people in the community sympathetic to your cause.

Some police labor leaders disagree with this tactic because they fear that your potential management adversaries will discover what the union is up to. But if you believe that almost every union communication won't wind up in the hands of a management, the authors have some prime beach front property in beautiful Yuma, Arizona that we would very much like to sell you at a premium price. Someone is usually going to tattle on your communications, so you may as well craft them in a format that puts the best spin on the issues of importance to the union.

The third purpose of communications is to build the union's image as a positive force in the community. Chapter 12 will explore image-building in greater detail. At this point, just remember that any union image-building program should be included in the union's communications arsenal.

The Topics That Should Be Included in Union Communications

There are certain elements that should absolutely be included in a union communication – each individual topic does not necessarily have to be in every communication, but these themes should find their way frequently into the union dialogue.

We have already discussed the importance of including your messages and priorities. The more your communications touch on message and priorities, the more understanding your members have about the union's direction. The greater extent that these matters are broadcast to the outside world, the greater the knowledge elected officials, administrators, and the public will have about your organization.

The other important points for inclusion in union communications bear repeating from our first book:

- **Organizational success.** If the union has done something remarkable, like negotiate a dynamite contract, win a grievance arbitration, or beat back an attempt to impose civilian review, make sure to blow your horn because no one else will!
- **We're politically involved.** As you will learn in a later chapter, the union's political program is at the heart of building and using power. Some of the points that might be covered are solicitation of PAC contributions; the union's process for endorsements; the union's endorsements and how members can help in a political campaign; endorsement victories; the correlation between the union endorsement and achievement, such as a good contract; or the spin on a losing endorsement ("Our candidate lost, but we met with the winner the day after the election and we are his new near and dear friend").
- **The "thin blue line."** There should be constant reminders about the dangers of police work and the effect it has on the families of officers. Stories about an officer's death or serious injury, as sad or grisly as that might be, will show the perils facing officers every day. Human interest stories about the stress and fear that family members face are also effective – the authors have found that the use of spouses and children of officers has a dramatic impact on the public's perceptions about the job.
- **We care about you.** Chapter 12 discusses image building; and your communications must be part of that effort. When the union holds its annual Shop-With-a Cop or other community feel-good event, it should be covered in depth. Every opportunity the union has to build up its reserve of positive community feelings toward your organization will come in handy whenever there is a confrontation that will inevitably result in negative backlash against the union.

• **The issue of the day.** There is always an "issue of the day:" the Chief changes the secondary employment policy from 20 to 15 allowable hours per week; the City wants to increase health care premiums and reduce benefits; community activists demand a police review board; the civic center administrator wants to reduce the overtime rate for officers working public events; . . . the list of issues facing the union are infinite. You must be on top of any issue, analyzing the effect on your members, taking a position, and communicating with members and the public. Your position is important and must always be heard!

Things You Should Not Do and Things You Should Not Say

Sadly, many police unions continue to communicate in ways that detract from their message, priorities and other essential matters discussed in the preceding section. If your union's communications contain any of the following blunders, you should re-think your communications strategy.

• **Too much clutter equals too little understanding.** The police union editor's nightmare of an overstuffed publication was discussed in a previous section. It is baffling how some of the largest urban police unions in this country spend so much time in their publications on irrelevant trivia: sports tournaments, bowling tournaments (sorry bowlers, the authors don't accept this activity as a sport), deer hunting (our apologies in particular to West Virginia police officers), movie reviews, the Police Spouses Club, *ad nauseum.* It is really difficult to extract the message and other indications of what the union is about when all of this extraneous information is thrown at the reader. Remember: the police union is not a social club – it is an organization whose sole purpose is to help its members achieve better benefits and working conditions. How does last month's article about the police union fishing tournament further this purpose? It is also important to remember that police union members are overloaded daily with information and messages from the media – advertising, news, editorials; and other places such as billboards, junk mail, and car leaflets. You must figure out how to break through all of this information clutter so that the union message is heard first and foremost.

- **Opinions about world events.** An editorial by the union president about why the United States should stay in Iraq so we can fight the War on Terror over there rather than on the shores of West Palm Beach might warm the hearts of some members and Bill O'Reilly, but what does it have to do with the priorities of the union? Remember that the union publication should be discussing issues that affect union members as workers and not personal concerns such as war, school prayer, gays in the military or abortion. So keep the focus on the union and away from personal viewpoints unconnected to labor issues.

- **Don't be a "raging bull."** A few police labor leaders continue to believe that the interests of the union are best served by continually lashing out at some real or imagined foe. They constantly and venomously attack the Chief, the Mayor, the City Manager, or the editor of the newspaper. Like Don Quixote chasing windmills, these leaders hammer away, day-in and day-out, not giving a thought to how their vicious attacks are perceived. There is nothing wrong with picking a fight when warranted; in fact, this book is filled with examples of giving some out-of-line public official a deserved whipping. However, your union cannot stand up to being on a war footing all the time – the members become worn out and tune you out; public officials and the public perceives the union leadership as a bunch of whiners and crybabies.

- **If you want a democratic communications strategy, go to work for the *New York Times*.** One of the authors was in the middle of negotiations in a Southwestern urban city in the early 2000s when a Letter to the Editor appeared in the police union magazine attacking the president and vice-president for certain actions taken they had taken. After EMS had been called to revive the distraught negotiator, he asked the editor why the letter had appeared, since the magazine was sent to the Mayor, Council members, and community leaders; and it gave the appearance of membership disunity. When the editor explained that the union magazine was run on a democratic basis and that any member could write in and get things off their chest, the negotiator became so overwhelmed that he was admitted to the Nervous Hospital for a brief rest but fortunately discharged very soon thereafter to continue, at least in the opinion of his most immediate family, a modestly distinguished career. The point is that any union communication will wind up in the hands of people who are not always your friends; and negative information will create the perception that the union is weak and disunited. The idea of controlled communications does not in any way imply that the union should be governed like totalitarian state – if a member has a complaint, he or she can always come to a Board or membership meeting and state their opinion and seek resolution of the complaint. Remember that communications are the place where the union puts its best foot forward, making the case that it is a player with a seat at the table with the other community power brokers.

• **First impressions are important, so dress for success.** Rightly or wrongly, many people judge others by outward appearance – how they are dressed at the initial meeting. The same thing is true of the union's communications. This chapter has already covered substance – the kinds of material that should be included in your communications. Your work product must also look good as well: the publication must be well laid put; every communication from the union office checked and doubled checked for spelling and grammatical errors; the web site must be user-friendly, understandable, and maintained with frequency. When the outward appearance is polished, the substance becomes even more impressive.

Get Ahead of the Curve and Join the 21st Century Internet Revolution – A Little Bit About E-mail Addresses

Two of the authors' childhoods were spent first listening to the radio and such shows as *The Shadow, Fibber McGee*, and *Amos and Andy*; and then later enjoying the luxury of television with exciting selections from only three stations such as *The Spike Jones Show, Lassie*, and that explosive hit *The Lawrence Welk Show*, featuring world renown accordionist Myron Florin and the lovely Lennon Sisters. Imagine the wonder of it all!

Given this context, there is no way that we could have envisioned the Internet revolution that was just underway as we completed our first book. Even the youngest of the authors – and that is a relative term in this crowd, could not have envisioned the impact the Internet would have on police union communications.

One of the frequent grumblings heard among police union members is that "We never know what is going on." One of the complaints voiced by union leaders is that "we have trouble effectively communicating with members." With the advent of the Internet, leaders and members should no longer have an excuse about communication.

It is baffling that almost every police union has all the members' home mailing addresses but very few have their personal e-mail addresses. Almost everyone in the work force today has a personal and/or business e-mail address.

Think about this scenario: You are in a heated fight with the City over the contract that has some controversial issues on the table such as the reduction of health care premiums and benefits and a City offer of a one-time cash bonus and no other waged increase. As in any difficult negotiation, rumors are flying all over the department about what the union is, or is not, doing. Up-to-date information is vital to keep members from making inaccurate suppositions about what is taking place. **With the stroke of one computer key**, you can send an e-mail letter to every member on a list-serve that tells them that the union absolutely will not accept a one-time bonus, and will accept only minor concessions on health care; otherwise the parties will be at impasse and go to arbitration, use a public campaign, or whatever the union impasse strategy may be. Facts are dispensed – rumors are squashed. How simple is that?

So let's go back to the point about getting personal e-mail addresses. In smaller agencies, this goal should not be a problem. In medium-size and large agencies, it is more difficult due to the numbers involved.

How do you go about getting these addresses? The most obvious place is to pluck the apple before it falls from the tree – the training academy. Many unions today have the right either by contract or administrative policy to speak to recruits in the academy about the union and to enroll them in the organization. Make sure to update the union application form to include an e-mail address. Being the obsessive-compulsives that we are, the obvious also needs to be stated: enter these addresses into your office data base.

To obtain e-mail addresses from veteran officers, some police unions have used a drawing with a nice prize such as a Glock or getaway weekend trip for two to a resort or other enticing location. The price for entering the contest is submission of the member's personal e-mail address. This tactic has met with checkered success.

In an effort to avoid all the hard work of obtaining personal e-mail addresses, some police unions have negotiated into their agreements the right to use the city or police department e-mail with messages sent by the union from inside the same system. This idea has limited merit because the public employer will want place the same restrictions on e-mail usage as exist for department bulletin board postings such as nothing political and nothing adverse about the City or its representatives.

Here is another idea worth exploring. In many states, public employee e-mail addresses, including police officers, are open records. Citizens will often send e-mails to employees for a variety of reasons. So if police officers e-mail addresses are open and anyone can communicate with officers from an external e-mail system, then nothing should preclude the union president from doing the same thing from his or her personal e-mail account.

Before you jump with joy and think that all your e-mail communications are solved and the hard work of obtaining addresses has been avoided, here are some serious caveats. Check with your union attorney to determine whether the public e-mail addresses of police officers in your City are open records. If they are, then run the idea up the flagpole as the old saying goes, by notifying the Police Chief and/or City Manager of your intention, and asking that you be notified if there is any legal impediment to this course of action. You will have covered your backside in case a ruckus is raised later by the Powers-That-Be. Also, some servers can block incoming e-mails, so in these cities your efforts might be for naught.

More Getting Ahead of the Curve – Creative Communications

The Internet Highway offers so many new ways to touch your members. Your newsletter or newspaper can now be published and posted on line – if the *New York Times* can do it, so can your union. If you now have all your members' e-mail addresses as discussed above, and want to insure a higher probability that members actually read the publication, send it by e-mail. The same programs that are used to lay out a union newsletter or paper can be used for the e-mail publication. These programs include *Adobe PageMaker*, *Adobe InDesign*, and the *Microsoft Publisher*, which is easy to use and often comes bundled with the Microsoft Office Suite. The economics of this change in publication methods make sense as well – the days of taking your publication to a printer and mail house are over for good!

Many police unions now have web sites, mainly used as a way to discuss recent activities and upcoming events, and post-collective bargaining agreements and other relevant documents. This first step should be done at a minimum, but there are so many other creative uses of the web site that will benefit the union and its members. Consider these ideas.

Discussion Forums

Many organizations outside of the police labor world now establish "discussion forums," where a topic is posted on the web site and members are encouraged to discuss it on-line. This method should be distinguished from web site "chat rooms," where a continuous stream of conversation takes place – chat rooms allow too much room for rambling and unfocused discussion as opposed to getting members to look at an important issue. Discussion forums get members involved and thinking about the organization and offering their views, some of which might be worth incorporating into a project or plan.

Here is an application to police unions: the union is negotiating a new contract and the City has proposed an increase in the health care deductibles and co-pays, and an increase in premiums by $100 per month. The union might post a topic on the website seeking members' opinions about his proposal. Beyond the fact that no member will like this proposal, there will at least be some developing view of what the members might be willing to accept and what they find objectionable.

There are some serious warnings about discussion forums. The first is that the union has to monitor the discussion and a union official should respond where necessary. When this idea was proposed by one of the authors to a major urban police union president, the leader's response was that no one on the Board has the time to monitor this activity. When it was called to his attention that his entire Board had spent an excessive amount of time over the past year monitoring the website of a rival union that was taking potshots at his organization, he at least conceded that it might be an idea worth pursuing.

Another caution is that there must be firm rules for any member participating in the discussion forum. Every member must identify himself or herself – if any member isn't willing to associate his or her name with a particular point of view, then it should not be a view worth considering. Any discussion must be respectful and avoid foul language – these limitations might seem a little odd in a world of high testosterone workers, but if civility isn't enforced, then mayhem will follow.

Web site "Meetings" With Union Officials

Here is a terrific idea. Once a week, month, or whatever time period suits your union's culture, notify your members (once again, accessibility to every member's e-mail address is significant) that on a given day and time, the union president, Executive Board member, grievance representative, attorney, insurance consultant, or other union representative will be available on a web site to discuss unions affairs, legal or insurance matters, or whatever the representative's area of expertise is.

This mechanism allows direct interaction and real-time "chat" through a written dialogue between members and union representatives. Members can have their questions and concerns answered. Union officials can identify areas where the union is deficient or whether membership needs are being met.

This idea can be especially helpful to a police union leader, who can post in an issue of his or her choice for discussion on a given day and time. Members can be encouraged to engage in the discussion by making comments, asking questions, or offering solutions to issues. This idea will allow the leader to build a relationship with members and also manage time by keeping the conversation within a specific time frame.

While this idea has considerable potential, you can't just set it up and expect members to show up for the event. The union must publicize the new system of communication between members and the leadership, show the benefits of the system, and generate enthusiasm that will result in members wanting to participate.

The union must also make it easy for members to join in the program. They must be given explicit and easy instructions on how to create an account, and how to post their own comments.

Another important point is that these written dialogues should be archived for future reference. A considerable amount of knowledge will be generated from these discussions and should be available for future leaders to read and learn from.

Live Webcam Membership Meetings

Some private sector unions have taken the Internet Revolution to a whole new level by conducting live webcam membership meetings. The Communications Workers of America has used this device to great effect for membership meetings in the context of national organizing campaigns.

This same concept could be used by any local police union for its monthly Board or membership meeting. The meeting would be held at its regular location, with the picture showing the leadership seated at its usual head table. Any members who attend would participate as usual but members unable to attend could call or write in if they have questions or concerns; and the leadership could respond on the spot. This arrangement extends the reach of members who can become involved in your meetings.

Blogs

One of the fashionable Internet systems now in use is the blog. A blog can be an individual's personal diary or thoughts; or it can be a place where persons with similar interests can go to share ideas. One envisioned use of a blog would be for the union President and other Executive or Board members to use it as a form of diary or communication, outlining issues and leadership concerns on a periodic basis that will allow personal interaction with other members. It is too early in the development of this concept to visualize whether it has other effective application to the police labor world.

The concepts discussed in this preceding section – discussion forums, web site meetings, webcam membership meetings, and blogs are all cutting edge in the police labor world. Some caveats are in order. Each of these ideas requires specialized software, knowledgeable leaders to operate the system, and members willing to use it. Special care should be given to which of these systems will work best for your union and how to implement them with the fewest glitches possible – technical help will likely be needed.

These Are All Great Ideas but Who is Going to Do the Work?

The good news is that this chapter has offered many ideas that your union can incorporate into its communications strategy. The bad news is that someone actually has to do the work.

Someone has to write and edit the publication. Someone has to monitor the discussion forums. And someone has to participate in the web site "meetings" and "chats." Internal and external communications are vital to the success of the union – you can't be a player unless you can get your message out to members and the outside world.

You have two choices. First, try to find a person or persons inside the union – there is always a computer geek among all those gun-carrying members, who will make a serious commitment to get the work done. If there is no one inside to do the work, then farm it out and pay an outsider – the result will definitely be worth the cost.

Chapter 10

MOBILIZING THE MEMBERSHIP

Reader alert! Reader alert! This chapter contains a false and misleading title that could get the authors into grievous hot water with the Truth-in-Advertising Police. A "mobilized police union membership" – now that's an oxymoron if there ever was one.

"Membership mobilization" is a hot buzzword among private sector labor unions. Whenever a labor-management conflict exists, these unions will attempt to generate membership excitement and unity over the issue at hand. This process can include such activities as wearing unity pins, hats, and/or shirts; demonstrations; carrying placards; telephone banks; and unity or block walks. In the private sector, membership mobilization does sometimes work; in the police labor world, it is more often than not a futile exercise.

When was the last time that more than 5 percent of your union membership turned out for an event such as a demonstration, informational picket, block walk or activity to the further the interests of the union and more important, **their** interests? Unless economic and working conditions have become so horrific, 10 percent of the work force is about to be laid off, or the City is about to raise health care premiums by 100 percent, membership apathy is overwhelming. The authors are unanimous in their belief that membership disinterest is the singularly most difficult problem facing police union leaders; and that solutions are difficult to achieve even on a good day.

Are you feeling a little depressed and ready to move on to the next chapter? Before you do, let's dig the hole even a little deeper.

Some Observations about the Members You Are Leading

Before a discussion begins about mobilizing your members, it would first be helpful to understand something about who you are mobilizing. Let's look at the average police union member and what this profile means in terms of your decisions to mobilize them.

While we leave ourselves open to criticism of blatant stereotyping, here is our take based on a combined 110+ years of police union experience on what a 35-year-old, 10-year police officer and union member might look like. If you have been reading this book carefully, you will have noticed that we have diligently strived to avoid any charges of sexism by keeping references to officers and/or members neutral in terms of gender. At the risk of drawing the ire of the Political Correctness Enforcement Squad, our average police union member will be a male for reasons that become immediately apparent.

He is on his second marriage, has two children by this marriage, has two kids by his first wife, and pays $1,200 per month in child support. He works twenty hours per week on an extra job to supplement his police salary and his wife's job. There is a house mortgage, car note, truck note and fifth wheel camper note, piano lessons and Brownies for the daughter, football and Scouts for the son, and all the other costs associated with a middle-class lifestyle. Quality time with the two children from the first marriage must be spent on alternate weekends. There is yard work, home maintenance, maybe an occasional golf or beer outing with co-workers, and Wednesday and Sunday church services. Mom and Dad and the in-laws both live nearby and demand constant attention. You can't own a fifth wheel without occasional three-day weekends to the nearest state park. There is constant tension with the wife about how ends are going to be met; and when the two of us are going to get away from this Rat Race for a little time to ourselves.

He thinks the job totally sucks. The Chief is a chicken____. The City doesn't understand police officers and is out to screw him at every turn. The public hates cops and citizens will do anything to see him lose his badge. He is already counting the years, months, days, hours, and minutes when his twenty years is over and done with.

He is apathetic about the union basically because, with the life we just described above, and the sour, life-stinks outlook, who has time to think about the union, or wants to help the union? So he never comes to a union meeting except when contract time rolls around; then he will sit in the front row of the meeting and yell at the negotiating committee about what a lousy job they did. But when the leadership asks him if he'd be willing to donate his time to block walk in order to talk to citizens about the need for a better pay raise, he will say that it's a bad idea, or he just doesn't have the time. When the union attacks the Police Chief, he writes a letter to the newspaper saying that the union doesn't speak for him.

He has Republican political values: his values are "law and order," pro-life, pro-school prayer, anti-gun control and anti-gay marriage; and believes that union political endorsements should have something to do with these issues. He thinks that when Sean Hannity, Ann Coulter, and Bill O'Reilly die, they will sit at the right hand of God. So when the union endorses a liberal candidate for a key City Council race, his reaction is apoplectic rage. The union is out of touch with the membership, he says; or the union leadership shouldn't be allowed to endorse candidate without a vote of the entire membership. Even if he supports the union endorsement, he might not be registered to vote; and even if he is, won't bother to show up on Election Day to cast a ballot.

Do you recognize this fellow? This profile of a typical police union member is grim and might dishearten even the most glass-half-full kind of leader. As a matter of fact, the person who invents the formula for handling this tough crowd and actually getting them involved with the union will get an immediate waiver on the 5-year waiting period for induction into the Police Union Hall of Fame. But do not despair – following are some ideas for how to tackle this problem so deeply rooted in the police labor movement.

Dues versus Bodies

When most police officers enroll as members of the union, their motivation for this decision is pretty basic self interest – they want an organization that will secure them consistent pay raises and benefits; fight for a safe and fair workplace; and when the administration levels a severe disciplinary action or the district attorney brings a criminal indictment, provide a high-powered lawyer at no cost who will get them out of a jam. There is nothing wrong with self interest – it is a part of the human condition. The trick is to turn that self interest into a positive force for the good and welfare of the union.

Most union members just want to pay their monthly, weekly, or bi-weekly dues and be done with it: don't call me, don't bother me, don't expect me to get involved because I've got much better things to do than waste my time with union affairs. So the dilemma is how to transform this apathetic, disinterested and cynical union member into someone who will become excited enough to do something that benefits the union and the member.

The union needs bodies for so many activities such as grievance representation, committees, communications, political action programs, demonstrations, press conferences, block walks, putting up yard signs, telephone banks, liaison with community organizations – the list of to-do's is infinite. The heart of the issue then is how do we get members to think beyond the mere payment of dues and feel a commitment to volunteer their time to help the union and themselves?

Why Do Members Volunteer?

The union leader should want to create a volunteer army, or at least a company or brigade, so there are bodies that can help out when needed. The first step is to understand why members volunteer in the first place. The reasons are many:

- **Ideological commitment to the principles of unionism.** Some members were raised in households where one or both parents were union members, maybe participated in a strike, and where the conversations around the dinner table often centered around what the union was doing and politics. This kind of member should be a slam dunk to volunteer because he or she understands the importance of the union in the workplace.
- **I've got nothing else better to do.** The best volunteer is often the member who has just come out of a sour marriage with no children involved – he or she has loads of uncommitted time on their hands! When this kind of member shows up at the union hall to help out, take full advantage of their availability, especially before they decide to get back into the dating game again.
- **The special expertise member.** Many of your members have extraordinary knowledge and/or skills on a particular subject, such as computers, active or retiree health insurance, pensions, legal representation rights, oratory, weaponry, uniform specifications, state licensing, or labor board requirements. You should

find out who these members are and rely on their knowledge when the need arises.

- **Self-interest – the prime motivator.** Many members will get involved because the issue at hand appeals to their self interest: the union is holding firm on a 10 percent pay increase; the City is proposing a 30 percent increase in health insurance premiums; the Chief intends to civilianize the dispatch center, property room, crime scene workers, or certain parts of traffic control. These kinds of issues can mean more or less money to members, or can result in their collective oxes being gored. The key is to tap into this self-interest for the benefit of the union and for their benefit as well.

Getting Members to Volunteer

Now that you know why members volunteer, let's look at how we get them to take that very crucial step of actually volunteering. First, you must be on the constant lookout for volunteers, even when things are quiet and there is no major issue on the front burner. The function of identifying volunteers is so critical that it might be wise to make a Board member or committee responsible for developing a volunteer list. This list should be part of a data base that includes members' contact information, specialized knowledge or expertise where applicable, and what civic organizations they belong to (more on this subject in the next chapter on coalition-building).

When a major issue comes up that necessitates the need for volunteers, your union's new and improved communications system outlined in the previous chapter will go into high gear. Through the newsletter, e-mails, direct mail and/or website postings, the message should identify the issue, the effect of the issue on members, the critical need for members to do their part by volunteering, and who to contact to register as a volunteer. This communication should be followed up by a telephone call to likely volunteers.

Another device for getting members to volunteer is the pledge card. A pledge card should be developed that acknowledges a commitment of time and/or activity on behalf of the union for a particular issue. When a member signs a pledge card, it indicates a moral commitment to assist the union. These cards can be distributed at union meetings or in one-on-one settings in the same manner as membership organizing is carried out.

Pledge cards are especially helpful when there is a major issue facing the union where many volunteers are needed, such as a staffing initiative or a crucial council race. If only the same old reliable few members volunteer and there is an insufficient showing of interest in signing pledge cards, it's pretty clear that your position on the issue is in trouble.

How to Keep Volunteers

A member who consents to volunteer for any project or activity must be treated as a valuable commodity. If you ever want to use this member in the future, there are certain basic principles that must be observed.

When a member shows up as a volunteer for an event, there must be specific, definable activities and instructions for him or her to observe. Otherwise, there will be goal confusion; and goal confusion equals member confusion. If the volunteer shows up and is made to stand around without any direction, he or she will become frustrated, give up, and go home. Do you really believe that if members are treated in this cavalier fashion, they will have any desire to come back a second time?

You must therefore follow **the volunteer bargain**. The volunteer bargain is: "Their time for your commitment to respect their time; train, manage, educate, and utilize them; and finally to reward them." This principle means that a manageable task must be given in a manageable amount of time, with clear direction, follow-up and follow through by project organizers.

Here is an excellent example. The union is pushing a staffing voter initiative and plans a block walk to talk to citizens about the campaign. When the volunteer member shows up at the union hall or other pre-arranged meeting site, he or she should be given identifying union paraphernalia (e.g., hat, t-shirt, jacket) and a packet that includes talking points, possible questions and suggested answers, hand-outs for the citizens, and the specific households to contact that contain registered voters. The member should be given a time limit to carry out this activity and then return to the original planning site for debriefing of the block walk, possible additional work, or release. Water, soda, and food should always be available for volunteers – the work is often tiring and sometimes done under inclement conditions.

One other piece of the volunteer bargain is reward. People like to be acknowledged for their efforts; and **every** member who volunteers should be recognized. A post-event gift such as a t-shirt, hat, or jacket might be given. Their participation should be mentioned on the website, in the newsletter, and at membership meetings.

You might even consider a Volunteer of the Year award, given to the member who has demonstrated the most consistent willingness to devote time and energy for the betterment of the union. You don't have to be parsimonious with bestowing this award – if more than one member has really gone above and beyond expectations, give credit to as many as deserve it.

Management Will Try to Create Division

One of the keys to management's ability to prevail in any conflict is to sow division within the union membership: young versus old; men against women; white against black. The union is composed of various factions, each of which has certain real or perceived interests to protect.

The leadership must be aware of the factions in its membership base and keep lines of communication between them. If the City proposes to reduce pension benefits and in return give a wage offset, there will be tension between the older officers who want and need the pension benefits and the younger officers who want the wages now. You must sit representatives of the old and young groups down and conduct a rational dialogue to find common ground – sometimes you will, and sometimes you won't, but you must make the effort. If you don't try at all, there will inevitably be membership disunity, which is a death blow to the union.

Some Parting Thoughts About Membership

When it comes to membership participation, it is best for the police union leader to have reduced expectations about what is achievable. If only 5 or 10 percent of the membership choose to give their time to the union, be happy with that and don't dwell on the unfairness of it all. If the percentage of involvement rises to 15 or 20 percent, it is all gravy – a union can climb the highest mountain with this higher level of participation.

Except for the most hard core union activists, members will come and go in their commitment to the union. Accept their time commitment for the period that they are active and don't begrudge their making the choice to invest time later in other outside activities.

Chapter 11

BUILDING COMMUNITY COALITIONS

The building of community coalitions places a close second to membership mobilization in issues that plague police unions. Union leaders generally understand and seek to deal with the membership problem; but any time that the authors speak to police union leaders about building coalitions with community leaders and organizations, their eyes glaze over and their minds wander. There is a general elitist, us-against-the-world mentality among police officers that carries over into union leadership. Any time there is a conflict with the City, the union leadership circles the wagons and fights the good fight without help from anyone.

This course of action is shortsighted at best, and at worst a prescription for disaster. Think about any major issue facing a police union today such as staffing or pay and benefit disparity that affects recruitment and retention. Police officers are not the only stakeholders in these issues – citizens have a concern about the delivery and quality of public safety services. It therefore makes a great deal of sense to convince citizens that the union is on the right side of the issue and then involve them in the public debate. It changes the debate from a police union issue to an inclusive community issue, giving the outcome a better chance for success.

There is a Southwestern police union in a mid-size city that has enjoyed collective bargaining right since the early seventies. The demographics of this city are approximately 60 percent black and 40 percent white. The leaders of this union – all white police officers, have over the years followed a conscious policy of avoiding any dialogue with black community leaders and organizations, viewing them with suspicion and disdain. Think about the folly of this position: whenever the police union becomes embroiled in a conflict with the city over a pay raise or any other concern, 60 percent of the community has, at least from the union point of view, been excluded from the debate!

The Biggest Mistakes Police Unions Make When They Finally Get Around to Asking for Community Support

Let's go back to the us-against-the-world attitude. Police unions will go for the longest time without seeking out help, then suddenly become embroiled in a nasty fight with the city, and decide that it's finally time to go to various community groups and leaders to enlist their assistance.

The first reaction among those being sought out for help is "Who the hell are you?" or "Why haven't you come around to talk with us before now?" Like any friendship, community coalition partners have to be cultivated. Showing up to ask for help on the eve of a major conflict appears manipulative and self-serving.

Let's say that a community environmental organization supported your drive for a big pay raise a few months ago. Now the leader of that organization seeks your union out to help in a fight with developers over building residential homes too close to a hike and bike greenbelt area. Unless those developers are also good long-term coalition partners, it would be strongly advisable to support the environmental group. You get help, you give help.

How Do You Go About Developing Community Coalitions?

The development of community organization and leadership alliances is a long- term – in fact a never-ending, process. When your union leadership sits down to discuss a strategic plan (see Chapter 7), identify the organizations and leaders with whom you have built or could build coalitions. This list could include business leaders, political activists, office holders, labor unions, minority organizations, neighborhood associations, or specific issue groups like MADD. The list of potential allies is virtually endless.

Coalitions can be long-term, or they can be transitory. Temporary alliances often arise when voter initiatives come up over subjects like single member districts or tax reductions. For example, many local

Chambers of Commerce are noted for their opposition to police union initiatives, so the Chamber might not be on your "Friends of the Union" list. However, a tax activist organization that is proposing a voter referendum on the reduction of a garbage fee that has been used for public safety costs might result in a temporary alliance between the union and Chamber, both of whom would have an interest in seeing the referendum defeated (a note for all you readers who are tax-slashing radicals: remember that your pay raises come from those taxes that you despise so much). Here's another example: in 2007, a suburban police union in the Southwest joined with the local Chamber of Commerce to pass a bond issue to build a new stadium for the metropolitan NFL team; and the Chamber of Commerce later endorsed a sales tax increase to add more police officers.

Police unions frequently overlook some organizations that have the potential of development as long-term coalition partners. Local labor unions and AFL-CIO Central Labor Councils are a great source of friendship development because these organizations are fighting the same workplace issues as police unions. There are some obvious obstacles such as lack of affiliation by the police union in the AFL-CIO and political differences. However, nothing should preclude the police union leader from keeping the lines of communication open with other local labor officials and giving and asking for help.

Another untapped source of coalition partners is minority organizations and leaders. Police union officials have traditionally been reluctant to pursue these partners due to obstacles such as charges of police brutality and differences over civilian review. However, think about this important point: citizens in minority communities want and expect good police service like anyone else, and are willing to have a dialogue about how this service can be achieved. This need should be the basis for a long-term relationship if a commitment is made by the police union leadership to make the effort.

The 2005 Austin Police Association Civilian Review Board Fight

The Austin (Texas) Police Association (APA) had a running battle in the mid-2000's with some elements of the minority community, the American Civil Liberties Union (ACLU), City Council, and *Austin American Statesman* newspaper over demands for a civilian review board. This ongoing battle is an excellent example of how a police union can develop relationships with community organizations and leaders in a high-profile fight.

After a series of serious police-citizen incidents, the City of Austin and APA agreed to a police monitor system. However, some minority activists, the ACLU and the newspaper continued to press for a full civilian review board. The culmination of the fight came when the newspaper printed a series of articles that manipulated traffic stop statistics trying to show that Austin police officers targeted minorities.

The APA began a campaign called "Whose Side Are You On," which included radio and television ads and also enlisted the support of community groups, all directed at making the City Council continue the police monitor system and not cave in to political pressure from vocal activists and the newspaper.

The list of organizations and citizens that came to the support of the APA was impressive: local and national labor unions, other law enforcement unions, businessmen and women, municipal and state political leaders, radio personalities, and even several minority community leaders. All of these groups and citizens were present at a major rally where more than a thousand people came, sending the City Council a powerful message that the current police monitor system should stay in place. The Council then did the right thing and decided to continue the monitor program.

When You Start Making New Friends, Make Sure to Educate Your Members

The old adage that "politics makes for strange bedfellows" has a great deal of application to the subject of coalition building, especially in the case of temporary alliances based on a specific issue. There are times when your union might become aligned with an organization or community leader that will raise the collective eyebrows of your membership and the Powers-That-Be.

Police unions have made coalitions with such organizations as the ACLU, the NAACP, churches (and ministers), liberal politicians, Project Acorn, student activists, and so on. Remember that us-versus-them view many of your members hold? Unless they are prepared for these kinds of odd political relationships, there will be considerable blowback from the membership that mistrusts any kind of dealings with "those kinds of people."

The answer is to prepare your members for your coalition decisions. With the new communications system that you have undoubtedly adopted after reading Chapter 9, clearly explain to your members the issue, why you need help from organization A or B, and what the benefits of the coalition mean to the members. It would also be helpful to invite a representative of the coalition organization to a membership meeting or participate in a website "meeting" as discussed in Chapter 9.

Establish a Coalition Data Base

Your union office should establish a data base that contains contact information for all of the community organizations and leaders that you have determined to be actual or potential coalition partners. This data base should be used for sending publications and contact letters or telephone calls; and should be constantly updated.

Coalition relationships come and go. An organization or leader that is your friend today could very well be your adversary tomorrow. That is why these relationships should be periodically reevaluated by the leadership to determine who your friends are.

Chapter 12

BUILDING THE UNION IMAGE

One of the inevitable outcomes of buying into the principles of this book is that there will be conflict between the police union and City officials. Conflict does not take place in a vacuum; it is a very public spectacle where people in the community pay attention.

Any time that conflict takes place, the union will be attacked by the power structure: public officials, businessmen, and the media. The union will be characterized as "power hungry," "unprofessional," "greedy," and other negative labels. The result will be a negative backlash from the community; and that is where image building comes into play.

Image-Building Puts the Union in a Positive Light

The union must develop high positives in advance of any future confrontations. You want to take the edge off of the union's rough-and-tumble image and establish the softer, "warm and fuzzy" side of the organization. By taking this important step, the union builds up a base of support, or "credit," with the public that can be cashed in with the public when the Big Fight takes place.

So what exactly is image-building? It is an activity that is designed to influence and shape public opinion regarding the union. Image-building can be accomplished in several ways. One is to inform the public about the police job so that there is no misinformation about the danger and stress of the job. The public gets their "education" about police work from watching television shows such as the various *Law and Order* and *CSI* programs. It is vital that you correct the misimpressions created by these sanitized versions of the job and provide the real picture of your work.

Another method of image-building is participation in charitable programs that give help to underprivileged or special needs citizens in the community. These programs can be as simple as a donation to a charity or more complex such as Shop-With-a Cop. Some union leaders engage in this kind of benevolent activity for the simple reason that it is the right thing to do. Others are more Machiavellian types who do it for the sheer calculation of the leverage benefit it brings to your union. Whether you are a purist or a cold-hearted SOB, image-building is an absolute must for your organization.

Teaching the Public about the Hazards of the Job

Your union should be proactive in getting the word out about how tough policing really is. This activity can be accomplished by promoting ride-along-programs or shoot-don't shoot exercises, particularly by media representatives and City Council members – then they can see how tough it really is out on the street. Public service announcements put out by the union about the job are especially effective and very inexpensive since only production costs are involved. Another great idea is to announce press advisories or a press conference any time there is a noteworthy incident involving officer safety, injury, or death – let it be known that there are serious consequences to being a police officer.

Another good tactic is to look for issues that highlight the problems that officers' face. For example, if the City is dragging its feet on vest replacement, it is a great opportunity to talk to the public about the life cycle of vests and the importance of periodic replacement of vests in order to increase the survival rate of your members.

The problem with all of these terrific ideas is that someone has to manage them, giving direction to the message and how the message is publicized. That is why you might consider appointing a leader to the position of press or public relations liaison to oversee this work. This subject is expanded upon in the part on the news media.

Some Charitable Image Building Programs That Work

There are many types of image-building programs that police unions use. In recent years, the Shop-With-a-Cop program has been employed with remarkable success. The union raises funds for the purchase of presents for needy children at Christmas (the one time that the authors reluctantly approve of solicitations by the way); and officers go with the children to toy stores to assist in the purchase.

Another winner is a program called fingerprint-photo ID. Members of the union go to grammar schools on a designated day to fingerprint and photograph children as a means of identification of an abducted child. There are now software programs that make this event a very simple process. Both school officials and parents appreciate and remember the event.

If these types of programs don't fit the needs of your union, there are many other options. There are boundless local charities that are looking for financial assistance that will be greatly appreciated.

You can also look for spur-of-the-moment events that lend themselves to charitable assistance. Citizens who are victims of floods, tornadoes, hurricanes – or for those California unions, mudslides – will need help in the form of financial aid, food, water, and shelter. You can be creative in the type of assistance that you provide.

Shevy Wright – A Story That Will Warm Even the Hardest of Hearts

This story is a classic use of charitable image-building by a police union. In 2007, Shevy Wright was a 9-year-old boy who lived in Chandler, Arizona. He was diagnosed with inoperable brain cancer that left him less than a year to live. The Make a Wish Foundation contacted the Wright family, and Shevy told Foundation officials that he wanted to be a Chandler police officer. The Foundation did not have the capabilities to provide such a wish so Shevy settled on a trip to Disney World.

Shevy's mother contacted Sergeant Keith Benjamin, President of the Chandler Lieutenants and Sergeants Association (CLASA), and told him about the boy's strong desire to be a Chandler police officer. CLASA then went into high gear to make Shevy Wright's wish a reality.

CLASA convinced City officials to declare July 18th Shevy Wright Day. Shevy was outfitted with a police uniform, badge, and other gear; and was escorted to a public ceremony by the Chandler Police Honor Guard. The Mayor read a proclamation announcing Shevy Wright

Day. The Chief of Police gave him an "Oath of Honor." He was then presented with a police quilt and model police charger. The entire ceremony was videotaped and given to the family.

After the ceremony, Shevy spent an exciting day taking a helicopter ride, performing FATS training, doing a ride-along, talking on the radio, and spending time with the K-9 and Bike teams. Sergeant Benjamin contacted a local car dealership and convinced the owner to donate a vehicle to the financially-strapped Wright family so they could take Shevy to his constant doctor visits. CLASA also sought donations from City employees to pay for one year of health insurance for the family and $1,000 in gasoline cards.

Keith Benjamin was truly moved by the whole experience. "The excitement on Shevy's face when I met with him and his Mom," Benjamin said, "and explained what was going to happen was beyond explanation." Benjamin felt that the Shevy Wright experience created considerable good will in the community and made every one of his members proud that they belonged to an organization that would do something so extraordinary.

Please note that our book is dedicated to Shevy Wright and every other officer who is a part of the police labor movement. Shevy Wright died before publication was completed.

When Your Union Does Charitable Image-Building, Blow Your Horn!

Many unions engage in these kinds of wonderful programs without an iota of public notice. While it is commendable to take a Mother Theresa-like approach to charity, the whole point is to get people in the community to notice what the union is doing.

That is why you must blow your horn whenever you do some noteworthy charitable act. Make it a media event that is preceded with a press advisory giving information about the what, when and where. Notify your personal press contacts and urge them to attend. Send out a post-event press release for those media organizations that were unable to attend. Also, post the information about the event on your website and put it in your publication.

Part III

POLICE UNION POLITICAL ACTION

Chapter 13

A KNACK FOR PACS – AN OVERVIEW OF POLITICAL ACTION

The ever-recurring cycle of federal, state, and local elections means that every United States Congressional representative, one-third of the U.S. Senators, many statewide political figures and too many local officials to count are up for election at one time or another. This election process means that political action must be the lifeblood of any police union.

Successful state and local police unions must be masters at passing legislation and killing unfavorable bills at the state level by staying politically active. Political involvement makes these unions powerful enough to stop the State Municipal Leagues from destroying a lifetime of benefits accumulated by the police. Successful political action at the local level means getting the wages and benefits members richly deserve.

Political action cannot be achieved or maintained without two things - members and money. Successful state and local police unions must donate money and time to candidates' campaigns. Each member must be asked to join the PAC, put out signs, make phone calls, work the polls and get out the vote.

When Your Union Becomes Involved in Political Action, Go All In

If your union leadership and members aren't convinced of the need to take an active role during an election year, or your participation in a campaign is lukewarm or indifferent, then your endorsement will be empty. The union will be viewed by political insiders and the general public as a paper tiger.

In fact, it is better to give no endorsement than to give an endorsement that is meaningless; because an empty endorsement is the worst of all possible worlds. The candidate who got the endorsement will feel cheated when the union fails to come through during the campaign. In turn, if the endorsed candidate is elected, he or she will know that they did it without the union's help. The candidate will not feel any debt of gratitude, and may actually feel hostile.

Should a candidate who did get the endorsement win, that individual will know that there is no penalty for going against your wishes because there is no tangible benefit to getting the endorsement. That same elected official will not hesitate to oppose the union in the future. If there are no consequences to taking a position contrary to the police union's interests, then there is no risk in offending law enforcement!

The result of an empty endorsement is that the police union will become a political laughingstock. Your organization will have absolutely no leverage with the politicians you were trying to influence today; and you may not have any in the future as well.

Set Up a PAC

Every successful police union will have a general purpose Political Action Committee (PAC) that collects and spends money on candidates. Elections are expensive, and every candidate needs all the money he or she can receive. Use the bargaining process to get PAC deductions in your contract, or use the credit union. If all else fails, raise funds by whatever lawful means are available.

How much money is enough? As an example, if each of the 70,000 Texas police officers donated only $1.00 per week to a police PAC, the resulting $3,360,000 per year could probably protect any benefit and pass any bill! Since that is normally unrealistic on a statewide basis, local police unions should consider a minimum goal of $1.00 per week to their local PAC.

This calculation is great if you have 800 members in the union. Over the course of a four–year election cycle you can bank over $166,000. It's not so great if you have 200 members in a suburban department where metropolitan media costs will inhale your entire PAC budget in a matter of hours.

Now you have a tough decision: do you limp along on the pennies and nickels members can contribute to the PAC (much like one–bullet–Barney in a gunfight) or do you expand the potential donor base by going outside the union?

Expanding the Base of Your PAC

If you want to be effective you expand your PAC base. Elected officials may not like it, but during their term of office they have to make decisions. Any controversial political decision leaves a winning side and a losing side. With a little work on your part, the losers could be your friends.

Here is a good example. In a major Midwest city, a police union got an early present from Santa late in the election cycle. The city council voted against a major real estate developer's plans to revitalize part of downtown. The NIMBY (Not In My Back Yard) crowd was able to defeat a project that represented hundreds of jobs and an almost $1 billion expansion of the property tax base.

The losing developer was furious and he sent an unsolicited $5,000 check to the union PAC in late September. The city council election was only weeks away and this contribution was an unexpected windfall, but it was not enough to have an impact. So instead of spending it, union leadership went back to the donor and said that they needed between $50,000 and $75,000 to have an impact on the elections. The president requested the businessman put together a meeting with potential donors so PAC leaders could put on a presentation and ask for contributions.

The key word in the paragraph above is "ask." Making a presentation at a meeting like that and then not asking for a specific amount from each attendee is a waste of your time and breath. Doing a little hand–wringing, feet shuffling at the end of the pitch and asking for "support" will get you nothing. The people at the meeting will define "support" as their vote, which costs them nothing and does nothing for your PAC.

Depending on your local election laws, the phrasing of your request for money cannot usually be a specific guarantee of how the money will be used. Most states interpret that as "coordination," which is against election law.

What you can do is tell potential donors what you've done in the past using case histories and election results. Then you can say that the union intends to do more of the same this election and if you want to know where the union stands on the candidates, then visit our web site to see the union's position on the issues and candidates we support. Advising how PAC money will be used in those terms conforms to most election laws and insulates your organization from charges of collusion.

You may not have a large, unexpected donor to get the ball rolling for your PAC, so you will have to do the identification work on your own. The good news is you don't have to be a politician to know where potential political money is to be found. All that's needed is the ability to conduct an investigation.

When looking at a crime, investigators search for means, motive, and opportunity. The search for political donors uses the same criteria.

You find the means by looking over the contribution reports for local candidates. You want to contact the donors that gave the maximum to the opponents of the officials you want to defeat; or donors that have given the maximum to candidates you want to support. If you are targeting a Republican for defeat, you can also look for maximum donors in your city or county who gave to Democratic state senate, federal and statewide candidates. Do the reverse if you are looking to support a candidate.

Motive can be found in a number of areas. Potential donors to your PAC can come from people who have given to opponents of someone you wish to defeat. Donors to candidates you support may want to maximize their participation by giving to a PAC that supports their choice. Businessmen who are angry after being rejected by the city council may wish to express their anger by contributing to your PAC. The same is true for homeowners groups or trade associations. You provide the opportunity when you ask for the donation.

Some Tips About Political Involvement

A police union with an active, well–funded PAC commands respect from elected officials. All politicians worry about getting elected, and then staying elected. Before a November election or a local city council race, schedule meetings with politicians running to discuss issues of concern to your membership. Politicians seem to have more time to discuss issues with police unions at election time.

Each union should host a political forum for all the candidates. Invite the firefighters, other public employees, the public and the media. Exposure to political reality awakens the sleeping membership. Also, it forces aspiring politicians and incumbents to make their promises in public.

Don't worry about picking a loser. There is a 50 percent chance of doing that in every election. Work hard for your candidate; and if he or she loses, approach the winner about what he plans to do for the police now that he or she is elected. A candidate's support at the state capitol or city council can always translate into police union support in the next election.

During one recent city council race a police union ran a comprehensive positive independent expenditure campaign in support of the incumbent. The PAC sent out mailings, did surveys, purchased radio time and made GOTV calls. On election night, in a tremendous upset, the incumbent was defeated.

Did this mean the union lost political power at city hall? No. The newly elected council member – impressed by the effort the union made on behalf of the losing candidate – called the president and asked for a meeting. During the subsequent discussion he expressed support for the union's manpower efforts and asked how they could work together in the future.

The key word is: **involvement**. Getting involved means building friendships, relationships and respect. This activity clearly translates into support for passing bills or approving good collective bargaining agreements. But police unions cannot win for the membership if the members do not work for the elected officials. A union that cannot provide manpower or PAC support (better yet, both) is a paper tiger that will not have respect and will not produce results for the membership.

REMEMBER our earlier Jim Hightower quote that the only things in the middle of the road are yellow stripes and dead armadillos. Endorse a candidate, and once endorsed, give the candidate your strongest support. One source of **real** police union power is in the political arena. It is the only place where the playing field is level between the police union and its opponents - the public employers and state municipal leagues.

Chapter 14

PRINCIPLES OF POLICE UNION
ENDORSEMENTS

Almost every police union endorses a candidate or measure on the ballot at some point in its history. Police union leaders who are active in the political arena understand that any endorsement carries with it a potential backlash. Every political endorsement is a two-edged sword.

Every time you endorse a candidate the whiners and naysayers within the union will predict that not only will your candidate lose; the winner will punish all the members after the election by making the entire union walk a beat on the midnight shift. Some union leaders are defeated for reelection based on the perceived damage done by failed endorsements. Proponents and opponents of political endorsements lash out at each other in union meetings and publications.

Political endorsements may cause internal dissent and disrupt the normal activities of a union. Members drop out over endorsements and attack the union leadership in the local media for being out of touch with the membership. Police management often speaks out against political involvement by police officers as being damaging to professionalism.

Then why do police unions endorse candidates and measures? Because politics is the essence of power, and power controls the political system that in turn controls the police profession. Unions that do not endorse candidates or participate in the political process are merely observers in the system that determines their livelihood.

The Effect of Endorsements

As long as crime remains an issue in politics, the endorsement of police unions will continue to be highly valued. Opinion polls repeatedly indicate that the endorsement of a candidate or measure by a police union has a 60 percent to 75 percent approval rating. Translated, that means 60 percent to 75 percent of the voters are more likely to support a candidate or measure endorsed by the police union. Contrast these numbers to lawyers and unions that generally have a 50 percent to 75 percent disapproval rating. A 2007 survey in Minnesota found that in selected wards voters were between 92 and 70 percent more likely to vote for police–endorsed candidates.

Regardless of whether or not your members believe it, that support is why candidates actively campaign for police union for endorsements. During the 1988 presidential race Bush and Dukakis fought for police endorsements. The news media was filled with stories highlighting both candidates receiving the endorsement of some police organization.

These endorsements give candidates third–party validation. The conservative candidate wants the endorsement to certify that he is a law and order politician. The liberal candidate wants the endorsement to in order to bring voter's perception of him to a position nearer the center of the political spectrum. With few exceptions, no politician is opposed to law and order. Both conservatives and liberals want the support of the police.

Educate Your Members on the Importance of Endorsements and the Credibility of the Endorsement Process

The police union leader must first sell the membership on the importance of endorsements. Many law enforcement officers feel that they should be above politics and politicians. They view the entire process with disdain, and are not eager to play any part in a campaign.

Yet this garrison mentality is very counter-productive, because it is those same politicians that pass laws or levy taxes that affect salaries, pensions, other benefits and working conditions. Your members must be convinced that if your police union purposely removes itself from having any influence on the process, then law enforcement professionals have no room to complain when politicians fail to give them adequate support and ignore their input.

Therefore, you must educate the membership as to what is at stake in the endorsement process. This education process should take place both at membership meetings and through union communications.

The illustration of the political process on members' economic interests is indeed very simple. Use a wallet as an example, and explain that the wallet's thickness or thinness depends in large part upon what politicians do and say. A Social Security card is another good example: ask your members if that is what they want to depend upon for retirement. Health insurance is a hot topic right now, and can also be used as an example of why participation in the political process is important. The police labor leader can also use on-the-job issues as examples, such as equipment, staffing and assignments. Every one of these issues is part and parcel of the political process.

In explaining the importance of endorsements, the police labor leader might consider using a circus juggling act as a good example of why endorsements are significant. Elected officials have to juggle a number of competing interests. They tend to catch the ones they are familiar with, or the ones who have supported them energetically in the past. The inactive or ineffective groups tend to get dropped when the juggling stops.

Another piece of the membership education process is to clearly explain how union endorsements will be made. Too many union leaders attempt to persuade the board or membership to endorse political candidates without this part of the education process. Unless the union has been politically active for some period of time, endorsements can be volatile situations.

The union should make absolutely clear how endorsements will be made. Members get upset if they perceive that the union leadership is trying to push through an unpopular endorsement. Police officers are suspicious by nature, so do not add to the controversy by using heavy–handed methods.

The Cardinal Rule of Police Union Politics: "The Friendly Incumbent Rule"

This rule should be the first part of the endorsement process that the union establishes. The Friendly Incumbent Rule simply states that as long as a previously endorsed candidate supports the union's issues by an established benchmark (four out of five votes; a "B" on the report

card; voted for the pay raise or whatever), that candidate will continue to receive the union's endorsement as long as they run for that particular office, regardless of who runs against them. The candidate will
only lose the endorsement when he or she fails the previously established union support test.

The endorsement is not portable, meaning that if a friendly incumbent city councilman decides to run for mayor, he does not take the
endorsement with him. He has to compete with the other candidates
running for the mayor's office. A new office means a new endorsement process.

Why is this rule so important? Because the rule establishes the union
as a dependable organization that stands behind its endorsement and
supports those who go out on a limb to support the union. Without the
Friendly Incumbent Rule you can find yourself in the same situation a
Florida police union recently did.

In an open city council race this union supported a female who
interviewed well and said she would support the union on the council.
During her first term she did just that and when she ran for re–election the councilwoman expected to get the endorsement again in
recognition of her work on the council.

What she did not expect was for a retired police officer, and member of the union, to file against her. Since the union did not have a
Friendly Incumbent Rule, the membership felt they had to support the
retired officer, so he got the endorsement and she didn't. In the subsequent election the councilwoman crushed the retired officer and
entered her new term as an enemy of a police union she considered
ungrateful and undependable. You do not want to be viewed as fickle
and unreliable, which is why that union now has a Friendly Incumbent
Rule and your union should, too.

A good example of a police union who always follows the friendly
incumbent rule occurred in Texas in 2006. The widow of an officer
who died in the line of duty won a seat on the city council. During her
two-year term she voted for the ratification of the police union contract when the majority of the council voted it down. However, she
made some mistakes and was targeted for defeat by certain groups in
the community. A retired officer filed against her and demanded the
union's endorsement because he was a member of the union and all
polls indicated she would be defeated. The union endorsed the incumbent female councilwoman and she lost. During the next two years the

former member voted against the union's interests, and the union endorsed a challenger who defeated the former member.

Endorsement Process

While every union does not have the time or resources to conduct each suggested step below, it is recommended that you attempt as many of the steps as possible. The best endorsement process involves having the candidates answer written questionnaires about issues of concern to the members. Second, ask the candidates to attend a union screening committee to answer questions in an informal setting. Third, the screening committee votes to endorse a candidate. Fourth, invite the endorsed candidates to a forum where the members can ask questions and then ratify the selections of the screening committee.

1. Written Questionnaires. While candidates often avoid difficult questions with evasive answers, a questionnaire does force a candidate to put his answers in writing. This step can be useful later when approaching him for delivery on his promises. Make the questions short and insightful.

2. Screening Candidates. Screening can be a very useful method in sorting out candidates. The informal setting will allow you to focus in on areas of concern. If necessary, explore the candidate's answers to the written questionnaire. Try to keep the questions asked of each candidate comparable so there can be no question of favoritism later. Record or videotape the session so that members can view the interview if they disagree with the screening committee's selection.

Use politically astute members on the screening committee to avoid sour grapes later by the candidate. Avoid confrontations. Remember: your objective is to educate the candidate about your concerns and to develop a relationship with the candidate if he or she wins.

3. Political Forums. Inviting candidates to debate before the membership is an educational process of its own. Unless you have a very large membership, consider inviting the public and/or special interest groups (i.e., fire fighters, city employees, union members). It is strongly suggested that you invite the media. The purpose of endorsing candidates is to gain political exposure for your union. Holding a forum does not bypass the screening committee. The forum is to display the union's power and prestige. It is not held so the membership can vote to endorse at the forum's conclusion.

4. Voting on Candidates. Who should vote on endorsements? While the methods vary, most unions endorse based on votes of the Board of Directors, Political Action Committee, or Screening Committee. While a few unions have membership ballots, it is strongly recommended that the membership **NOT** vote on candidate endorsements. Letting the general membership vote on endorsements too often means the endorsement is made based on the personal political concerns of whoever attends that meeting, rather than which candidate is better for the union on union issues. Instead, present the membership with the recommended slate of endorsed candidates at a general meeting and have the members vote to approve the list. That way no one can say the endorsements are the product of a group of insiders that ignore what the membership wants.

Organizational Goals versus Individual Interests

Few issues are more controversial than political endorsements. The union is an organization composed of individuals. The organization's goals and the individual members' interests may or may not be the same. The number one priority of the union leadership is to propel the organization toward its goals.

Too many leaders allow individual interests to misdirect the union from achieving organizational goals. The goals of the organization should be improving the living and working conditions of the membership. The individual member may care most about hot–button issues like gun control, abortion, national security, crime or the death penalty, which are not union issues.

Once the union starts making endorsements based on the individual interests of the majority, the goals of the organization will become skewed. The differences may be slight at times, but they may be critical in determining whether the organization reaches its political peak.

Endorsements say that the candidate supports the **GOALS** of the organization. Individual members can vote any way they want. If you clearly identify the organization's goals to the candidate, members and the public, it should lessen controversy.

Conservative Versus Liberal

Most police officers are politically conservative. Day-to-day contact with reality on the street will do that to you. They tend to rant and rave about liberal politicians. However, liberals have traditionally given the organization the majority of its goals (i.e., pay, due process, collective bargaining) because liberals support unions. Conservatives tend to vote against labor issues while supporting law and order issues.

Police unions should endorse candidates based on the candidate's position on the organization's goals. Whether the candidate is a Democrat or Republican should not be an issue. Unions affiliated with the AFL-CIO may have to follow the endorsements of their national, state or central labor council.

More About Yellow Stripes and Dead Armadillos

Jim Hightower's famous expression has great application to endorsements. Endorsements require a decision. No endorsement is a decision.

Unless special circumstances exist, the union should endorse only in key races. Nothing requires that the union endorse in every race. If an office has no impact on the union's goals, then there is no reason to issue an endorsement. This means that both school board races and presidential elections may not merit the union endorsing. Other races that don't rate an endorsement include contests where none of the candidates support union goals; races where the incumbent is anti–union but the challenger has no chance; or incumbents are running unopposed.

Union leaders must stand tough in making endorsements. You cannot satisfy every member. Forget about whiners and naysayers. They always want the union to take the path of least resistance. Remember that there is no middle of the road in this game: leaders make the tough decisions for the organization because that's what they were elected to do.

More on Yellow Stripes: Endorsing Losers and Winners

It seems members are always worried about endorsing a candidate who may lose. Remember: the winners will love you and the losers will appreciate your support. The winning candidate that you did not endorse may want your support next time. Unless he is an absolute idiot, he will not be a sore winner.

No guts, no glory. If you never participate in the political process, you can never experience the rewards of victory. The political process requires that you participate at each step. You cannot expect to pass legislation at the state level or win benefits at the local level if you do not endorse candidates and help them win election.

The political process is the American Way. Police unions cannot achieve their goals without getting out of the middle of the road and taking political risks.

Chapter 15

HOW TO ASSIST THE CANDIDATE

There are five basic ways that a police union can assist a candidate in an election: letter of endorsement, media support, money, manpower, and information. This chapter will look at these five methods of assistance.

As you decide what to do for a candidate beyond an endorsement, the police union leader must first think about what the membership can and will do. The crucial thing to remember is that you should never over-promise to a candidate. The police union's failure to live up to its assurances can equal betrayal in the fevered environment of a campaign.

Letter of Endorsement

If this is all you do for the candidate, you have not done much for the campaign. There may be races where you have only a passing interest, and therefore, the union may not want to invest time and money in the election. It's ironic that the larger the race is, the more important a letter–only endorsement is. For example, if your union is the largest in the state, then it may make sense to endorse in the governor's race. A campaign contribution of a few hundred dollars will disappear without a trace in a multi–million dollar governor's campaign chest, but your endorsement letter is unique and priceless.

This kind of endorsement is sometimes called the auto-pilot endorsement and it has the least impact of any union contribution to a campaign. A mere endorsement is better than nothing, but not by much. An endorsement with no other union contribution has little impact, because the candidate's campaign has to do all the work. Your union is too weak to do more than issue a press release and the political insiders know it. The candidate will accept and use your endorsement, but the campaign will also remember how little effort you put in to support it.

Media Support

Media support is something that a police union can offer to a candidate that is as valuable as money and just as memorable after the election. In fact in the most expensive campaigns, media support can be more important than money.

Media support means that the union leadership will be out front and visible during the entire course of the campaign. The leadership must be willing to appear in endorsement press conferences, issue press releases and even conduct opponent attack press events. And these aren't necessarily one-shot affairs – in a statewide race, police union representatives may have to travel on a press caravan to get the message out, hitting a number of media markets in a single day.

This kind of support can mean much more to a candidate in a well-funded race than a $500 check that he may never personally see. The union's $500 dollar contribution wouldn't buy the paper clips for a gubernatorial campaign, but its public endorsement and involvement with the campaign is priceless and unique.

One important warning: don't confuse media support with allowing the union's name to be used in an ad. This passive approach to candidate support won't earn you any points with the candidate after the election.

PAC Money

Political campaigns are propelled by three things - money, money and money! If your union has political action committee money, you have potential power. Every candidate needs money to get his or her message out to the voters.

Remember: money talks. Power is merely money and/or people. Raise PAC money any legal way you can get it. Do not let the non-political members prevent the union from raising and spending money.

- **Direct Expenses.** Use your PAC funds to buy yard signs, direct mail pieces, phone banks and other direct campaign material. You might want to purchase radio or television spots for the candidate as part of an independent expenditure.
- **Indirect expenses.** If you have a union hall, let the candidates use it for their campaigns. Put in phone banks to save the candidate money. Hold a fundraiser and buy the food and drinks. Note: check state campaign laws about reporting indirect expenses.

Manpower

Many police unions and their members don't like to get involved in the day-to-day work of a campaign; but this aloofness will be costly after election day. After the election, candidates recall who helped them get where they are; and those groups that were visible on a day–to–day basis and provided manpower to the campaign will be rewarded.

The reason that firefighters have had so much influence at city halls and state capitals throughout the country is that they own the yard sign franchise in many localities. Every year, candidates are getting yard signs printed, and in many cases installed, by firefighters.

Police unions can do the same thing. Obvious areas where volunteers can make a difference are door-to-door canvassing, working the phone banks, or helping out at campaign headquarters. If union members aren't keen on these activities, then they can volunteer, make an in-kind contribution, and stay in uniform by providing free security at campaign events. This volunteer effort can include guarding the proceeds at the ticket office, crowd control, or directing traffic.

The use of union members to serve in a security capacity will save the campaign a significant amount of money. Also, the union can have a visible role in the election; and your members will be doing something that is familiar to them.

Manpower does not always mean union members. No campaign is going to check for a union membership card when the volunteers arrive. Family members and friends are also valuable as long as they wear the union t–shirt while they help.

Information

Knowledge is power, and lack of knowledge can be a weakness in any campaign. Along with an endorsement, the police union can function as an independent source of information concerning law enforcement in your city, county or state. Police union leaders can often give candidates information that they otherwise cannot get from the city manager, the mayor, the city bureaucracy or the chief. Police union leaders know where the bureaucratic skeletons are buried.

This kind of inside information is priceless to a campaign where crime is an issue. Challengers are particularly grateful for this knowledge, but incumbents who are on the outs with the establishment and candidates who are being misled by government bureaucracy are also likely targets. The best thing about information is that it is free, and can have a big impact on the issue side of a campaign. If your membership is too apathetic to get involved, then information can often take place as the union's contribution to a campaign.

Chapter 16

AN IMPORTANT QUESTION TO ASK ABOUT ENDORSEMENTS: WHOM DO WE ENDORSE?

The question of whom your union endorses largely depends on determining where the endorsement can do the most good for your organizational interests. In the long run, does your union benefit more from helping your friends or hurting your enemies? These questions must be asked and answered before making any decision to step into a particular race. Otherwise, you will make ill-advised endorsements that could have disastrous consequences for your union.

Helping Your Friends

Any police union has two categories of friends: current or future. Your current friends are incumbents. These officeholders have been supporters in the past and you want to continue to have their support in the future. What's more, protecting incumbents may involve so much work that your efforts are limited to them alone.

Fortunately, incumbent endorsements are the safest for the union to take because year in and year out, most incumbents are reelected. Unfortunately, the incumbents know this fact, too. Consequently, the impact of your support is reduced.

The endorsements that produce the most influence for your union are those that have the most impact. For example, an early endorsement of a candidate in a multi-candidate field can give him or her credibility with the fund-raising community and the press. This kind of endorsement has great impact and can be a building block for the campaign.

Helping Future Friends

The early, credibility-building endorsement is most often found in a race for an open seat where there is no incumbent running. A successful endorsement in a race for an open seat can produce future friends, and can get you in on the ground floor of their political career. As the officeholder's power and influence grows, law enforcement's voice becomes even stronger.

But you must remember to choose wisely in races for open seats, because if your candidate loses, you have a problem. At the very least, you will be viewed with suspicion by the winner for the first term and at the worst, you'll have made an enemy for the course of a political career.

An endorsement in an open race can also be an attempt to take charge of the future. In your situation, it may not be so much that there is a great candidate that you want to support, but rather one candidate is so bad that your union can't afford to have that person win. In this instance, the police union's efforts are devoted more at one candidate's defeat than the other's victory, which is simply choosing between the evil of two lessers.

Endorsements as Western Union

Your union can use an endorsement to send a message to an incumbent by supporting the opponent. And you don't have to win the election for your message to be received loud and clear.

By supporting the opponent, you show an unfriendly incumbent that there are unpleasant consequences to being on the bad side of law enforcement. If your union is smart, the leaders and members will work very hard for the opponent, and make this election a living hell for the incumbent, assuming he or she wins. If the incumbent loses, so much the better!

After the experience of a tough campaign against your union, a reasonable incumbent may decide that voting against your interests is more trouble than it's worth. This former enemy may be more open to your position in the future, because he or she has seen firsthand what can happen otherwise.

But you must avoid becoming irrelevant. If you send a message, make certain that it arrives. The union must marshal all of its resources for the campaign and must be enthusiastically supported by the membership. Otherwise, your follow-through will be weak; your union will be embarrassed; and this enemy will write you off forever.

Endorsements as Absolution

There are candidates that need your union much more than you need them. These candidates have a problem. They can be incumbents, challengers or running for an open seat; but all of them have a hickey on their political record that a police union endorsement will do a great deal to cover. Examples include a former ACLU attorney running for district attorney, an incumbent with a driving under the influence conviction, or a former Operation Rescue member running for anything.

When your union endorses this type of candidate, you are more or less absolving the candidate of his or her political sins. The union endorsement tells the voters that in spite of this earlier transgression, law enforcement thinks that this candidate is qualified, worthy of support and deserving of forgiveness.

When you endorse a candidate for absolution, make sure to extract a price. This candidate needs you much more than you need him or her. Get this candidate's binding promise to support the pay raise, new collective bargaining agreement or whatever else is your top issue before you make the endorsement. Then remember to collect on the promise after the election.

Challengers: Another Way to Build For the Future

Incumbents don't often lose, but when they do, it gets everyones attention. A visible effort by the police union on behalf of a successful challenger sends the entire political community – challengers and incumbents alike – a message. Your power and leverage will increase geometrically as a result of this one victory.

If a loss is closer than expected – flying in the face of the so-called conventional wisdom – it will have much the same effect. Supporting a credible challenger with potential may not pay off the first time, but the second race – oftentimes a victory – will bear dividends. And while a good challenger may not win an election on the first attempt, he or she may surface victorious somewhere in the future.

Chapter 17

ANOTHER IMPORTANT QUESTION: WHEN DO WE ENDORSE?

When the police union endorses is a matter of timing that has to balance when the endorsement will do the most good for the candidate; when it best serves the purposes of your union. Remember that your goal is not simply to elect people – if it was, you'd be a political consultant. The goal is to maximize your group's influence on the political process by influencing voters; and by electing or defeating candidates.

There are basically four times that your union can endorse: early, late, both, or at the candidate's discretion. In order to have the most potential influence, your union must have an internal endorsement mechanism in place to begin interviewing candidates and determining how to distribute your support before the campaign season begins.

If there are primaries in the races your union is concerned with, the group must start identifying potential candidates weeks before filing deadlines. This process might mean that the leadership will start looking at these campaigns the year before the election is held.

What's more, your union may make primary endorsements and then endorse again in the general election. This can be complicated. If you endorse in both the Republican and the Democratic primaries and both endorsed candidates win, then you have a real problem in the general election. A joint endorsement for the general election looks namby–pamby and endorsing one over the other makes people – candidates included – wonder what your primary endorsement is worth. It's much less complicated to wait until the general election and issue one endorsement then.

This entire process takes time and organization that must be in place, and agreed upon, weeks before it's time to decide on a particular endorsement. It doesn't do a challenger who needed an early endorsement in May much good to finally get your blessing in September. A police union that can't properly time its endorsements isn't going to have a great deal of impact on the political process.

Early Endorsements

Early endorsements are most valuable to challengers, candidates in a crowded field, and first-time candidates. For challengers and first-time candidates, your endorsement provides credibility. These candidates can use your seal of approval to begin the process of persuading others to join their effort.

The early endorsement tells editorial boards, political activists and contributors that this candidate is credible. It also puts your union in at the beginning of this candidate's career. You automatically become one of the core supporters, a member of the inner circle and someone the candidate turns to for advice and listens to when it comes time to vote.

An early endorsement helps a candidate in a crowded field to stand out from the rest. It gives them a point of distinction and something they can use as an issue or advantage when they contact voters and contributors.

In an election year when crime or law enforcement-related issues are paramount, this early endorsement gives your candidate a great advantage over the opposition. Other candidates have to scramble to get endorsements from other law enforcement groups in order to negate your candidate's early advantage or they risk losing this important issue.

When your union chooses to make an early endorsement, it's best if that event isn't the last contact with the campaign. Stay in close contact, be an advisor or offer some of the other facets of an endorsement that has been discussed earlier. In short, be a presence for the duration of the campaign.

The Late Endorsement

Done properly, a late endorsement can tip the scale and put a candidate over the top. It puts your group in the position of being a king (or queen) maker as you provide this last bit of organizational and public help for a campaign. Unfortunately, it's hard to time this type of endorsement properly.

For a late endorsement to work, the union has to carefully judge the available options in the race. You are choosing late, so you must choose well. This race should be carefully handicapped, and that means you have to do your homework. A late endorsement can be a very public event, so backing the wrong candidate can result in a very visible failure.

But in an evenly matched race, a strong endorsement package can determine the outcome. This scenario won't happen too often in a congressional race, because too many variables are at work. But in a city council or mayor's race, and particularly in a judicial race, a late law enforcement nod can be crucial.

Early and Late Endorsements

These types of endorsements are for highly organized law enforcement groups. This combination means that you do the early endorsement events with accompanying press conferences and public appearances. Then the campaign takes the ball and runs with it.

At the close of the campaign, your union appears again, this time with some form of paid endorsement support – either a television spot, radio commercial, direct mail piece, block-walking or members at the polling places with slate cards to remind the public who your chosen candidate is.

This kind of effort also serves to remind the candidate of just how crucial your support was to his or her victory. And it also will pay big dividends later when your issue comes before that officeholder.

Candidate's Discretion

In this situation, the candidate decides when and where your endorsement will do the most good. Your group can earn plenty of points for being cooperative, but there is a danger in letting your union be taken for granted.

This candidate's discretion arrangement works best with candidates that your group knows and whose judgment you trust. This option is not recommended as the choice for first-timers or candidates with whom you have not had a relationship in the past.

Chapter 18

THE LAST IMPORTANT QUESTION: HOW SHOULD THE UNION ENDORSE?

Another important question is: how does the police union make the public aware of its endorsement? If it's an auto-pilot endorsement, the candidate's campaign will take care of notifying the voters. But if you've decided to determine your own fate, the methods by which your union makes voters aware will depend in large part on the size of your budget. There are several ways of getting the word out to the community: television, radio, direct mail and print ads. Let's look at each of these methods.

Television: Large Impact – Large Expense

Television is expensive for two reasons. First, it costs more to produce the advertisement. Production of a fairly basic television spot can cost $2,000. A more creative effort can run more than $5,000. Second, television is a mass medium – which accounts for its impact – and buying time can be expensive.

Given the considerable expense, it's important to consider ways to make TV ads less expensive. On a cost-per-thousand-voting-age-population basis, TV can cost a half of what a direct mail piece does. In congressional races, where there is a great deal of wasted coverage, a candidate can broadcast three television spots for a cost per thousand of less than $200, compared to a mail cost per thousand of $350 to $400.

So why don't all candidates use TV instead of mail? Because broadcast television has only one list (i.e.; the entire TV market), so you have to buy everyone on the list; that is, you're buying the entire voting (and non-voting) community that watches television.

For a community of 200,000 at $200 per thousand, the cost is $40,000. With mail, you can choose any number of lists that vary by size; so instead of trying to reach 200,000 voters, your union might mail to only 10,000 voting households for a total cost of $3,500.

Cable TV: Using the Television Alternative

Cable television can cut the size of the TV list down to a manageable size. Even in a city that's 100 percent wired for cable, a spot will cost much less than one broadcast over the airwaves. This situation makes cable a good compromise that still gives the impact of TV, with less cost than broadcast TV. However, you must remember that the union will be reaching fewer households.

In an area that has less than 50 percent cable market penetration, cable subscribers are usually upper income residents. When cable penetration exceeds 50 percent of the market, the make-up of the cable subscriber universe begins to accurately reflect the demographics of the area.

Radio: Broadcasting Without the Bite

If your union can't afford television advertising, then radio will become the broadcast medium. Costs in this instance are much less for both production and time. However, it's difficult to reach as many people as you do with television advertising.

A typical radio spot costs under $600 to produce and a 60-second commercial is usually much less than the equivalent spot would cost on TV. What's more, your union can target potential voters fairly precisely and with less waste, since radio stations have different formats and listener profiles.

For example, the union won't reach many voters when it puts its endorsement on a heavy metal station; but the same ad on a news/talk station will hit thousands of potential voters each time it is broadcast.

If the union is going to use either radio or TV, plan on a minimum two-week buy. Any less time will not allow your message to penetrate the market. If your union has the money, three or four weeks is the most effective time period for your endorsement buy.

Mail: Hitting Them Where They Live

If your union can't afford radio or TV, then mail is your last really effective mass contact alternative. It's best to keep your mail message simple and direct. You don't need to do an entire brochure to tell why your police union likes candidate X. The candidate should have told his story long ago. All your union should do is tell voters that it supports the candidate and his/her program. An oversized endorsement postcard in the last two weeks of the campaign will accomplish this goal nicely.

Your toughest decision will be who should be targeted for the mail. The largest possible list is registered voters in your area of both political parties, but this will be expensive and not target efficient. This universe can be reduced by mailing only to voters who voted in the last primary or last municipal election. Ideally, the candidate who's receiving the endorsement can give you the mailing list where the endorsement will do the most good. Then all the union has to do is buy the postage and print the materials.

If the candidate can't supply the list, then the union will have to purchase it from a list broker. These brokers will charge you based on the size of the list and how much trouble it was to compile the names. Once you obtain the list – usually in the form of labels – the union can deliver the labels, the mail and a check to a mail house for delivery to the target voters.

Print Ads: The Last Alternative

Print ads are expensive, and they require as much repetition as broadcast advertisements. If your union is going to use print ads, don't do any less than a one-half page ad and plan on running it three or four times.

To reach the most voters, you should request that the ad be placed in the metro or city section of the paper, or in the sports page. These placements may cost a little more, but are worth it.

If you do a print ad, get a professional to design it. Don't run "An Open Letter to the People of Metropolis," because these ads are dead letters. The only people that read them are you, the candidate and the opponent. A clean, well-designed layout will pay off in increased readership and impact at the polls.

Endorsing Candidates on a Shoestring

If your union doesn't have the money for any of the above advertising programs, but you still want to do something visible, then push cards and volunteers are the last alternative. Call the candidate and find out where the most important target precincts are.

Line up enough volunteers to cover precincts on election day. Then print up a small card with your endorsement on it and pass these cards out to voters as they approach the poll.

Uniformed officers will have the most impact at the polls, but in jurisdictions where law or regulation prohibits wearing a uniform for political activity (probably most states), use off-duty or retired officers in your union's jackets or ball caps. It's a personal touch that can help persuade the undecided and remind the already decided.

Part IV

DEALING WITH THE NEWS MEDIA

Chapter 19

UNDERSTANDING THE FOURTH ESTATE

In a book filled with advice on every manner of labor relations, contract negotiations and political action, many readers might wonder why we devote an entire segment to the media and its role in the fortunes of police unions. The answer is simple: the failure to understand and tame the media beast can be devastating to your reputation as a labor leader, your union and your members.

Positive media coverage enhances the power and prestige of your organization, can bring significant pressure on elected officials to give you what you need at the bargaining table, and help generate public support for your members. Negative press can destroy your reputation, discredit your members and your profession, and make your union appear weak and ineffective in representing the rank and file. For these reasons, we want to explain the nature of the media beast, its organization and psychology, and teach you the skills you'll need to deal with reporters, especially in a media crisis.

The "Fourth" Estate

Everyone (at least everyone who reads this book we hope!) is familiar with the three branches of government, executive, legislative and the judiciary. All three branches (or estates) decide virtually every aspect of our lives. On the national level, the president (executive) and the congress (legislative) pass laws that literally determine life and death issues for our nation. The third estate, the judicial system, acts as a check and balance on the enormous powers wielded by the other two. On the local level, the city manager (executive) and the Mayor and Council (legislative) are supervised by local courts (judiciary). It's a system with built-in checks and balances so that no one estate dominates, and there is accountability for their actions.

There is one other branch of government, the "fourth estate" which has absolutely no checks and balances and damn little accountability for its actions . . . the news media. Snug and secure in the protective cocoon of the 1st Amendment to the U.S. Constitution guaranteeing freedom of the press, today's news organizations wield enormous power to destroy the lives and reputation of ordinary citizens with virtually no consequences should they "get it wrong." History is replete with examples of media frenzies that turn out to be dead wrong, yet very few reporters or their employers are called to account. It is therefore not surprising that such unbridled power often results in arrogance, egotism, and a media beast that displays little conscience for those trampled in its wake.

News Organizations Are Big Business – The Myth of the "Liberal Media"

It has become a staple for right-wing talk radio to rail against the "liberal" media and its perceived bias against conservative causes. It's a sexy notion that has provided plenty of red meat for the far right. Although individual reporters may have a left (or right) leaning bias, it is important to point out that the news is big business.

Take a look at who owns the "liberal" media. CBS is its own enormous corporation; ABC is owned by Disney; and NBC is the product of the mega defense contractor General Electric. Are we seriously to believe that the Board of Directors of these capitalist titans is populated by left-leaning, tree-hugging apologists for the liberals?

These corporations are out to do what all corporations do: make money. They make money, not by reporting news fairly and accurately, but by dishing out as much prurient sensationalism as they can find. The big three haven't quite stooped to the tabloids' level of the "Three-Headed Baby From Mars," but they're close. This explains the recent media frenzies over O. J. Simpson, Paris Hilton and whatever couple likely murdered their kids lately. Is this "hard news" that we need to stay informed on the major issues of the day?

Hardly, but it sells soap. What also "sells soap" is accusations of police brutality, racial profiling, sex scandals in the police station, and department corruption. The day-to-day truth of police officers risking their lives just doesn't have the "sizzle" to move products. It is not a "liberal" bias but rather a "commercial" bias that motivates news corporations to breathlessly report the difficult childhood of a cop shooter and the reasons they are so misunderstood. That stuff sells . . . at your expense.

Reporter Psychology 101

There is a famous quote "Know thy enemy as thy know thyself" that is more often used when discussing political rivals, management, or groups or individuals who, for whatever reasons, hate law enforcement. We don't often view the news media as our "enemy" but, in a real sense, some reporters and editors with a hatred of the police can be our most formidable foe. We won't try to explain the psychological pathology of these people. Maybe their mommy didn't hug them enough or they wet their beds well into their teens. It doesn't matter. What matters is our ability to "get inside" the minds of the average reporter. Why did they choose journalism in the first place? What are their motivations, intentions and potential bias against you and your union? Where is this story going? What is the potential that your organization is going to get the worst of things?

Why Reporters Chose Journalism in the First Place

People who seek a career in journalism must be prepared for an expensive college education that lands you a job that pays less than a journeyman carpenter. They must be ready to commit to long hours, weekends, holidays, and assignments at three o'clock in the morning. They have to move, many times, to bigger and better news organizations to have any kind of career at all. Don't forget also that the media is a cut-throat business and that any cub reporter is more than expendable.

It has to be the money . . . right? But according to a fall 2005 survey by the National Association of Colleges and Employers in Bethlehem, Pennsylvania, communication majors with a Masters Degree earn $31,879. Recent graduates earn an average annual salary of $29,962, News assistants at television news organizations earn an average annual salary of $25,000, according to a 2005 survey from the Radio-Television News Directors Association in Washington, D.C.

Sports reporters at radio-news organizations earn $21,400 in average annual salary.

The average annual base salaries (weighted by newspapers) for entry-level reporters and copy editors are $28,234 and $30,687, respectively, according to a 2005 survey of 519 daily newspapers by the Inland Press Association, a trade group in Des Plaines, Ill. The following is the median annual salary (i.e., half of these graduates made less than the salaries listed below) according to the type of media organization they joined:

- Daily newspapers: $26,000
- Weekly newspapers: $24,000
- Radio: $23,000
- Television: $23,500
- Cable television: $30,000
- Advertising: $28,000
- Public relations: $28,500
- Consumer magazines: $27,000
- Newsletters, trade publications: $28,000
- Web sites: $32,000

Would you invest six years in college to land a job at these salaries given all the other drawbacks of a career in the news media? So what accounts for the steady stream of eager young reporters flowing into America's news rooms?

The Pen and the Mighty Sword

We are convinced that the vast majority of journalism graduates enter the field for one reason . . . altruism. Altruism is defined as "the notion of self sacrifice, selflessness in the service of humanity." Among these young graduates there is a sense that, with this pen as my mighty sword, they have the power to right all the wrongs that beset society. They will expose the wrong-doers, challenge the power elite, and make society better for the effort. Their vast intellect and sense of right and wrong will carry them to a Pulitzer Prize and the riches and respect they so rightly deserve.

What happens after ten years at this noble cause? What have they come to realize mid-career? What has become of their idealism? What have they become?

They have become mean, ornery, cynical bastards. Why? Because many mid-career reporters begin to realize one simple fact — it's all a lie. Everyone lies. The corporations lie, the president lies, the bureaucrats lie, and the most professional liars are politicians. Cops are corrupt. Firefighters abuse their spouses. Corrections officers are brutes. Probation Officers let murderers prey on our families while they play golf. Everyone lies.

They have come to believe that there is no "truth." There are no sincere people. Folks act in their self-interest and only for their own personal gain. There are no saints, no good guys, and no hope for humanity.

They also take a look at their current station. They have moved from town-to- town, paper-to-paper, or network-to-network, clawing their way to the top. It has becoming glaringly obvious to them that their station in life is limited and not likely to improve very much in the near future.

In short, they will sell their grandmother for an "above the fold" story that will make them famous and, hopefully, get them the hell out of their present predicament. Don't think for a minute that selling you and your members out is off the table.

Sounds harsh, doesn't it? We are not saying that all journalists are in this frame of mind, just the majority for all the reasons explained above. What is important is that you realize this is the type of person you are likely to deal with when the media comes calling.

Chapter 20

WORKING WITH REPORTERS – SOME BASIC PRINCIPLES

First and foremost always remember that reporters are **NOT** your friends. They will **NEVER** be your friend. Sure, the nice reporter visiting your office is polite, witty, and appears sympathetic to you, your position in the matter, and your cause in general. Don't buy it for one second! One of the key talents of a good reporter is the ability to put the victim at ease, to cause them to drop their guard just long enough to divulge their inner secrets. It is a dance with the ultimate cobra charmer, smooth and subtle yet inches away from a savage and often fatal bite. So when a reporter is sitting across from you, its dukes up all the way. Stay on guard and always watch what you say.

The Pre-Judgment Principle

When the reporter shows up at your office, he or she has already written their story. It takes only the first few questions for the trained observer to know exactly where this reporter's story is going. If you listen carefully to these first few inquires, the general direction or "angle" the piece is taking can be determined. Like all humans, reporters tend to come to a conclusion and then research the story to arrive at where they wanted to be all along. Along the way, many discard inconvenient truths that do not support their preconceived notions. Pay attention and you'll know where the story is heading.

We often think of a reporter as someone seeking information, something original from you based on your position as a labor leader, police officer, or other professional qualification. The truth is a reporter rarely asks questions he or she has not asked everyone else involved in the current matter. They have probably researched the issue on the internet, have asked independent sources for their take, and have posed the same issue with your opponents. Why then, if they know the answer, are they asking you the same questions?

They are looking for inconsistency. They are sniffing for blood in the water. Should your answer differ, even slightly, from the other sources they have queried, then the chase is on. Someone is lying or someone is fudging the truth. You have to assume that reporters know the answer, have heard the responses from the other side, and are testing **YOU** to see if there are any inconsistencies to exploit. Once again, be on guard.

Develop Your Message In Advance and Stick To It

You have already learned a great deal from the comprehensive chapter in this book about message. Given the manner in which reporters go about developing stories and the ever-present need for a consistent message, it is critical that you prepare your take on things in advance and stick to it. We will provide a message development exercise in a later chapter that will help you frame your issues as you intend them, as well as advice on how to "stay on message" once defined. You have a song to sing, and it is critical that you write the verses and deliver the melody on your own terms.

Never Lie To a Reporter – And Never Means Never!

Remember, reporters are smart people. More important, the one thing you must guard jealously is your integrity and reputation for straight talk. Reporters depend upon reliable sources and deeply resent those that try to deceive them. Here is a great analogy to illustrate this point: Most folks hate lobbyists and all they represent. But the truth is that a lobbyist's currency of trade is credibility. As a lobbyist for any cause, if you are caught in a lie, your credibility is forever destroyed. As much as the general public looks down on lobbying as a profession, its credo is "truth first" no matter how intense the current legislative competition may be.

In our media crisis chapter, we will make the case that everything that can be known, will be known no matter how hard one tries to hide the truth. If it can be known, a good reporter will find out, maybe not today but at some time in the future. If the truth is ultimately found out and you have been shown to be a bald-faced liar, the reporter will regard you as a union leader not ever to be believed. So guard your credibility like your own children . . . it is just as precious.

Never Argue With a Reporter – You'll Never Win

It's natural for you to believe passionately in the police union cause – it is your life and you represent the men and women who risk their lives every day. It therefore follows that, when encountering a reporter who exhibits opposing views, you have the urge to engage in a Harvard debate. Resist the temptation, because you can't win.

There is an old adage that you should never get in a fight with someone who buys ink by the barrel. The media can pound you and your organization into bits over many weeks. A television reporter can take your one-day story and begin a series of blistering reports that make you look like a baboon. Unless your union has unlimited, and we mean unlimited, ability to buy print and air time to respond, you simply can't win this contest.

Don't argue with these people. It is better to respectfully present your views using the tactics we have given you and let the chips fall where they may.

What To Do About a Reporter Who Treats You Unfairly

It is inevitable that you will from time-to-time be misquoted or mistreated by a reporter. The temptation to go above the reporter's head to the editor should be resisted. This tactic typically backfires. Ask yourself how you feel when a citizen or coworker takes an issue to **your** boss rather than deal with the matter directly with you. A reporter is likely to resent this affront, and whatever relationship you have developed will probably evaporate. So the advice on an **occasional** lapse by a reporter is to discuss it with him or her one-on-one.

This situation should be distinguished from the "rogue" reporter – someone who consistently and deliberately misrepresents the facts, misquotes you, and slants articles to put you in the worst possible light. When faced with this problem, first realize that reporters who conduct themselves this way with you and your organization probably treat their other sources likewise. Second, remember that all members of the news media traffic in one vital commodity: information.

In this situation, it is definitely warranted to go over the reporter's head and seek a meeting with his boss – the editor. Before meeting with the "rogue's" editor, document each and every incident in which you were misquoted or the reporting was not factual. Then tell the editor that your union will respond to any other correspondent at his paper but will not, under any circumstances, continue to work with this particular reporter.

You freeze the offending reporter out of obtaining information, and if other organizations do the same, his or her career is on the way down. It's hard to be an effective correspondent if no one will talk to you.

Chapter 21

NEWS ORGANIZATIONS AND A REPORTER'S WORLD

There is another famous adage (we have a bunch of them in this book!) that you can't understand someone unless you've walked a mile in their shoes. If you want to truly understand the media beast and how to deal with it, then you must become immersed as much as possible in the day-to-day media world.

Hard News versus Editorial

The first important distinction in journalism is the wall between "hard news" reporting and the editorial staff in the print media and, to a lesser extent, television news programs. The two entities live in very different worlds, don't necessarily like each other, and bring an entirely different focus to the news they cover.

"Hard news" reporters are proud of the fact that they are on the crime scene at 3 a.m. where the blood spills and the victims scream. They are the "nuts and bolts," "just the facts" types that derive great satisfaction going "live" from the field.

The editorial board is a different breed of journalism. The team that makes up the editorial department at most news organizations considers themselves above the "nuts and bolts" crowd and actually pities those poor devils trudging through blood and guts day after day. They view themselves as great thinkers, prolific pontificators, and the source of all knowledge.

This distinction is important because when dealing with hard news types, you give them the nuts and bolts – just the facts. When presenting your side of an issue to the editorial board, be ready to paint the "big picture" – how this issue affects the community at large.

Under the Gun – Using Deadlines to Your Advantage

Let's be honest for a moment. Very few of us have solid, unbreakable daily deadlines. Sure, childbirth and taxes can't be pushed off to another day. But most of our lives allow for a little leeway, the opportunity to push things off for at least one day, maybe more.

This luxury does not exist in the fast paced, highly competitive world of news reporting. In fact, the average reporter not only has a drop-dead time each day to submit their work, but carry weekly assignments for the Sunday supplement and even a multi-week five-part series. In short, these people are very busy and face the unusual pressure of "pumping copy" each and every day.

Why is a deadline important as part of your media relations strategy? Because shame on you if you don't make things easy on these people. That's right. Let's make life as uncomplicated as possible for our dear friends in the media.

We are continually amazed to hear stories from police union presidents who lament about the lack of positive coverage they receive from their local newspapers or radio/television stations. Yet very few of these union leaders take the time to make covering their stories effortless for the reporters that cover them.

Given their hectic lives, reporters are simply unlikely to take your news "lead" and translate it into a positive piece on your issues. In fact, that's your job. Say you have a pension issue coming up before city council. Doesn't it make sense to provide the media with a well-written press release, with documents supporting your position, well in advance of the city council vote? If you give them the tools they need to cover your issue, you'll have a lot more success not only in getting more ink but more importantly the right angle on your story. The bottom line is: make life easy on your reporters by doing their homework for them.

Be THE Authoritative Source For News

When an incident involving public safety, good or bad, occurs in a community, it is a shocking fact that the press usually calls the Chief, the Mayor or the City Manager but rarely contacts the head of the union. Can you imagine? Local media come to management first, not representatives of the rank and file, for comment on issues effecting your membership. It is inconceivable that the union would, by routine practice, hand the public microphone to representatives of management to have their say while the union remains on the sidelines. **This should never happen!**

YOU should be the **FIRST** source for comment on issues that affect your membership. You accomplish this goal by establishing a solid working relationship with the reporters that cover your issues. You need to be their most credible source for news information about local police issues . . . **NOT** management.

About Radio Talk Shows

From time to time, you may be invited as a guest on the "Angry Radio." The radio talk show circuit is typically dominated by conservative commentators that generally support law enforcement officers and their mission. Many police union members are regular listeners and are sympathetic to the messages and issues discussed on these programs.

There is a temptation to feel that these are "friendly" forums for law enforcement. Think again. These shows, above all others, attain their ratings at their guests' expense. People tune in to hear their favorite hosts lambaste some poor sap who never saw it coming. You should view these programs with a jaundiced eye. Sure, it's exposure . . . but at what price?

As a program note, if your adversary is dumb enough to appear on one of these programs, shame on you if the phone lines aren't flooded with questions they don't want to answer. This opportunity is excellent to put your adversary in the cross hairs and expose the flaws in his or her position on a given issue.

Some More About Talk Shows

As you can see, we are not big fans of talk show formats for the reasons cited above. However, you will receive invitations from time to time that merit an appearance and offer an outstanding opportunity to present your position on issues. Here are a couple of tips to help you evaluate whether to accept or decline an offer to appear:

- **What is the format?** Before agreeing to expose yourself to public ridicule, ask the station manager what kind of format will be used for the interview. A one-on-one interview with prepared questions is much easier, and less dangerous than an "open mike" with listeners calling in to take pot shots.
- **Who will be asking questions?** Fielding questions from a local personality is one thing. Going toe-to-toe with a Mike Wallace or Chris Mathews is another matter. Are potential adversaries going to be present or allowed to grill you, unprepared, on air?
- **Who is the likely audience?** Who is going to be listening to this stuff anyway? Despite all the hype, radio talk show audiences are notoriously small, highly partisan with sharply defined opinions you are unlikely to change. Before accepting the invitation, ask yourself how "persuadable" these people really are toward your position.
- **What is the upside for the union in going on the show?** How will this appearance benefit your members? How does it fit into your overall campaign plan? Does your appearance support or distract from your message? These are essential questions that need answers before you commit.
- **What is the potential downside?** All interviews with the media are dangerous. While interviews can often allow you to present and focus on your positive message, there is always the danger that you will step on your verbal tongue. A well-known police labor leader did a radio interview in 2007 to discuss a new law giving collective bargaining rights to sheriff's deputies. It was an hour-long session where dozens of tough questions were successfully asked and answered but the labor leader managed to step on a land mine anyway. When asked about how ready these deputies were for collective bargaining, he responded, "Politically it's like they have been living in caves." The next day their Sheriff held a news conference accusing the union leader of calling his deputies "cave men," and that was the way the rank-and-file saw it as well. Not good.

Chapter 22

DEVELOPING A MEDIA RELATIONS STRATEGY

The Russians don't take a dump without a plan, son.
Fred Thompson
Former Senator and television actor
Quote from the movie,
The Hunt for Red October

He's absolutely right. A union president has no chance of success with the press without a well thought-out plan. Following are a few first principles for your media strategy:

Speak with ONE voice

This single most important rule is yet the one most often violated by police unions, sometimes to disastrous effect. There should be one person, typically the union president, who is responsible for interacting with the media. This individual should have a strong appearance, a bubbly personality, and solid credibility as the "voice" of your union. He or she should attend professional training seminars (especially our PFLI sessions – another crass and commercial plug!) to develop and polish their media skills. Their most critical role is to nurture the personal relationships with reporters that cover your union and to do so long before facing a media crisis. The worst possible scenario is the member who happens to be cleaning up the union hall taking a call from a reporter.

Here is real life example of why it is imperative that only **YOUR** designated spokesperson control the message. A southern police union was in a major fight with a local state attorney over his zealous and mostly bogus prosecution of officers/union members. Everything went well in the beginning: the message was clear and the union had received some excellent press. The leadership decided to push the envelope by holding a press conference in front of the state attorney's office to ratchet up the campaign against him.

Just as the press conference was about to begin, a carload of off-duty officers pulled up, park illegally in a tow away zone (mentioned later by the media), sporting handmade signs calling the state attorney the "antichrist." Needless to say, every future story about this fight began with "the union that called the state attorney the antichrist." It was later discovered that these dummies were not even members of the union!

Have a Procedure For Handling Press Inquiries

First and foremost, your union should create a media contact form that includes the following important information:

- Date/time of the call;
- Reporters name and contact number;
- Deadline they are working under; and
- Exact subject matter.

Never take a call from a reporter without gathering the information above. There is a famous story about newly elected Congresswoman Corrine Brown of Jacksonville, Florida. A smart aleck reporter from *Mad Magazine* decided to call the newest batch of recently elected members of Congress to see if he could trip them up. He called Congresswoman Brown's office and the call went directly to her with no notice or preparation. The conversation went something like this:

Reporter: "Congresswoman, how do you feel about the ethnic cleansing going on in Fredonia?"

Brown: "I'm appalled at the loss of human life and, as one of my first acts in Congress, I will urge the President to commit U.S. forces to stop it."

There was one big problem with this exchange: there is no such country as "Fredonia." Sure, ethnic cleansing was underway in Bosnia but not "Fredonia," unfortunately for the Congresswoman. This incredible lapse would never have happened had she and her staff used the contact procedures we advocate.

You should also probe to learn exactly what the reporters are after. Do not accept "we want to talk about the budget" because the real subject could be "allegations of police embezzlement." Tell them you need to know as much as possible so you can be prepared to answer their questions intelligently.

Any press inquiries should be answered promptly, but you are under no obligation to answer them immediately. The distinction here is between a prepared response and an "off the cuff" remark that can doom you and your union. Take the time to get your facts straight, develop your message, and anticipate counter messages (discussed later) before returning the reporter's call. Don't ever "wing it."

Getting Good Press

There will be occasions when you want to aggressively seek out media coverage of your union and pending issues. But there is a right way and a wrong way to go about the matter. The first question you should ask is; "Is the issue newsworthy?"

There is a four-part test to answer this question. If your event doesn't include at least two of these factors, you probably don't have a news story sexy enough to attract attention.

- **Immediacy.** As discussed previously, reporters operate on daily, sometimes hourly deadlines. If your event is a week or more away, it is simply a "lifetime" away for a harried reporter. Unless your event is within 24-hours, it does not meet the requirement for immediacy.
- **Controversy.** There is an old media saying; "If it bleeds, it leads." Reporters are attracted to conflict as sharks are to blood in the water. Someone has to win and someone has to lose in order to pique their interest. Many police unions are frustrated that the media does not cover their good deeds, donations to charity, or youth outreach programs, but the media doesn't sell advertising covering feel good events. The more that controversy is involved, the better your union's chance is for attracting the sharks to your tank.

- **Saliency.** This is a 50-dollar word for "what folks are talking about." Keep a close eye on events happening nationally such as the early release of Paris Hilton, dogfighting and Michael Vick, or fatal shootings at schools? These events that everyone is talking about often offer opportunities for a "tie in" for your union. Comparing a local politician who got a light sentence to the Paris story, a new task force investigating dogfighting rings, or stepped up police efforts to protect schools are good examples.

- **Local Impact.** This point is the "what's in it for me" factor. Remember when President Clinton proposed adding 100,000 new police officers around the nation? Your local audience wanted to know, "how many are we getting?" Any time you can "localize" your story improves the chance of getting good coverage. Remember the old adage, "The closer your issue is to my front doorstep, the more I'll pay attention."

Chapter 23

HOLDING PRESS CONFERENCES

Once you have determined the newsworthiness of your event, you may want to call a press conference to get your point across. There are some important principles that you must observe in order to have a successful press conference.

Do a "Pre-Press" Notice

Send a notice alerting the press no more than 24 hours in advance of your event. You should include the who, what, where and when of your event, but don't give them all the details. Give the press just enough "red meat" to pique their curiosity but don't give them so much information that they don't feel the need to come to your press conference. Remember the adage: "If you give them the cow, they won't buy the milk."

Always Use a Visual

Newspaper people are visual people. The typical press conference gives television reporters a "talking head" spokesperson, which is good for about 5 to 10 seconds of on-air time for your issue. By creating a visual aide that summarizes your message, you can earn an additional 5 or 10 seconds, thereby doubling your exposure time.

A press event scheduled to focus on proposed cuts to a Florida city's police budget hit a snafu when a professionally produced visual got lost in the overnight mail. The union leaders improvised with a "stick man" holding a book (budget) that was drawn by hand on the way to the press conference. Incredibly, the "stick man" visual appeared on all three local networks that night.

Get Lots of People Involved

One of the great advantages of running a police union is the multitude of people you can mobilize to your cause. Keeping in mind the visual nature of television, you always include dozens of supporters, in tee-shirts and carrying signs summarizing your message or call to action. Camera crews will "pan the crowd" giving you even more air time and reinforcing visually the verbal message you are delivering. (Program note: Be sure to brief your participants on the need to maintain message discipline at all times!)

Best Time and Place for Your Event

Experience has taught us that the best time to hold a press event is on a Tuesday at 10:00 A.M. This day and time is optimal for catching the "top of the news cycle," and by holding the event mid-morning, you give reporters time to recover from their hangover in time to attend.

The worst time to hold a press event is any afternoon (you'll miss the midday and often the nightly news that day), and on Friday or Monday mornings. Friday gets you in the Saturday edition (the least read), and Monday means you notify on a Friday making it difficult for the press to make your event.

Always hold your press conference at a location that is both convenient to the press and reinforces your message. Holding a press event in some out of the way place will guarantee low attendance, and does not bode well for getting your message out.

Do the Advance Work

You should always check out the location of your event the day before. If you are doing a power point presentation or plan to play a radio commercial, make sure there is electricity available. Scouting the location beforehand can help you avoid unpleasant surprises that can ruin your event.

The Things You Say, and Don't Say, at a Press Conference

Many police union spokespersons has been tempted to present their personal version of *War & Peace* at a press conference. If you've ever witnessed such an event, you'll notice that the reporters wait impatiently for the tirade to finish so they can ask their questions.

It's smarter to first read a brief five-sentence statement summarizing why we are here today. There is a rule for press conferences that you speak to television first, radio second, and the print media last. That is why the first sentence or two of the press conference should always include a dramatic sound byte that will make a good clip for the 6 and 10 o'clock television news.

After you finish the statement, then take a lot of questions. There will be a time after questions when the print media might want to stay for a more in-depth briefing.

Follow-Through is Critical

As we mentioned in an earlier chapter about developing a working relationship with the press, your reputation for reliability is king. If you promise to give more detailed information to reporters at your press event, do it. Your follow-through says a lot about you as a credible source of information.

Press Releases – A Forgotten Art

Very few police unions send out press releases with any regularity. This state of affairs is puzzling because a press release is literally your chance to write the news on your issue.

Press releases can be used in the context of a press conference. Hard copies can be distributed at the event to reinforce the information you are discussing. For those representatives of the media who do not show up at the press conference, you can fax a copy of the release to their office.

Sometimes an incident or issue does not call for a full-blown press conference, but still might be sufficiently newsworthy to send out a release. For example, an officer seriously injured in the line of duty and hospitalized would be worthy of a press release to call attention to the dangers of the job. It might then interest someone in the media to follow-up with an interview of the officer, his family, or the union leadership. There is no reason why your union should not send out press releases with regularity – you are creating news!

The first paragraph of your release should include the five "W's" and the "H." By this we mean Who, What, Where, When, Why, and the How. The How paints a visual picture of the scene and makes your event more real for your readers – the How is the toughest to write, but it spruces up your effort.

Here are some examples.

1. The Tucson Police Association (Who) held a press conference in front of City Hall (Where) today (When) to protest threatened cuts to police services (What).

2. A bugler played taps and police widows covered their hearts as the Tucson Police Association held a press conference in front of City Hall today to protest threatened cuts to police services (How).

Include Quotes in Your Message

Reporters are leery of making changes to written quotes provided in a press release, and this gives you a great opportunity. You should always include the gist of the message in quotations or comments from union leaders. This technique guarantees that your message will be delivered as you intend it.

Always Include A Photo

Whenever possible, include a photo with a caption summarizing your message with every press release. Why? Because space considerations often make running your story impractical for the local paper but there just might have space for a picture and your descriptive caption.

When taking photos, try to avoid the standard "grip and grin" shots typical at awards banquets – they're boring. Try to involve "action" in your photos and be aggressive, get in close and get the shot. Your caption should describe the action in the photo, identify participants from left to right, and always give credit to the photographer. Many times the police union's release will end up in the trash can but the accompanying photo runs on page one.

Chapter 24

FRAMING YOUR MESSAGE FOR THE NEWS MEDIA

So far, this part of the book has examined news organizations, reporters, and techniques to get your message out. Now it's time to turn to developing your message, anticipating counter messages, and learning how to stay on track.

We live in a fast paced, ever-changing world and are constantly bombarded by messages from a variety of sources. This barrage of information is called "white noise:" television advertising, the internet, radio ads, billboards, mail appeals, political ads and even family pressures compete for the public's time and attention. It is therefore not surprising that Americans have an ever shrinking attention span, and more and more organizations are trying to "punch their messages" through the noise.

Remember that your union is one of those organizations. It is vital that your message on any given issue can saturate all of this "white noise" so that it is heard loud and clear. Otherwise, your voice and your message will be lost in all the informational clutter. For these reasons, it is important to remember the axiom: "Brevity is next to Godliness."

If Your Message Can't Fit on a Postage Stamp, It's Too Long

You have to work very hard to take your broad message and distill it down to one or two key phrases that sum up what you're trying to say. People simply do not have the time or inclination to sift through complicated facts to arrive at the point you are trying to make. You have to keep the message simple, uncomplicated, and as direct as possible if you want people to remember what you are trying to convey.

The more complicated the message, the simpler the terms need to be. And in labor relations, we often have some pretty complicated concepts to argue before the public. Esoteric issues such as pensions, multipliers, pay steps, and cost ratios cause the average person to roll their eyes back into their heads. For example, if we are arguing for a 3 percent increase in our annual pension multiplier, the message would be framed around "rewarding officers for a career of risking their lives to protect the public." Let the lawyers argue about the details.

The "Rule of Threes" Principle

When framing a message, ask yourself, "What three things do I want the public to remember about our issue?" This question can best be answered by the "Rule of Threes" and this concept works extremely well for virtually any issue you are trying to pitch or defend. Here's how it works.

First, you begin with an "umbrella" statement, one that encapsulates your message and the goal you are trying to achieve. Going back to our pension enhancement, the umbrella statement would read like: "We need to reward these veteran officers who have risked their lives for 25 years to protect us, and the best way to do that is to pass the 3 percent special risk benefit. It's only fair."

Now that you have staked out your broad goal or justification, you then give the public three reasons to support your position. "Giving the 3 percent increase in pensions for our officers makes financial sense, says 'thank you' to our existing veterans, and allows us to recruit and retain new officers because they know they will be taken care of down the road." The public gets the message that we want to reward veteran officers, we can afford it, and it makes sense in the future as well.

You will find this structure works for practically any issue you are trying to convey. Try it the next time you make a public pitch to the city council during budget sessions or during contract negotiations. You'll be amazed at how functional this technique is for distilling and framing your messages.

Here's a great example of this principle involving financial fraud committed by the old guard of a union that had been recently voted out of office. The new team was facing a barrage of bad press regarding some pretty extravagant and, even illegal, expenditures by the previous administration. The old guard certainly did live high on the hog including trips to Las Vegas, rented yachts for fishing trips, girly magazine subscriptions, and lavish dinners. The public was outraged that their donations had supported such nonsense.

The new union leadership held a press conference and delivered the following message: "We apologize for the actions of the previous administration and want the public to know that we do not condone such behavior. Here are three things we intend to do to make sure this never happens again: public audit of our books, hiring of an accounting firm, and putting safeguards in place regarding the expenditure of future union dollars." The press scrutiny fizzled, and the public was satisfied.

Message Development Exercise

The authors have spent many collective years in this business, and have come to realize that there truly is nothing new under the sun. Human nature being what it is, we can make some very accurate predictions of what folks are likely to do or say on an issue or in a political campaign. The following innovative issue development model is an excellent method for making reasonably precise calculations about your position and your opponent's position.

You set up a grid with the following questions and gather your leadership team for a brainstorming session to answer them as honestly as possible.

- **What are WE going to say about OUR position?** This question is where you get to "sing our song." You list each and every reason to support your position, dissect your argument, and list supporting facts to prove your case.
- **What are WE going to say about THEIR position?** This question is usually the fun part for the team. You tear the opposition's arguments to pieces (a lot of fun really), and list all the reasons why they are greedy, uncaring worthless scoundrels for not giving us what we want.

- **What are THEY going to say about THEIR position?** Hey, the opposition has a song to sing too. You must anticipate their arguments, and the reasons and data they will offer in support of their position. You need to be brutally honest at this point. Try as hard as possible to put yourself in the position and mindset of the opposition. Be their attorney and you'll discover the most effective arguments working against you.
- **What are THEY going to say about OUR position?** The opposition isn't dumb. Sure, they will offer some very solid reasons to support their argument, but they will also take the next step in tearing down your castle. Again, you have to be totally honest about your weaknesses to make this step effective. Only when you frankly consider the reasons **NOT** to support your position will an effective defense emerge.

Inoculation Strategies

Using the message development exercise above, you have discovered a number of weaknesses that the enemy may exploit. You may have a problem that you are sure will emerge during the campaign and don't know how to address it.

The truth is that none of us are perfect. We all have our warts, and just because we have displayed a lack of judgment in the past doesn't mean that we have to pay the penalty in the future. When confronting a problem that has the potential to destroy your campaign, it is often necessary to "immunize" or inoculate yourself or your campaign before the enemy uses your problems against you. Following are some inoculation principles to bear in mind that apply to any campaign situation.

Always Concede On Principle

All issue or political campaigns usually boil down to a single, underlying moral principle. This statement sounds extreme, but you will be surprised by how easily you can gain a deep understanding of a situation simply by identifying the fundamental principle that is being debated.

For example, take the explosive issue of racial profiling. Virtually every police agency in the country has had to confront accusations that its officers specifically target minorities for a tougher brand of law enforcement than whites. It goes without saying that the overwhelming majority of law enforcement officers do not support or condone the use of racial stereotypes when enforcing the law.

The danger in confronting these accusations is to immediately buy into the underlying principle the opposition is trying to advance; specifically, that law enforcement officers are racist by definition and that they willingly dispense unequal justice to minorities. If you find yourselves actually defending the practice of using racial profiles to enforce the law you are, by default, accepting the opposition's view.

The real principle at work here, and the one that should be debated, is that every American is entitled to equal justice under the law. Your union will never, ever allow the opposition to seize the high ground like that. You simply will not willingly allow your adversaries to "profile" us as racists who use the law for evil purposes. Sorry, we are not buying into it.

You begin this kind of debate by defending the rights of every law-abiding citizen to be safe in their homes, businesses, and on the streets regardless of their race, sexual orientation, or religious preference. Now, you can debate all the societal ills that have led to an unconscionable number of minorities ending up in our prisons. Or you can talk about the roots of poverty, such as our substandard education system or the deterioration of the family. You can even discuss preventive measures, such as record keeping, to ensure that some rogue cops aren't targeting specific groups. But what you will not accept is the premise that justice for some and not others is the law of the land.

Better to Define Yourself Before the Opposition Does It for You

As a child, you learn very quickly the principles of inoculation. When you mess up at school, you know that Dad's ass whippin' will be far less severe if you tell your side of the story to him first. You don't want for him to hear it from the principal before you put your "spin" on the situation.

The same is true when confronting a problem that you know will become an issue in an issue or political campaign. It is far better for you to acknowledge the problem, put your spin on it, and hopefully diffuse the issue before it grows legs and becomes a bigger obstacle.

Here is a great example involving a candidate for a state senate seat. He had a sparkling resume, a beautiful family, and deep roots in the community; and he was 100% pro-law enforcement. Internal opposition research revealed, however, a bankruptcy and several financial judgments against him twenty years ago. It was obvious that his opponent would make a major issue of his money management skills as a disqualification for office.

Instead of waiting for that attack to happen, the candidate opened the campaign with a tear-jerking account of how he struggled through poverty, suffering these setbacks along the way, to eventually emerge as an American success story. The opposition likely gasped at the "leading with his chin" opening but the story effectively inoculated him on this issue. He won the seat and has consistently supported law enforcement ever since.

Anticipate Criticism . . . Shine a Light on Your Problem

Do you remember George W. Bush's cocaine problem in the 2000 presidential election campaign? The issue of past drug use threatened his bid for the presidency. Early in his bid for the White House, reports began to surface that George was a bit of a bad boy during his college years. While talk of his drinking and carousing were legendary, no hint of past drug use, particularly cocaine, had come to the attention of the media. Then a number of individuals began talking to the press about George's use of marijuana and cocaine; and there were hints that some of these folks were willing to speak on the record.

How did the Bush campaign respond? They at first refused to acknowledge the rumors at all. They then pursued an even more bizarre strategy by declining to discuss drug use during his college years (they even specified which years they would not discuss). What this effectively did was define for the media the years in which George had used drugs. The issue began to snowball but, because no individuals went public with their accusations, the storm subsided and Bush was elected.

While it clear that the Bush campaign would not ever have sought our advice, the authors believe that this response could have been handled in a very different and more effective way. We would have had George W. hold a press conference immediately to convey this simple message: "There has been much discussion as to whether or not I experimented with drugs in my youth. I am here today to acknowledge they are true. That's right. I made some serious mistakes in judgment as a young man that I am not proud of, and I am sincerely sorry. But that's not what is important here. What is more important is the fact that I am the son of a President of the United States. I was raised in a privileged environment, had a loving family, and enjoyed all the benefits of the American dream. If someone like me, the son of a President could be enticed into drug use, how are poor children in our inner cities to resist this temptation? If you elect me as your President, I will do everything in my power to remove the scourge of drugs from our streets."

Instead of endlessly confronting these rumors, why not "shine a light" on your problem and use it as an advantage? It goes against human nature to admit a problem but doing so can be a powerful inoculation strategy.

It's Hard For Someone to Hit You When Your Fists Are in Their Face

The authors have all developed a reputation as aggressive, "in your face" combatants. We are quite proud of that fact. Our attitude stems from the fact that our team is right and theirs is wrong (well, usually anyway). It's just that simple.

So we don't hesitate to take the fight to the enemy. This tactic is particularly true when we think the bad guys are about to hit us first. If our side has a problem or weakness that the enemy is about to exploit, we hit them first. It is called "blowing up their rocket on the launch pad;" and it involves striking their weaknesses fast and hard. Instead of waiting for their punch, we will launch a multi-pronged attack on their camp, get them on the defensive, and make any counter-punch by them appear to be an act of desperation.

An example best illustrates this principle. One of the authors represented a Southwest police union where the police administration was making every effort to destroy the union through intimidation of union leaders and members. The management staff began reassigning union leaders, questioning members about what took place at union meetings, and requiring members to sign a document supporting the administration.

The union began a campaign of pushing back – getting in the employer's face, by first sending a series of letters from the union attorney calling attention to management's actions and the possible legal consequences of these actions. Then the union held a press conference where the leaders announced that they had had hired an outside consulting company to do a job satisfaction survey of its members. This press conference was of course preceded by an advisory and followed up with a press release. Another press conference took place when the survey was completed to announce the findings that there wasn't a whole lot of job satisfaction among the members. In between the two press conferences, the union made a public information request for travel and training records involving the management personnel. Just remember that it's hard for the opposition to hit you when you are in their face first.

Chapter 25

HANDLING A MEDIA CRISIS

Despite all of the advice in this section of the book to help you avoid negative press, it is nearly inevitable that your union will face a media crisis. If you have worked hard to develop the media skills described previously, things won't be as tough. Still, there is some important strategic advice that will help you, your union, and your members emerge hopefully unscathed.

First of All, Keep Your Cool

Anyone who has lived through a major media crisis will never forget the experience. These crises seem to explode out of nowhere, and the pressure generated by the blast is white hot. The media are in the union hall lobby demanding comment, the phones are ringing off the hook, the Chief is on line one, the mayor on line five, and your members are gathered around like scared antelope yelling for you to "do something!"

Under this extraordinary pressure, you may be tempted to lash out, to wing your response, or to do something rash to relieve the stress. **Don't do it!**

As a union leader, you must be the eye of the hurricane, calm when the winds are fierce all around you. You above all others must keep a cool head and lead the frightened antelope away from danger.

Take Time to Develop Your Strategy

If possible, step out of the line of fire long enough so that clear heads will prevail. Take the time necessary to craft your response and anticipate counter-messages using the techniques discussed previously. Begin by remembering the various audiences that are watching your performance.

- **Your members.** Your members expect you to stand up for them; and they will hold you and the union brutally responsible if you don't. Your response to any crisis has to bear their feelings and impressions in mind. Will the response strategy instill confidence in the rank-and-file that you are ready, willing and able to defend the herd?
- **Political leaders.** The political elite in your community will be watching to see how skillfully or clumsily you handle this crisis situation. They will make judgments about the effectiveness of the union and your leadership skills. Remember, the politically connected community is small and incestuous – everyone knows everyone else's business. How you respond to the crisis can greatly influence their impression of the power and effectiveness of your organization. What are the politicos thinking about this event?
- **Voters.** The frequent voters in your community decide elections and are most feared by politicians. They are the ones you always turn to when the mayor or sheriff needs to be put back in their place. How they view the crisis will have enormous implications for your reputation among this critical group. How do ordinary citizens feel about the situation?

Don't "Hunker in the Bunker"

Once you have taken some quiet time to get your message straight, go ahead with a media event to get your perspective on the record. One of the worst things you can do is to hide from the media, take overly long to respond or, worst of all, offer "no comment." The longer you take to respond translates into suspicion by the media that you have something to hide.

Cast the Message in Your Terms and Stick With It

Once you have developed your message – your take on things, stick with it. The media will do everything possible to get you "off message" by discussing or defending something that is not part of your planned message response. Don't take the bait. Stay on message.

When in Doubt, Get it Out!

Invariably, you will be in possession of information that the media does not yet have. Very often, it is damaging to your cause, and there is a tremendous urge to conceal this bad news from the press. Don't do it.

The fact is, if you know about some harmful information, it can and will be discovered eventually by the press. These guys aren't stupid, and when they discover the truth and your attempts to hide it, you're cooked. Watergate was a story about a break-in, yet 35 years after the fact, people remember the cover-up.

When in doubt, get it out. Take your lumps like a man and resist the urge to conceal the truth, no matter how ugly it may be.

It's Okay to Say "I'm Sorry"

Perhaps one of the most powerful and least used political weapons we have ever seen is the apology. Most of us hate to admit when we are wrong, and have a tendency to go to great lengths to justify and explain our actions. What is amazing is how powerful simply saying "I'm sorry" for a deed can be in diffusing a situation and how rarely we use this devastating weapon.

Here is a nasty political race years ago that involved a young, hot-shot challenger taking on an elderly, well-liked, and respected senior member of the State House. The young buck was plowing away at the old man and running a very aggressive, in-your-face campaign. He crossed the line, however, with devastating results. It seems the legislature was working into the wee hours on the last day of session and the old geezer was photographed by an AP camera man laid out in his big fluffy chair. The young challenger seized on this opportunity, thinking that this was the "silver bullet," and held a press conference the next day accusing the old bird of sleeping on the job.

The backlash was spectacular. The press asked the senior gentleman if he was indeed sleeping at the time photo was taken. His response was that he was "stretching his arthritic neck," and even the photographer confirmed he was awake at his post. The local citizens were outraged and flooded the challenger's campaign office with angry calls, a ceaseless stream of letters to the editor, and even a protest in front of the young man's campaign store front.

What did the young gunslinger propose to do in response? He suggested that a nationally recognized sleep expert be hired to hold yet another press conference challenging the old man's account! The young client was told, however, that the meal for the day was "crow," and that he was going to eat every bit of it, beak, feather, talons and all. He apologized and the crisis faded. He didn't beat the old man but came back later in another political incarnation. But that's another story.

It's Okay to Beg

The authors are unapologetic prostitutes when it comes to defending rank-and-file officers . . . period! That means we will readily swallow our personal pride and beg a reporter to not run a story that is likely to harm an officer and his family. It doesn't happen often, but we have successfully appealed to certain ethical reporters' sense of fairness and have headed off stories that would have harmed our members and their reputations. Humility can go a long way when you have developed a solid, working relationship with the press that covers your union.

Chapter 26

EFFECTIVE TECHNIQUES FOR DEALING WITH THE MEDIA

This part of the book has run the gamut of news media issues: understanding the Fourth Estate, working with reporters, the world of news organizations, a media relations strategy, press conferences, message, and handling a media crisis. This last chapter will look at some effective techniques when you come face-to-face with a reporter.

Handling Tough Questions

In any exchange with the press, you can expect to face tough questioning. The interview may begin with "soft balls" but usually evolves into hardball questions that are a challenge to answer yet stay on message simultaneously.

To those union leaders with little face-to-face experience with reporters, an upcoming interview can be nightmarish. It's like being called to the principal's office in grade school. On the way to the administration building, you think of all the bad things you've done lately and try to anticipate what the big guy wants to scold you for this time. You really whip yourself into a frenzy asking; "what will he bring up?" or "what if my parents find out?" By the time you reach the principal's office, you are in a cold sweat of terror. This is **NOT** the frame of mind to approach an interview with the press.

Worse, once you enter the briefing room, you feel like a boxer beginning a match. You sit there wondering where the next blow will land, and while you deal with that, you get hit again and again. Too often, you feel like a victim, helpless against the barrage of media questions. This state of affairs just doesn't have to be so.

Don't approach any contact with the press as a victim. You should not feel helpless or fearful of this confrontation, but instead should welcome it. You should feel powerful, confident, and eager to get your chance to go *mano y mano* on **YOUR** issues.

Always Think Before You Speak

One of the authors' dad, God rest his soul, spent 27 years in U.S. Army Intelligence and a lifetime safeguarding sensitive information. He had an extremely irritating habit that served our nation well but was very frustrating to us civilians in day-to-day conversation. He was a big fan of the ponies and the young teenager would ask him something as innocent as "Hey Dad, what do you say we go down to Calder Race Track and watch the ponies run?" He would acknowledge the question, but what would follow was a protracted pause before he gave an answer. What he was doing as the result of a lifetime of mental training was processing the request, checking it against his internal database for national security clearance, and then formulating an answer that was exacting a well within military protocols. This technique certainly didn't make him the hit of the party.

The point is that you are not required to instantly respond to a reporter's question. Take a breath, ask him to repeat the question, restate the question yourself, anything to buy yourself that little extra time to formulate your answer.

Staying on Track – the Art of Bridging

As we've described previously, you don't approach an interview with the press like a sheep, but more like a lion. You formulate your message in advance and hone it to a razor's edge. But what do you do when the reporter constantly drags you "off message" with questions that you don't expect? How do you stay "on message" and not get drawn into subjects and debates that are not to your liking?

The solution is the art of bridging, which are effective techniques that you can use to keep the discussion focused on your issue. Here are some useful phrases with some observations as to their use:

- **"Let's keep things in perspective."** This comment works well when the reporter is hurling fireballs about just how big a problem or incident is. A good example is the number of adverse shooting incidents in the community. Thankfully, there are not many so when a reporter overly-hypes the situation, you should ask them to keep things in perspective.
- **"But the real issue here is. . ."** This one is good because no matter what issue the reporter wants to discuss, you simply say, "No, that's not the issue, the real issues is the one I came to talk about!"
- **"Another important point I want to make. . ."** This statement is a soft ball but can be very effective in shifting gears back to the topic you were addressing.
- **"Let's cut to the chase here."** This comment is used mostly when you are getting a barrage of questions or statements that simply cloud the issue. "Let's cut to the chase" breaks through the chatter and gets you back to the soul of the issue.
- **"I can sum this up in three words."** This phrase uses our "rule of threes" to the extreme. Simply stop the questioner in his tracks, hold up your hand and say "I've got three things to say here" and re-take charge of the interview.
- **"What my opponent is trying to say is. . ."** This remark is an all-time favorite because it really irritates the opposition. You can almost hear the Mayor demand "How dare you presume to speak for me!" No matter what your opponent is saying, what he really means is up to you to define.
- **"The bottom line is. . ."** This classic closer is used as the interview winds down to reinforce or put an exclamation point to the discussion.

All of these phrases put you, not the reporter, in control of the message. Practice these techniques with a mock debate with your executive board. See if you can formulate a message and stay on track. It's a lot of fun and will make you a real pro when dealing with your next encounter with the Fourth Estate.

On Camera Skills

The final stage of preparing to face the press is to brush up on some practical on-camera skills to help you deliver your message effectively. Let's start with your physical appearance. Many men enjoy sporting beards, feeling they lend an air of distinction and sophistication to their appearance and convey credibility and confidence. We hate to burst your bubble. Think about it. What other famous person sports a beard? How about the Devil, Satan. You know: the Anti-Christ. The truth is that folks don't trust folks with beards. Psychologists suggest that the covering of face conveys mistrust. Either way, you may want to consider losing the goatee if you are the face of your organization.

Now let's talk about your wardrobe. There are proven television "friendly" colors, and those that distract viewers and hurt their ability to focus on you, the messenger. Light blue is the most advantageous T.V. color followed by a soft pink (yes, we said "pink") and a light non-offensive brown. Colors that don't work are bright red, yellow or black. These are considered "hot" colors that distract the viewer on camera.

Another thing to avoid is "patterns" in your clothing. This means lose the striped shirts and "busy" ties that look electric on television. Single color shirts and subdued ties are the rule.

Finally, male union leaders should buy some knee-high socks. This suggestion sounds weird, but you should see what your enormous hairy leg looks like to viewers when you cross them. It distracts from your message to say the least.

When on-camera, you should watch your gestures. During the 70s, the art of reading body language was all the rage. There were countless books on the best sellers list about how to use unconscious human gestures and body postures to your advantage in everything from winning over the opposite sex to succeeding in business. A lot of these techniques were over-hyped but there are some negative body gestures to avoid and some positive body language to help you communicate more effectively.

- **Crossed arms and legs say "stay away."** It is a natural tendency for folks to cross their arms or feet, sometimes both at the same time, as an instinctual defense mechanism. This response is particularly true when the questioning gets rough, but you don't notice that your body is communicating a defensive posture. Just be aware of what you are doing with your arms and legs and you'll be okay.
- **Violent or deceptive hands are the work of the devil.** The most threatening gesture in human communication is the

"point." Look in the mirror and point your figure at yourself. Do you see just how menacing and hostile that gesture can be? A better tool to help underscore your point, without pointing, is what is called "the rock." You simply close your hand into a fist and lay your thumb on top. Use this "rock" just as you would your pointed finger to emphasize what you're saying . . . it works. Check out any stock footage of President Bill Clinton giving a speech – he made the rock a staple for media training professionals.

- **"Open palms, open hearts."** A very positive technique is called "open palms, open hearts." If you've ever watched a preacher spread his hands in the pulpit welcoming the faithful to prayer, you have a good example of the open palms method. By opening your palms and extending your arms out to viewers, you are saying "Come, join me, and let's share the love." It is very effective.
- **"The Bridge."** Another negative hand gesture is called "The Bridge." This gesture is where you lace the fingers of both hands together and place them over the bridge of your nose. This motion effectively covers your face and conveys a sense of dishonesty (see objections to beards above).

The minute you sit down for an interview and the camera and lights go on, your body subconsciously has already begun the "fight or flight" response. There are a number of common physiological changes that happen: sweaty palms, tightening of the throat muscles, and the like that can seriously hamper your ability to calmly present your case.

This natural nervousness is actually healthy because it helps animate your presentation; it gives your responses some zing. If you were truly relaxed and felt no pressure, your performance would be "flat" and frankly, boring.

The one downside to the fight or flight response is that you talk faster, sometimes so quickly that people simply don't get your message. Be conscious of how fast you are speaking, make an effort to slow down to ensure you are getting your points across, and don't forget to breathe! In other words, when it comes to word traffic, slow it down Nellie!

You will be tempted to look into the camera as each and every question is asked. More than likely, the interviewer will discourage you from doing this as it is a real distraction to viewers and, frankly, looks kind of silly. Maintain eye contact with the reporter until you are ready to spring the trap; that is, when you are ready to make your critical point (i.e., your overall statement and the three things you would do about it), turn to the camera to dramatize the moment.

Part V

GETTING TO YES OR ELSE: CONFRONTATIONS AS A MEANS TO MAINTAIN RESPECT

Chapter 27

ABOUT ETHICS, CONFLICT, RESPECT
AND TACTICS

Conflict has long been the way that people and groups have changed the system. Nineteenth century black activist Frederick Douglass had this comment about conflict: "If there is no struggle, there is no progress. Those who profess to favor freedom, and yet depreciate agitation, are people who want rain without thunder and lightening. They want the ocean without the roar of its many waters."

In the twentieth century, one of the most famous advocates of conflict as the method for organizations to achieve their goals was Saul Alinsky. While Alinsky's philosophy was discussed thoroughly in Chapter 3, a few of his principles should be restated here as a reminder of the inevitability of conflict and confrontation that police labor leaders face:

1. Change comes from power, and power comes from organization.
2. The first step in community organization is community disorganization.
3. The leader must simultaneously breed conflict and build a power structure.
4. No one can negotiate without the power to compel negotiations.

There is no point in re-hashing the entire Alinsky philosophy in this part of the book, since that task was completed in Part I. It should be strongly emphasized, however, that no police labor leader can really succeed in achieving organizational goals without anticipating, and at some point, facing some degree of conflict and confrontation; and no leader will feel comfortable in this role without an understanding of Alinsky's principles.

Conflict for the sake of conflict is self-defeating. Some union leaders strive on continuing to battle with the chief or elected officials long after the conflict is resolved or should have been resolved. Confrontations should be viewed as relationship adjustments. Relationships with management and elected officials oftentimes get into a rut, and the degree of respect needed to sustain the relationship is diminished. It takes a lot of energy and a willingness to create a strained relationship for a period of time to get that respect back.

The number one recurring problem faced by all police union leaders is that they believe that recognition **OF** the union is the same as respect **FOR** the union. Disrespect of the union by management or elected officials must have consequences. If a husband shows disrespect for his wife, and the wife does not stand up for herself, will the husband have more or less respect for his wife? If the disrespect continues or grows worse, the couple will get a divorce or the wife will demand respect to readjust the relationship to one based on mutual respect.

There is no divorce in the relationship between the police union and management or elected officials. Almost certainly the city will continue to exist, the officers will have a union, and people will get elected to the governing body. Since there is no divorce, the union must constantly demand respect from management and elected officials. Management and elected officials must know for certain that any disrespect will cause an appropriate reaction from the union.

Maintaining relationships based upon mutual respect is not easy and requires constant adjustments. Many police union leaders are too lazy or too afraid to upset the status quo even when they know they are being disrespected. Understanding confrontations and how to use them effectively is the focus of these chapters. Police union leaders can decide if they wish to be a lap dog or a pit bull. We believe the pit bull gets more respect, and everyone knows for certain what will happen if you kick one.

"Principle-Centered" Negotiations and Impasse Arbitration

A great deal of attention has been paid in recent years by academia and public sector management associations to the concept of "principle-centered" negotiations and leadership. Unfortunately, the real world does not find an abundance of principled management negotiators and public leaders – decisions are more often than not made on the basis of trade-offs, *quid pro quos*, business and political relationships, and other factors totally unrelated to sound public policy.

It is tragic that many police labor leaders have bought into the notion of "principle-centered" negotiations without giving their acceptance to the idea some thought. In states where collective bargaining is permitted, this path of least resistance results in lukewarm negotiations, mediocre wage and benefit offers by public employers, and oftentimes, mediocre settlements mandated by third-party neutral impasse procedures. These arbitrator-driven settlements are safe; that is, decisions that will not greatly offend employers or the public. Police unions rarely have the opportunity in this process to break out of the pack with a significant wage settlement or a new benefit, because state bargaining laws normally require arbitrators to adhere to a strict wage and benefit "comparability" standard.

Any police union leader who feels smug that his or her state bargaining law is all that is necessary to achieve the interests of the membership is sadly mistaken. There are an untold number of police union leaders throughout the country who have been condemned and driven from office by frustrated members who felt that the contract settlement or arbitration award was insufficient to satisfy their economic needs.

If the police union is going to break through the maze of backroom power brokering, ivory tower decision-making, and lackluster contract settlements that often disregard the needs of union members, then conflict becomes inevitable for the successful police union. It is the essence of what will bring the union to the center of power.

Using Conflict and Confrontation for the Benefit of the Police Union

There are three things that the successful police union leader must do to achieve the short and long-term goals for the membership. First, conflict must be accepted as an essential component of any success you might achieve. Second, the leader must understand when and how to engage in conflict. Finally, conflict must be used when it becomes necessary.

Conflict does not, however, always have to be severe – a stern, well-publicized letter to the mayor or city manager protesting certain actions of the city can sometimes achieve the desired goal. At the same time, a pitched political battle against an incumbent mayor who has not been the union's friend, or a high-visibility referendum against an anti-employee city manager, might become necessary as well.

The police union leader must always be aware that conflict for the sake of conflict will wear thin with your members, with the public, and even with your political allies and friends; and in the end, will prove to be unproductive. The police union leader must have a strategy that centers on calculated risks that will achieve calculated gains. The organization should pick the fights that are vital for the achievement of short and long-term goals.

The use of conflict and confrontation is a touchy business – it's an art, and definitely not a science. This part of the book will examine how to go about using conflict and confrontation in the police labor leader's arsenal: how to conduct referendums; how to gather public support for police wage and benefit issues; how to select political consultants who can assist your group in waging high-visibility conflicts; using other pressure points; and finally, understanding that in all fights, there inevitably must be a winner, and a loser.

Chapter 28

THE BATTLE IS FOUGHT IN THE COURT OF PUBLIC OPINION, NOT AT THE BARGAINING TABLE OR AT THE COURTHOUSE

There have been at least two Northeastern police unions within recent years that became so frustrated with pay and working conditions that they have taken the fight public. Coincidentally, both groups used billboards to make their displeasure known. And just as coincidentally, nothing has been heard from either group after the first billboard.

The general view on billboards among political consultants in any type of public and political campaign is very simple. There are only two really effective locations for a billboard: one is outside your candidate's bedroom window; the other is outside the opponent's bedroom window.

But the goal here is not to make it harder for the billboard salespeople to make their house payment, or to pick on those two police unions, both of whom should be commended for trying to do something. Instead, what should be emphasized is that if your police union is planning a public pressure campaign over wages, benefits or working conditions, then it must be fully planned **BEFORE** you go public.

This chapter will look at how to effectively bring public pressure to bear on the politicians in order to improve police compensation packages and working conditions. And for those readers who bargain and think that they don't need to read about the use of public pressure to get things which you normally negotiate for, think again. Both of the unions cited above who used billboards had collective bargaining laws and were located in states with compulsory, binding arbitration laws!

There are three elements which a public pressure campaign must contain if it is to have a chance for success: a clearly defined goal; an evaluation of what tools you can bring to bear in the coming fight; and control over the outward appearance of the campaign.

Number One: Defining Public and Private Goals

The decision to go public means that the police union is embarking on a political campaign. Successful campaigns have a central theme or message that drives the entire enterprise. If you're really serious about being successful, then you'll devote a great deal of time to this stage of the process.

Union members may simply want a raise, but let's face it – a campaign based on "give us more money" isn't a campaign. It's no more than a ransom note.

Your job is to frame the pay raise argument so that the public is willing to take money out of their pockets – sometimes in the form of higher taxes, and to put that tax money in your pocket. This task is not easy during unstable economic times when the public is facing layoffs, declining health insurance coverage, and loss of defined benefit pensions. Too many officers believe that public support **OF** the police automatically translates into a vote **FOR** higher taxes to give the police higher salaries and benefits.

After September 11, 2001, scores of Texas police unions placed wage increases on the ballot for a vote. All of the unions lost. The heroism of 9-11 did not translate into a positive vote for higher wages. The public still had great respect for the job of a police officer, but when voters closed the ballot box curtain, they voted against higher taxes and not against the police themselves. Higher wages for police officers in and of itself is not about the public – it is about an officer's desire for more money.

The first step in this definition process is to get specific – simply asking for a pay raise is not enough. You must know exactly what you want, and what the members will accept. For example, you might take the position that you want a 5 percent pay raise to make up for the erosion in paychecks since the last pay increase; and you want shift differential pay increased by one percent to keep pace with what other comparable law enforcement agencies are making.

Once You Know What You Want, Find Out How to Pay For It

The city or county's response will normally be: "We can't afford it." So the next step should be to find the money.

Hire an outside economic expert or get a friendly professor at a nearby college to analyze the budget and find money that can be redirected to the police department. Show how eliminating the city staff's take-home cars, cellular phones, and fitness club memberships will free up some funds. You're not making a stock offering here, so the numbers don't have to stand up to SEC scrutiny; but it is nice to give your reasoning a little academic camouflage.

If the numbers don't completely add up, add a small tax or fee increase to the package. Earmarking the funds – that is, dedicating them specifically to law enforcement, is a nice touch which shows the taxpayers that the money won't be lost in the general fund.

The Next Step is to Define Your Public Message

It's crucial to remember that the public's **PERCEPTIONS** about the economy and their lives have a great deal of bearing on how they react to your message, and therefore how successful your campaign will be. You must wrap your pay raise in a message that will be accepted by taxpayers who might be worried about keeping their jobs, to say nothing of their concern over a pay raise from their boss.

The downside to *Misery Loves Company* is that miserable folks don't like the idea of someone doing better than they are. If you want a raise when John and Jane Q. Public aren't getting one at their office, then there has to be some perceived benefit for the public before they'll support you. That new bass boat you've had your eye on won't do it.

That's why you also have to define your public goal, which may differ in emphasis from the private goal your members are seeking. While local conditions vary, here are a few ideas for positioning your pay raise or working conditions request:

1. Upgrade the force. To reflect the growth and complexity of modern law enforcement, we need to attract the best and brightest to the force. We can't attract quality applicants with our current bargain basement pay scale. Adjusting the pay scale and benefits will attract quality applicants. The public wants professional police officers and seeking higher wages and benefits to attract only the best qualified applicants to your agency is a matter of public concern.

2. Stop the exodus of trained officers. We're losing trained, experienced officers each year to other departments with more realistic pay scales and benefits. The result is that the city is wasting hundreds of thousands of dollars in training costs to replace these veterans. Adjusting the pay scale and benefits would retain these officers, cut training costs, and give the taxpayer better protection than with a rookie-heavy department. One California police union has t-shirt made to resemble a tour by a rock band. The union's *Exodus Tour* t-shirt lists all of the agencies that have hired officers from that department.

3. Put more officers on the street. Based on national statistics, our force is currently understaffed by X number of officers. If we are to have any hope of stopping the rising tide of crime, we must have more police officers. The solution is to add X officers each year *and* adjust the pay scales to attract the kind of applicant we need. The number one concern of citizens in most communities is their personal safety. Police visibility lessens the public's fear of crime. Police management and elected officials tend to dwell on crime statistics. That is just hogwash and the public could care less about crime stats. The public's *perception* of their own well-being is all that matters.

4. Envy of low self-esteem. Our police are the lowest paid in the county, state, and probably the world. Why, just next door in Richville, police officers are paid 25 percent more. If we don't raise our pay scale and benefits to parity with Richville, our crime rates will go up, and Richville will get all the new business and tourists. Business people, the Chamber of Commerce and civic boosters all want to maintain the reputation of a safe community. It is bad for business for people to believe the city is unsafe.

In your city or county, you can mix, match or come up with an entirely different message. The important thing is to think like a taxpayer. If you're paying taxes in your town, would this argument convince you to dig a little deeper?

You've Got to Plan Your Campaign Well

Any campaign that has a chance of succeeding must be well-planned, because you will be using intangibles to attempt to force someone with real power to do what you want. City Hall already has the votes; otherwise you wouldn't be unhappy in the first place. To get the governing body to change votes will require a carefully orchestrated plan of action.

Here are some basic principles: Spur-of-the-moment protests and one-shot displays simply won't work, because the opposition can wait you out. The police union must have more than one arrow in its quiver, or it goals will become irrelevant. Governments can adapt to pain or insult, just as the body can.

Let's take the billboard example we discussed previously as an example of these principles. The morning the billboard appeared attacking city hall on pay or working conditions, it was a slap in the face. The mayor talked about it, the newspaper covered it, radio talk shows discussed it, and your members wanted to act as if it was your fault. The next day an editorial ran in the newspaper wringing its hands, and urging the police to work within the system. The third morning, the billboard was discussed in a city council meeting where members of the council said they were deeply hurt by this attack, and that they had always been strong supporters of law enforcement.

The next week, the powers-that-be looked at the billboard and said, "Is it still there?" Then they went on about their business.

When You Get in a Fight With City Hall, Escalation is the Key

Your union must have a plan with options for escalating the intensity and/or direction of your pressure. Here's an example of public escalation from the political campaign in a mayor's race. The female candidate was a woman who was trying to force her opponent to debate during a two-week runoff election for a vacant mayor's seat. The opponent was currently the sheriff, and had been running a macho, law enforcement campaign against the woman.

The first step in the female candidate's attack was to run a full-page newspaper ad with a headline reading: "SHERIFF ANDY TATE: COME OUT AND FIGHT LIKE A MAN." The press thought that the idea of a petite little woman challenging a gun-toting sheriff was great! She got coverage on every news media vehicle known to man.

Step two was interrupting Andy Tate's press conferences. She drove up outside his campaign headquarters in a mobile home, got out and erected a table with a large sign that said, "DEBATES ARRANGED

WHILE YOU WAIT." At the same time, her representatives sat in the waiting rooms of his campaign headquarters and asked for the members of his steering committee. Each of her representatives had full authority to negotiate debate terms. Her people sat there all day and tied up his organization. Again, she received massive news coverage.

Step three was never taken. It would have been another full-page ad that read: "FOR A GOOD DEBATE, CALL 555-1026." [Andy Tate's campaign headquarters.] But the ad never ran because the other candidate caved in and agreed to debate.

Why did he agree? Because the woman candidate continued to escalate the pressure, and the other side finally had no choice. The opposition's campaign simply couldn't function. And that's what your police union must do in a public campaign.

Your goal must be to set up such a flood of events and distractions that the pressure becomes unbearable. You want city hall to become so frustrated that the political leaders will give in or agree to negotiate just to have some peace.

Here's a Practical Example of How to Use Escalating Tactics

Now let's go back to where we started, with our billboard that caused the one-day sensation. Billboards do have some advantages for a public campaign, assuming that you get the right location. This site can be near city hall, near the mayor's house or business, near the city manager's house, near the newspaper editor's home or business, at the city, county or state boundaries or any other location which provides a daily irritant to those you wish to influence and affords some public visibility. Billboards can be especially useful if you can get them donated to your cause for a few weeks by the owner.

So here's the situation. Your union has secured two donated billboards, one in a location that's across the square from city hall and one on the main road into town. Your budget is so low that you won't be running full newspaper ads; and your membership is apathetic and only good for one rally. Is there any way you can have a sustained, escalating campaign?

In this situation, the answer is yes if you just keep changing the billboard message. You could start with a message that says: "Welcome to Hooterville. Home to 635 Registered Sex Offenders. Be Safe and Drive Carefully. The Hooterville Police Union," The second week, you can update the figures using a ceremony that provides visuals for media coverage. At the council meetings on the third week, you can bring in a large map with red pins indicating where the 635 sexual offenders reside.

To the public, it's a public safety issue; to your members it's a pay increase; and to the union, it's a way to go public that increases pressure, doesn't use much money, and doesn't require 100 percent participation from the membership. And it all started with a billboard and some planning.

Remember That When You Begin to Apply Pressure, You're Going to Get a Dose of Your Own Medicine

When your police union runs a successful pressure campaign, the plans will include a number of events calculated to increase pressure on city hall, and to keep the opposition off balance. But remember that for every action there is a reaction. Always keep in mind that pressure works both ways, so you must prepare the membership for a little squeezing too.

While your union applies pressure to the mayor for a pay raise, the police chief is going to be leaning on you and the rank-and-file to stop the campaign before you've achieved your goal. And the chief won't be alone – he'll be joined by other pillars of the establishment and status quo who will tell you, your board of directors, and your members that this campaign is hurting the whole city, and will backfire on you with the voters.

The pressure will be intense. And since police forces are hierarchical organizations, the members are accustomed to taking orders from the establishment. Many of your members will be uncomfortable with defying authority.

You will also encounter this pressure when you meet with the editorial board of your newspaper, or the board of directors of the local chamber of commerce. These people are the movers and shakers with influence in the community, and you must meet with them. So while you are at the meeting, never lose sight of the fact that these guys and gals are cheerleaders for the establishment.

These self-appointed Judges of *What's Right For the Community* will wring their hands, shake their heads, and "tsk, tsk" during the entire meeting. With pained expressions, they will urge you to be a team player and work within the system.

But the point is, going public with your desires is part of the system too. And once the pressure from above starts to build, you have to remind your members that there's nothing wrong with public conflict. The members must be resolute in the face of this pressure, or your campaign will fail miserably.

One Alternative for Confrontations That Doesn't Work Very Well – Job Actions

Now that you have issued Kevlar drawers to the members and are prepared for the fight, what can be done to draw attention to the issue? One of the first suggestions might be a job action; but this approach is problematic for cops because it's so easy to be accused of abusing your authority.

Take traffic tickets for example. If officers write citations for *every* violation of the speed limit, then the public is going to be hot, and that's who you want to support your position. If you announce that you won't be writing any tickets, then the public is happy, but at least as far as the public is concerned, there is zero pressure. In fact, the public may want police officers to stay unhappy so you won't go back to doing your job.

So let's say that you don't write tickets, but you don't announce it either. Instead, you wait for the administration to see the drop in revenue and respond. This process takes much longer and exposes your organization and members to a number of variables: state laws that call for firing public employees and union officials involved in a job action; and ticket quota systems that can be applied in performance review or disciplinary settings.

For a job action campaign to succeed there must be absolute membership solidarity, which is at best a questionable pursuit in the police labor movement. If management pressures officers to start writing traffic tickets and makes life impossible for traffic unit officers, then there must be some other response, like refusing voluntary overtime assignments.

As you can readily see, the police union's options are limited because you can't appear to do anything which makes the city less safe for the taxpayers. This scenario means that the administration can play dirty and your side cannot.

That's why job actions are a difficult road to success. However, if any readers have had a successful job action, the authors would like to hear about it. What's more, we'll write an entirely new book devoted to your clear thinking and strategic insight!

Three Types of Public Pressure With a High Likelihood of Success – #1: Embarrassment

Once you've excluded job actions from your arsenal, there are three types of public pressure left. These forms include *embarrassment, political,* and *drama.*

Embarrassment is just that: the police union discloses information about your enemy that is embarrassing to them when made public. Contrasting the city council's refusal to implement a manpower program with the $125,000 they spent on a trip to Aruba for a planning retreat is a powerful public comeuppance.

Examining the city manager's car phone records and listing the private calls he made at taxpayer expense are good ideas. Then release the manager's car phone number, and ask the public to call him on that number and tell him to quit wasting money. That tactic will get some attention at City Hall.

The number one source of information on elected officials is their campaign reports. It is surprising how often you will find a direct correlation between a campaign contribution and a later vote by the incumbent. Many candidates hire their spouse and family members and pay them outrageous salaries.

Go over all the opposition's expense accounts and office accounts for suspicious spending. These items are public records and available for your amusement and edification. Have a certified public accountant go over the budget with a fine-tooth comb and point out any waste. Ask for management and elected officials credit card receipts after a junket to some seminar or conference. Look for alcohol purchases, expensive meals, porn movies charged to their rooms, and other suspicious expenditures. Make the council justify spending money on the chamber of commerce or convention center, and not on law enforcement.

The term "blowing the whistle" didn't come from basketball – it came from English Bobbies who used to blow whistles instead of sounding sirens. Make your goal to blow the whistle on waste and recruit whistleblowers in government who will help your cause. After two city commissioners in one Southern town complained about police brutality and called the officers *Nazis,* the police union found records showing the two city commissioners had ownership interest in a towing company with the city contract. The radio ads produced and aired by the union attacked these two elected officials for this improper relationship. The two commissioners quickly agreed to measure their words in the future when complaining about the police.

Examine all the records and see what looks fishy, or what the public would question. Decide your timetable for release, and how to do it in the most effective and embarrassing manner; and then get to work.

More About Successful Pressure – #2: Political Pressure

Political pressure is probably the most powerful tool. Elected officials may challenge the union when they think the union is weak or they think the public is more supportive of the city's position. The key is to take control of the issue and escalate the pressure on management and elected officials. Many actions by management and elected officials can be overturned by the public using initiative and referendum.

A common political pressure point is to petition the government. Many states have state and local initiative and referendum provisions that allow the public to petition and change state laws, local ordinances and so forth. If local ordinances permit, and you are organized enough to gather names, these petitions are a very useful lever. Some petition options include binding arbitration for impasse or discipline, recall of elected officials, pension options by the city or just for the purpose of registering a protest over an issue. Check state laws about the legality of petitioning on the issue. For example, Texas law makes it a felony for a labor organization to participate in a recall election.

Your first move is to gather names. This step shows power and public support. The next move is threatening to file the petition. You may win here, but since city hall might not respond to your threat, *don't make the threat unless you are prepared to carry it out!*

The third move is to actually file the petition; and it is here that things start to get complicated. Once you go to the mat, you either have to win, or come within a whisker of victory. A big loss is fatal at the time, and even worse, the hangover can linger for years.

That's why your best bet is to get what you want without the election. Even if the city thinks it can win, elections do cost money and staff time, and the outcome is uncertain. Such an election can be a distraction the city may not want, so the police union could get a useful compromise at this point.

Going for an election when the police union has not done its electoral homework can be a disaster. If the city wins big, your goals will disappear for a decade. If the city wins by a whisker, you're in better shape to get petitions again. The second time, you may get a compromise without an election.*

And Even More About Successful Pressure – #3: Drama

Going the drama route, you'll soon discover that public pressure equates to media pressure. Obtaining media pressure means that what the police union does has to be interesting enough to merit coverage. Any activity that lends itself to a photo or dramatic television event has an even better chance of making the news.

The key is to recognize opportunities and act upon them. A policewoman who was a single mother contracted cancer and was off work for a year. Her leave was about to expire and the police union asked the chief if officers could work for her until she could return to duty. The chief said he had a no light duty policy. The union prepared a radio ad and set a press conference the next day that would have brought tremendous pressure on the chief and embarrassed the city manager and elected officials. A new light duty policy was created immediately and the officer was given time to recover and return to work.

You should plan press conferences and activities with an eye toward producing an interesting picture. Some of these activities include distributing leaflets at shopping malls in your town, warning of crime dangers for holiday shoppers, and/or dressing your officers as Santa Claus warning about crime. One police union hired an actor and dressed him in a police uniform (without a gun) and had the actor march around city hall during work hours with a sign reading, "Will Work for Food." The media went into a frenzy over the story and caught the mayor watching the event from her office in city hall.

You can also take out newspaper ads in other cities warning about crime in your city; or pass out flyers at malls in other towns warning shoppers not to come to your city. Off-duty officers can distribute flyers at the airport warning tourists and business people of crime dan-

---

*Author's Note: See more about referendums in the following chapter.

gers in the city or downtown area. This idea is an escalation that builds even more pressure. These boycott and crime warning actions come with a huge backlash from the media and business community. Scores of unions have started them and had to back down as soon as the crap hit the fan. Use extreme caution before choosing one of these options and weigh the backlash.

Support for your cause can be generated through appearances at city council meetings where the wives and families of officers killed in the line of duty ask why the council is abandoning law enforcement. The police union can hold a press conference with injured officers as the centerpiece.

You can recruit other organizations to speak out or hold press conferences on your behalf. These groups might include neighborhood organizations wanting police coverage, the downtown merchant's association, veterans groups, the National Rifle Association, or any organized group with some clout who will join your effort.

Hold a media event where you make chalk outlines representing every murder in the city during a certain period of time (week, month, year, etc.). If it suits your purpose, make it look like a crime scene, and have the outline represent injured or killed officers.

If you have the budget, use radio ads for real impact, or even cable television. Union leaders can write op-ed pieces for the newspaper. Have officers and their families write letters to the editor. Put spouses, parents and children of officers on radio, television, or cable talk shows.

But keep in mind that you always have to control the message. So any time you are dealing with the media, be prepared for trick questions, and stay on the themes and points that are central to your campaign. *Always* be professional and well-organized when dealing with the media.

Chapter 29

INITIATIVES AND REFERENDUMS AS A CONFRONTATION TACTIC

The use of initiative and referendum is often overlooked as a political tactic by many police unions. Police labor leaders often do not realize that by forcing a public vote on an issue, they are using the ultimate tactic of confrontation – they are taking power away from the public employer to control events, and placing it in the hands of the police union to control its own destiny.

The use of the initiative and referendum does not have to be limited just to police labor issues. It can be employed as well for other issues; and the police union's participation then sends a *message* to the employer that the organization is not pleased with some aspect of the labor-management relationship.

Initiative and referendum options have a long history among activist groups in this country. Very simply, initiative and referendum is the process of petitioning voters to require public officials to place a particular issue on the ballot for a single-issue election. The terms "initiative and referendum," "voter referendum," and "single-issue election" will be used interchangeably throughout this chapter.

The Legal Framework

The first question that any police union must always ask is whether or not initiative and referendum is permissible in your jurisdiction. Each state and/or local law empowers the initiative and referendum process in a different way. Here are some of the methods found throughout the country:

1. State laws on charters and ordinances. Many states provide for a specific method by which voters in home rule cities or other political subdivisions may petition to amend city charters or adopt new ordinances.

2. State laws on specific police issues. A few states permit initiative and referendums on very narrowly defined labor issues, such as binding arbitration, civil service, pay raises, or the right to collectively bargain. These often apply to municipal and county law enforcement employees.

3. City (or county) charters – charter change. The charters of many home rule cities (and some counties) provide for a system where voters can petition for amendments to the charters. Such provisions will sometimes have specific restrictions on the type of amendments that may be brought (e.g., no amendment may be initiated that requires an appropriation of money).

4. City (or county) charters – adoption of ordinances. Some charters provide that petitions may be initiated for adoption of city (or county) ordinances. This approach can be very limiting, because there is usually a time period – often one year, after which the ordinance may be modified in any way by the governing body.

Remember that the question of how a voter referendum may be set into motion is complex. Competent legal counsel should **always** be consulted when evaluating your options to use initiative and referendum.

Preparing for Initiative and Referendum

Any issue that is brought to the voters will be controversial to some interest groups in your community: the local governing body (i.e., city council, county commissioners); minority groups; taxpayers associations; senior citizens; and so forth. The decision to carry through with a voter referendum will, by the very nature of this adversarial process, put your association at war with a certain segment of the community. And like any war, **the failure to prepare in advance of the voter referendum virtually guarantees that the police association will be defeated at the polls.**

A police union should **only** use the voter referendum system when the union is sufficiently prepared to go forward. Following are some key preparation tips that will give your union a strong foundation once the commitment is made to proceed.

The two easiest things that the police union can do are (1) vote to seek a referendum; and (2) collect the signatures on the petition. For the unprepared union, the referendum starts going downhill from that point, because the police union leaders have failed to understand the political system that they have now entered.

Let's restate the cardinal rule for all police union referendums: Public approval **OF** the police does not translate into a vote **FOR** a police issue on the ballot! Voters can, and will, vote against pay, civil service, collective bargaining and other labor issues and still visualize themselves as "pro-police." The burden lies with the union to run a **POLITICAL** campaign, and not necessarily a **PUBLIC RELA-TIONS** campaign.

A police union that is considering an initiative and referendum should seek **professional assistance** before it is too late to turn back. It will be too late to turn back when the leaders or members become emotionally charged, and vote to seek a voter referendum that they have given no previous thought to winning. Or, the police union might file a voter petition that is legally inadequate; and the public employer challenges the legal sufficiency of the petition, delaying the election for several years while the attorneys argue over minute points of law.

Professional consultants should be sought out **before** the decision is made to seek a referendum to educate the police labor leader about your options, and to help to develop an effective political strategy. Your chances of victory will be increased.

Therefore, the wise police labor leader seeks two types of professional assistance before deciding to embark upon a voter referendum:

1. Legal. As discussed above, competent legal counsel should be consulted as to the proper statute and/or charter provision to follow; and the legal sufficiency of the petition should be carefully analyzed before circulating it among voters.

2. Political. A political consultant with polling expertise should be retained to perform a survey poll that will give the police union some feel for the public's attitude toward the police in your community; and the issue being considered. A decidedly negative public view as to public attitudes toward the police or the issue itself should make the police union reconsider the timeliness of an initiative and referendum. It would also be good to initially retain a general political consultant who can give some sound advice on preliminary matters.*

---

*Note: See the following chapter for an in-depth discussion of political consultants.

The last preparation tip is to realize that all successful political confrontations, whether involving candidates or single-issue ballot measures, require four essential elements. These four elements are money, membership participation, membership commitment, and expertise.

Sample Voter Referendums – Labor Issues

The initiative and referendum can be used to raise any number of issues that are directly related to police labor concerns – binding arbitration, manpower, wages, civil service, collective bargaining, work week, pensions, and so on. The process can also be used for other issues that, while not directly related to labor matters, are of immediate public concern and can bring the police union into coalitions with other community interest groups. Such non-labor issues might include single-member districts, term limitations, and governmental restrictions on use of tax money (e.g., prohibition against construction of a new city hall). Following are illustrations of labor issues:

1. Minimum staffing. A minimum staffing petition is an excellent option for a police union where the law enforcement agency is suffering from a marked personnel shortage that can be easily demonstrated through unacceptably high response times or threats to officer safety. If your population is increasing, it is recommended that the police union petition for a minimum number of police officers per 1,000 population (e.g., 3.0 police officers per 1,000 population). This approach might even include a graduated scale, such as 2.0 in 2008, 2.5 in 2009, and 3.0 in 2010. If your population is stable or decreasing, then it is recommended that the union set a fixed number of police officers for the agency (e.g., a minimum of 100 officers).

One important consideration in staffing petitions is to insure that the petition guarantees that the city or other governing body cannot lower or reduce the hiring standards or qualifications, or reduce the wages and benefits of officers because of the fiscal impact of implementation of the minimum staffing election. Otherwise, your union's sweet victory at the polls will turn sour later by an employer looking for ways to avoid the intent of your proposition.

2. Pay increases. In states where a public sector collective bargaining statute exists and a *binding* impasse procedure is in place, the use of pay increase referendums are of dubious legality and negligible value. However, in any state with no bargaining law, or bargaining with a non-binding impasse procedure (e.g., fact-finding), the possibilities for voter referendum pay raises are endless! City charter amendments can be proposed that will seek the following: a one-time across-the-board percentage raise; annual raises tied to the Cost of Living Index (COLA); a wage formula (i.e., future raises tied to percentage raises given to officers in comparable cities); or a restriction on future employee salary reductions.

There are two cautions when analyzing the wisdom of pay raises. First, a wage increase is a pocketbook issue, and voters know that it might cause a tax increase. The local economic conditions are **the most** critical factor in deciding whether to seek a pay raise election. If the voters perceive that times are hard, they will vote against anyone else receiving a pay raise. Careful polling before initiating a voter referendum on pay will let you know the public perception.

Second, there is a downside to seeking a police pay increase, because it impacts other government workers and projects. The city or county will calculate the pay increase based upon every other worker receiving an equivalent raise, or the reduction in government services (e.g., "meals on wheels" to the elderly). A perception of greed by the police always lingers in the background of pay elections, and can quickly strike a blow to the campaign.

3. Civil service or due process. A voter referendum is an excellent way to deal with civil service or due process rights. This option would not likely be available in states where a state-wide civil service system already exists. Initiative and referendum could be used to petition for a comprehensive civil service system (i.e., hiring, promotion and discipline); strengthening of a weak civil service system (e.g., replace the commission with an independent hearing examiner in discipline cases); a fair grievance procedure, including an independent final resolution of grievances; or creating a job property right for employees in at-will employment systems. Police unions in two Texas cities have won voter approval for city charter amendments granting police officers binding arbitration for disciplinary actions. Two Texas firefighter unions have been successful in amending city charters to require binding arbitration for contract impasses.

If at all possible, the police union should include all city or county employees in the petition for civil service. The employer will raise the issue of an elitist, police-only election if you do otherwise, and the other employees will be unnecessarily alienated.

4. Collective bargaining. In states where there is no state-wide collective bargaining law, but collective bargaining is permitted on a local option basis (e.g., Arkansas, Louisiana), there is a wide-open opportunity for the police union to propose a bargaining law through voter referendum. The beauty of this concept is that you will be able to draft a bargaining law that suits your needs entirely, so long as it can be sold politically to the public. Even in states where a bargaining statute is in place, initiative and referendum is available to petition for any number of impasse options. These options can include compulsory arbitration, fact-finding and/or public referendum. There is even legal authority in some states to tinker with an impasse procedure mandated by state law through local voter referendum.

5. Pension benefits. While most pension plans are regulated under state laws, these laws often provide for various options that employers might not choose. The police union may be able to initiate a voter referendum to require the city or county to pay maximum benefits. Another approach is to propose a prohibition against the city or county from using tax money to fund deferred compensation plans for department heads; or where a local pension system is in place, prohibiting the system from loaning money to the public employer (a financing system that has been on the increase in recent times).

6. Work week/overtime. If your employer is regulated by the Fair Labor Standards Act (FLSA) only, and there is no bargaining agreement in place, you may want to petition for change of the following matters by initiative and referendum: creating a 40-hour work week instead of the FLSA 28-day cycle, getting paid overtime after 8 or 10 hours of work, changing the work cycle to 4 day-10 hour or 3-day-12 hour, or eliminating non-productive hours to get overtime compensation based upon hours paid for (as opposed to actually worked).

7. Residency requirements. If the city or county has a residency requirement by ordinance or charter provision, you can petition to modify or eliminate the requirement. For example, the police union might propose to eliminate residency as a condition of employment, but require that an officer live within a 30-mile radius of the police department. Here's a cautionary note on a residency proposition: you will be asking the residents of the city or county to allow you to move out and cease paying taxes. This proposition makes for a tricky political argument, so be prepared to campaign on the issues of fairness and the United States Constitution.

Sample Voter Referendums – Non-Labor Issues

There are a variety of non-labor issues that are susceptible to initiative and referendum proposals. Many of these voter referendums are not directly related to the immediate needs of police officers, but they are matters of public concern that can unite the police union with other political activists in the community. And it obvious that many of the referendums listed below will strike fear in the hearts of public officials.

Consider some of the following options:

1. Term limitations. It is currently popular to campaign for term limitations on political offices. If your city or county has no such limitations, your police union might want to amend the charter to set limitations. It should be noted that there will be a tremendous political backlash from incumbent politicians if this issue is brought to the voters. You might consider assisting a taxpayer's group, and playing a secondary role. Term limits are a two-edged sword. Police unions may have friends in elected office that they would lose to term limits and decide to oppose term limits.

2. Single-member districts. In a city where council members are elected on at-large basis, there is a distinct advantage to the police union seeking a change to single-member districts. It is much easier for the union to reach and influence a smaller constituency than a larger one; and therefore to bring more pressure to bear on local political officials. Single-member district incumbents know that the police union can upset them if they get into conflict with the union.

3. Lobbying with tax money. If your city or county is using tax money to lobby against you at the state capital, your union might consider a petition to prohibit the use of tax money to influence legislation. As a prelude to such a campaign, use the Open Records Act in your state to find out how much the city or county is paying for lobbying activities (e.g., food, drinks, travel, entertainment, professional consultants).

There are also a number of other miscellaneous non-labor propositions which, under certain conditions, might be wise choices for an initiative and referendum. For example, in a situation where a city council is demanding employee salary reductions, give-back concessions, or layoffs, a charter amendment to reduce the salaries and other perks of Council members would find a great deal of public support, particularly in hard economic times. Remember that politicians are generally not trusted or respected by the public; if your union can make a case that police officers are willing to suffer the effects of tough times, but the politicians must do so as well, your proposition will receive a great deal of enthusiastic support!

Here is a specific example of how a non-labor issue can work to the police association's benefit. The City of Galveston, Texas and the Galveston Municipal Police Association (GMPA) were in a bitter collective bargaining dispute, with both sides taking hardened positions on wages and benefits. During this same period, the City decided to eliminate its Sanitation Department, and contract out for garbage collection – this decision was going to cost the jobs of more than 100 Galveston sanitation workers, most of whom were African American.

The GMPA developed a charter referendum amendment that would prohibit the contracting out of city services to private contractors without a vote of the citizens. This action was taken to send the City a message that there would be a heavy price for the City to pay for its inflexible position at the bargaining table. The GMPA then worked with African American community activists to gather petitions and campaign for passage of the initiative.

City of Galveston voters approved this charter amendment! And today, the City of Galveston cannot contract out sanitation or any other City service to private enterprise without first getting voter approval. This victory won over African American sanitation workers and community activists that the police union was sympathetic to their interests and concerns, an important factor whenever the GMPA would need political assistance on future issues.

How a Police Union Referendum Can Succeed

By the time that a commitment is made by the police union to proceed with a voter referendum, the police labor leader should already have a complete understanding of the many critical factors that spell the difference between winning and losing an election. These factors might include available referendum options; union resources; membership commitment; the community political and economic climate; possible opposition groups; possibility for compromise; and the potential backlash from losing. Once the police union is ready to proceed, there are a number of factors that go into making a police union referendum a successful venture: **membership education; coalition-building; strategy; campaign tactics; and get-out-the-vote.** We will now look at each of these factors.

Membership Education

The union will commit a fatal error by not educating the membership about the referendum issue. While pay referendums are self-explanatory, other issues are much more complex. Many members do not always support the referendum issue the police union leadership is proposing; and some members have false information about the issue.

A divided membership is the kiss of death to a union political campaign! Many police unions have split over an election, and killed any chance of its passage. A recent election to adopt civil service protections for the police department was defeated at the polls because all of the sergeants and above held a press conference and opposed the measure. Their rationale was that the Chief would not be able to fire "bad" officers.

It takes time, money and energy to educate your members. A workshop or training session is crucial to educating members and winning their support. At these programs, union leaders should attempt to win over members to the proposition, or to at least neutralize any opposition. The union newsletter can also be used to provide factual information.

Finally, a voter registration drive among your membership and their families should be a part of the union education process. It is amazing how many union members are not registered to vote! One police union conducts a raffle after each election using the names of members who voted in that election. The percentage of members voting has risen dramatically.

Coalition-Building

We have already discussed the importance of the police union having formed relationships with other special interest groups; and these relationships become critical prior to the election. This activity should be directed toward educating these groups about the referendum issue; and either neutralizing them to not oppose the referendum, or convincing the group to endorse the issue.

There are several key groups that should be targeted by the police union:

1. The political leaders. Political leaders (e.g., city council, commissioner's court, sheriff) will remain neutral if they understand the union's referendum issue. Neutrality is as good as an endorsement from political leaders!

2. The media. The news media in any community sees itself as the protector of Liberty, Truth and the American Way of Life. In fact, many newspapers, radio/TV stations are owned by biased individuals who are opposed to your exercise of power. To the extent that you are able to recruit respected community opinion leaders, the more likely the police union will get fair coverage from the media. An attempt to persuade the editor of the paper or station toward your issue should **always** be made.

3. The power structure. Every community has a power structure, which includes elected leaders, business owners, bankers, civic activists and other **movers and shakers**. If this group of people is not neutralized, they will be the ones to fund an Opposition Group against the police union. Seldom, if ever, will the power structure endorse your effort to seize power at the ballot box; but these people **must** be contacted prior to publicizing the referendum in order to keep as many of them neutral as possible.

4. Labor organizations. There is a vast resource of support for your voter referendum among various labor organizations in your community. These groups include firefighters, organized labor groups (AFL-CIO or CTW), teacher unions, and other general city/county employee organizations. In the case of firefighters, AFL-CIO or CTW groups, and teachers unions, they can be a source of political activism, knowledge and assistance to your campaign that is invaluable. But each group must be courted and convinced that your issue is worthy of their support and commitment. In the instance of general city/county employee organizations, they must be sought out because the city or county government will tell these people that your referendum will cause layoffs or reduced benefits! The majority of the governmental work force must be convinced to be on **your** side, and not in the opposition's camp.

Planning a Strategy

There are a number of long-term strategy questions that must be discussed and planned at the outset of a voter referendum campaign. Following are highlights of the most important considerations:

1. The petition. As noted earlier, competent counsel should be consulted to prepare a legally sufficient petition. Otherwise, the campaign is doomed from the outset.

2. The petition drive. The best method to gather the required number of signatures is to target an election date as the day the police union circulates its petition – since every person you contact at the polls is a registered voter, you can often obtain all the signatures necessary in one day. Remember to use spouses and children and have all volunteers dressed in colorful union t-shirts with the campaign message embossed on them.

3. Timing of the election. There will normally be some requirement in state law or local charter as to the dates upon which a voter referendum may be held. Among the timing issues that must be looked at are: how much time to leave for the petition drive and validation of signatures; when the proposed measure would take effect; and possibility of other ballot measures or candidate elections that might help or hurt the union's campaign.

4. The pledge. Before starting any campaign for a specific purpose election, the police union should require each member to sign an individual pledge or petition committing themselves, both financially and time-wise, to the campaign. If the vast majority of members do not pledge to support the referendum with money and/or time, **DO NOT PROCEED!** You will lose the election.

5. The internal campaign. There must be internal responsibility for conducting the referendum. A union member must be assigned to coordinate the day-to-day activity – this person should be a police officer who can best motivate other members, and handle the pressure generated from an intense campaign. A campaign committee of police union leaders should have the responsibility for planning and supervising the general campaign activities. A separate campaign office and campaign bank account are also recommended.

6. Money and the budget. Here is the major key to referendum success: **Money is the driving force of any referendum campaign!** There are three sources of campaign financing: dues (unlike for candidate elections, most states do permit the use of dues money for single-issue campaigns); special assessments of members; and contributions from citizens and businesses. Once the finances are reasonably fixed, a time-line budget should be set establishing when each event or activity will occur, and the amount of money needed to fund it.

7. The professional consultant. If the financial resources are available, the police union should hire a **general consultant** to manage the campaign; and hire **special consultants** on an as needed basis for such projects as direct mail, polling, media advertising, and fund raising.

8. Database computer files. Regardless of whether a specific purpose campaign is planned, your police union should collect computer files for political activity. The union must be able to communicate with all aspects of the community; and voting lists can normally be purchased from county clerks or the Secretary of State's office.

9. Specific purpose PAC. Most states require PAC registration and reporting for single-issue referendums. These requirements normally vary from candidate elections; so consultation with an attorney, political insiders, and appropriate government officials is encouraged.

10. Citizen's Committee. Your opposition will form a "Citizens Against the Police Issue," which lends credibility to the opposition's position. In order to counter this tactic, a "Citizens For Committee" should be formed to take a position in support of your issue. This group should be a cross-section of the community; and can issue news releases, attend civic meetings, write letters to the newspapers, and generally defend the issue.

Campaign Tactics

The **entire** purpose of the police union campaign effort is two-fold: get-out-the-vote (GOTV) during early or absentee voting (as applicable); and GOTV on election day. Every effort and activity by the police union must be *only* to accomplish these two purposes. If you fail in your GOTV effort, you lose!

Set forth below are some campaign tactics that will assist the union's GOTV activity. Remember that where possible, these activities should be undertaken with the help of a political consultant. Also, all tactics should be geared toward sending a simple, understandable message to voters.

1. Direct mail. Mail pieces to voter's homes can be helpful, particularly to targeted groups where a **working class** issue will be received well. Also, use the union bug for all direct mail – union members will usually notice the absence of a bug.

2. Newspaper advertising. The usefulness of newspaper ads in a political campaign is debatable. But in smaller communities where the newspaper owners are generally a part of the business community that will oppose your proposition, a newspaper ad can somewhat neutralize the editorial pages.

3. Radio spots. Many police unions find radio advertising to be an effective campaign tactic – it is relatively inexpensive and reaches a wide audience, and can target people more likely to vote.

4. Television commercials. A large police union in a market with television stations might want to consider TV advertising. It is expensive, but reaches a large audience in a visual society. You cannot, however, "buy" an election through television. It should only be one of the tactics in your arsenal. Do not overlook using local cable stations where you can target most likely voters by the channels they watch and advertising is inexpensive. Cable allows suburban cities to use the local company and avoid using the metropolitan media stations.

5. Telephone banks. Volunteer telephoning is inexpensive and highly effective. Telephoning voters should be taking place from the beginning of early or absentee voting, all the way through election day. Voters who are called and indicate a preference FOR or UNDECIDED about your issue should be recontacted prior to election day.

6. Door-to-door. This tactic is absolutely one of the best campaign tools. The personal touch, especially by police officers who have a stake in the campaign, convinces voters that you really need their support. Households where voters live should only be targeted for your door-to-door campaign – this approach requires a great deal of preplanning.

7. Other Campaign Tactics. Some other activities that might be successful, depending on the number of union workers and its financial resources, include a Speaker's Bureau, press releases (cheap, but often of limited effect), bumper stickers, billboards, yard signs, and bus bench advertising.

Some Final Thoughts

The initiative and referendum is an excellent method to accomplish union goals that can't be reached through more conventional means. Remember that most single-issue police referendums are controversial; and experience has shown that the election will usually be won or lost by a slim margin. The campaign must be geared toward getting one more "yes" than "no" vote through the application of principles discussed in this chapter.

Chapter 30

EVERYTHING YOU NEED TO KNOW ABOUT POLITICAL CONSULTANTS

The two previous chapters have looked at how a police union attempts to convince the public that the union's position on a particular issue is valid. It could be a pay referendum, manpower issue, tax rollback, adoption of civil service, or collective bargaining vote. Your goal might be winning an election in a city the size of New York, or pressuring two city council members to change their vote. Regardless of the situation, your chances for a successful outcome become stronger if you have the proper political guidance from the beginning.

The need for political advice means hiring one or more political consultants to shape and direct your effort. It's axiomatic that law enforcement professionals tell civilians not to chase thieves, not to confront armed suspects, and not to take the law into their own hands. But all too often, when confronted with a political problem, those same officers will take off in hot pursuit of a potentially deadly issue without the least bit of political backup.

Consultant as a Generalist

The consultant you are most likely to have had some contact with in the past is the campaign manager/general consultant. These individuals are the jack-of-all-trades of the industry. It's a prized position in most campaigns because a big part of the job description is acting as the gatekeeper.

The general consultant assembles the entire campaign team, and suggests who the union should interview in connection with their particular problem. He or she also sets the basic guidelines for what kind of campaign should be run, and what constitutes a realistic fund-raising goal and campaign budget.

In a traditional candidate campaign, the general consultant plans overall strategy, directs message development, allocates resources, and works directly with the candidate. But in an issue campaign like the type that police union leaders will sometimes be running, it's more common for the general consultant to be what is called a **hyphenated consultant**. In other words, the lead consultant will most likely be a media-general consultant or polling-general consultant. Without a candidate to baby-sit, and a headquarters staff and volunteers to organize and direct, the generalist role in an issue campaign is a good place for one individual to fill two slots.

Media is Still the Message

Since an issue campaign or referendum is mostly message, it's only natural for the media consultant to function in a dual role as general consultant. However, a media consultant's primary duty is to oversee the development of the campaign message.

This message or theme is a part of every communication effort your campaign has. This theme will be the foundation of the paid media, free media, and any speaking engagements that occur in connection with the campaign. It will, in fact, dictate the entire direction of your campaign. Only the budget has an equal impact on what you do to communicate with the voting public.

The media consultant must ruthlessly cull any extraneous ideas or slogans from the communications efforts, because these only distract voters and defeat campaigns. The hands-on portion of his or her part of the communication effort is writing and producing the radio, television, and print advertising. At the same time, the media consultant will direct the association spokesperson in the free press strategy (see below), and recommend other campaign specialists for your union to interview and possibly hire to join the effort.

The media consultant your union selects **absolutely** has to be able to take an issue that is important to your group as law enforcement professionals, and to put that issue in a context that is relevant to voters who may have a very different set of priorities. Otherwise, your campaign is guaranteed to fail.

Voter Contact: Retail Politics

While a media consultant's messages reach large numbers of voters simultaneously – in a wholesale fashion, the **voter contact specialist** touches voters on an individual basis through the use of direct mail, phone banks, or door-to-door canvassing.

A limited budget may dictate that mail is your union's only paid form of contact with the electorate. Or a larger budget can allow your group to use mail in a mix with electronic media to give your message an even greater impact. Either way, your voter contact consultant must be able to express the theme in each of the individual contacts with voters regardless of whether it's a brochure, a phone call, or knocking on a door.

Voter contact firms that operate in what can be best described as a one-stop shopping operation will provide phone banks, targeted direct mail, recruitment of block captains for walking door-to-door, and getting out the vote. In a campaign effort where money is at a premium, this type of operation may be all that your union can afford; and in the end, all your group might need to win the election.

Press: If Only Free Media Was

The newspapers and television stations may not charge you when they cover your press event, but your union must still work very hard to get them there in the first place, and must also make sure that the press leaves with the correct story. What's more, there is a big difference between standard public relations and political press relations. The most obvious difference is that at the end of the public relations campaign, the audience is not asked to vote, but at the end of a political campaign, the audience does vote.

The free press message is therefore very important to any issue campaign. As a matter of fact, it can be the single most important factor in determining the outcome of an issue campaign with a limited budget.

With so much at stake, it is crucial to have someone who knows what they are doing – a person with press contact responsibilities (i.e., called a **press secretary**). Since free press sometimes has to take the place of paid media, it is important for the press person to be capable of thinking visually and creatively, so as to generate maximum coverage. Although the press secretary must be creative, he or she must also be willing to stay in the background and let the designated members of the union be featured in the news coverage.

Finally, the press operation, regardless of the overall campaign budget, must be expressing the same theme that appears in the paid media and other voter contact methods.

Polling: The Pulse of the Electorate

The pollster provides research for the campaign that is vital to message development and election strategy. The **benchmark poll** is where the campaign begins. Here is where your union can determine the existing state of mind among the electorate. What are the voters supporting? What will they vote against? What messages will work to your union's benefit in the campaign? What attacks will you have to prepare to deflect?

The benchmark poll becomes the knowledge base upon which your group builds the rest of its issue campaign. The numbers here are used as a baseline to judge if your campaign is progressing according to plan, or falling behind.

Polls taken later on the campaign are called **tracking polls**. These are brief snapshots of the electorate that tell you about the union's message. Is the message working? Does it need to be adjusted? Does your union need to spend more money to gain greater voter penetration?

In addition, a polling firm may recommend that the campaign conduct **focus groups**. These are small groups of six to ten people who are interviewed as a group for one or two hours. In a focus group, the union can learn how voters discuss the issue. What language do they use? How deeply do they hold their issue positions? And can their minds be changed?

How Many Is Enough?

In a small issue campaign, the police union may hire only one or two political consultants, while a large referendum may have one of each type directing campaign efforts. How many, and what kind are determined by your campaign budget, the size of your electorate, and how strong the opposition is.

Hiring a Political Consultant – The Three "E's"

The best advice for hiring a potential political consultant is to follow the three "E's:" **Experience, Expertise and Enthusiasm**. If you hire one, or a group of consultants who qualify on all counts, your chances of success in your political campaign are greatly improved.

1. Experience. Everyone has to get experience somewhere, but the question for you is: Do you want it to be **your** campaign? There is nothing like working in political campaigns to give political experience. Corporate public relations are not political experience; teaching political science at the university isn't political experience; labor organizing isn't political experience; and covering the crime beat for the newspaper isn't political experience. The foregoing backgrounds can be useful when combined with political experience; but by themselves, these activities aren't as useful as political experience.

If your potential consultants all have over ten years as either heads or members of their current political consulting firms, that's great. But this fact should not automatically rule out the person who is just starting a new firm. Although the particular company may not have been in existence long, the principals could be veterans.

Or there could be a situation where a long-time administrative assistant to a congressman or local official decides to go out on his or her own as a general consultant. This person might not have a great deal of experience as a general consultant, but would have a wealth of political knowledge.

2. Expertise. There is a big difference between the consultant who has ten years of experience, and the individual who has one year of useful campaign experience that he or she has been using for the past ten years. Your potential consultant with ten years experience would likely have been learning something during each of those years, while the person with one year ten times would be of less value. Whichever person you are considering, your goal is to discover that individual's skill level, and the ability to apply those skills in different political situations.

The best way to evaluate a consultant's expertise is to look at the person's work. Media consultants and voter contact specialists are prepared, even eager, to have you look at what they've done in the past, and to dazzle you with their footwork.

But keep your budget situation in mind as you examine their work. The fabulous commercials done for Senator Foghorn's reelection campaign probably had a bigger production budget than you will be offering. And the spectacular four-color mail pieces may have a lot of impact, but if you can only afford black and white, can the consultant do equally effective work? Consultants accustomed to lavish budgets may suffer from creative constipation when asked to work with a smaller amount.

Another question to ask is: Does all the work look the same? If the consultant's style dominates the work to the extent that it interferes with communication, that's bad. Or if the spots all look or sound so similar that the only difference is the name of the candidate or committee, that's bad too.

You want to avoid at all costs being caught in your media/mail consultant's rut. You deserve to have work created especially for you, not material already in the can that has been resuscitated for one more campaign.

Polling firms are something of an exception to the "showing samples" rule, and might have a problem when it comes to showing past, and probably confidential, work. When dealing with pollsters, you will have to judge them based on presentation and client references. There is a similar problem with general consultants – they have few work products, so you should ask to see a copy of the campaign plan for former clients and be energetic in following up on references.

With respect to **all** consultants, the police union should do some detective work. Check on the consultant's reputation, and whether it is good or not so good. This research should be done not only in your city, but other areas where the consultant has worked as well. Persons to talk to should include local newspaper reporters, political party officials, other clients, and political experts.

3. Enthusiasm. You may think that this term is out of place, and that the authors are reaching desperately for an "e" word that would fit. But in fact, you want a political consulting firm which views your account as important, and not as an "overhead" account; that is, an account which the firm is not excited about, but sees as payment of the monthly light bill.

You want your phone calls returned quickly. You want the work done for you to be original. And you want the advice and strategy suggestions you receive to be thoughtful and timely.

That's why you want to know how many other campaigns the consultant will be working on during the three to six months that your effort is peaking. If the consultant has ten statewide campaigns, four congressional elections, a big city mayor's race, and your issue, guess who will be at the bottom of the totem pole?

There are only so many hours in the day, and a consultant who is stretched thin doesn't do very good work. You deserve to have a reasonable share of the consultant's time, and shouldn't have to fight to get it! A firm with too many races is too busy for you.

Interviewing the Political Consultant

Your police union will be in the market for a political consultant whenever is it involved in a single issue campaign such as a pay referendum, manpower issue, tax rollback, adoption of civil service, or collective bargaining vote. You can narrow the field to a manageable number of possibilities without ever seeing any of the consultants face-to face.

Your decisions can be based upon how professional the firm's proposal is, how interested they seem, and any pre-interview research you do with the consultant's former clients. But eventually, it will be necessary to schedule an interview, either in your city, or possibly in Washington, D.C. or New York City, where a large number of political consultants are located.

During the interview, all the potential consultants should be judged according to the three "E's" discussed above: **Experience; Expertise; and Enthusiasm**. With these guidelines in mind, you are ready to begin the interview process. Each firm deserves a reasonable amount of time to make their case. Anything less than one hour cheats them, and turns your meeting into a cattle call.

It helps to have a question list or meeting agenda so you can structure each session as equally as possible. Now you'd think of all possible groups in the United States, police officers would be the least likely to feel uncomfortable asking tough questions during an interview. But it does happen. Like most suspects who won't confess without you first asking a question, the majority of political consultants won't volunteer unfavorable information unless you ask.

So now that you know why asking a question is important, here are a few of the questions that should be asked; and more important, **answered** during an interview.

1. How long have you been working in politics?
2. How long have you been with this firm or had your own consulting business?
3. If the consultant has changed fields (e.g., gone from campaign

managing to media consulting), why did he or she make the switch? (The ability to charge 15% commission on the media buy is **not** an acceptable answer).

4. If this campaign is the consultant's first political race, why should you be providing on-the-job training and paying for it to boot?

5. What races or campaigns in the past have you had that are similar to the police union's campaign, or would have given you experience that will be valuable in our situation?

6. Did you win that campaign? Or, if you lost, what did you learn?

7. Will you give us the names and telephone numbers of the principals in two winning campaigns and two losing campaigns for recommendations? If he or she will not provide names, **WATCH OUT!**

8. What samples of work do you have that are applicable to our campaign?

9. Exactly what was your role in the production of these samples?

10. How well known are you in your industry? Do you participate in professional organizations? Have you been a speaker at industry conferences?

11. How many campaigns will you be participating in during the next three to six months when the union will be the most active? Please include both candidate and non-candidate campaigns.

12. Of these active campaigns, which is the most important, or the largest?

13. Who will be the primary contact person in your firm for our campaign? If they aren't at the interview, why not?

14. Who will be doing the actual creative work on our campaign, if any? If they aren't at the interview, why not?

Coming to a Decision on Who to Hire

Once you get some answers, how do you know that you have the right ones? In many instances, you will have to trust your own instincts. Was the consultant forthcoming, or did he or she appear to be threatened by your questions? Did the consultant seem evasive, arrogant, or condescending during the interview? Is the consultant the type of individual you can trust and rely upon for the next few weeks or months?

These impressions are judgment calls. If you're lucky, someone on the union selection committee, or an advisor, may have had past campaign experience that will help you during the interview/evaluation process. The references that you obtained during the interview might possibly fill in any blanks you might have.

Finally, if you are still in a quandary, talk to other police unions about the candidates; or ask the other unions for references of qualified consultants who might be able to advise you on your choices.

Put It on Paper

Once you get answers that you like, make certain these answers stay to your liking throughout the campaign by having the political consultant put it in writing in a contract. Have the names of the client contact person and the creative person in the contract.

Also, ask the consultant to include anything else that you feel is important in the contract. If they refuse, find out why. If the reason is acceptable, fine. If not, then continue the interview process. It's better to take enough time to do it right the first time, then to try to find the time to do it over later.

Finally, don't make your search criteria too narrow. Hiring consultants who have only done your kind of campaign – pay raise referendums in cities between 100,000 and 250,000 in population occurring in the last quarter of an odd-numbered year, means that you are going to eliminate very good, creative consultants who have had similar, useful experience, but not the exact type of experience as your situation.

Chapter 31

THE DOWNSIDE OF DEMOCRACY:
THE POLICE UNION CAN LOSE

Winning is over-emphasized. The only time it
is really important is in surgery and war.
Al McGuire

In these chapters on politics and confrontation, you have been given
a wide variety of tools, techniques, and ideas that can be used to
increase your police union's impact in the political arena. You can
vary the application of your political power, giving one candidate a
simple endorsement and permission to use the union name, while
another one gets a donation and volunteers. Or you can jump head-
first into an initiative and referendum campaign to improve wages,
increase staffing levels, or achieve some form of employee rights. Or
you can take on the Chamber of Commerce in a bond election.

But anytime that there's an election (read: war), there will be a winner, and unfortunately, a loser. And the odds are 50 percent that your
union members and you will have grim faces after the final votes are
in on election night.

What Happens When The Union Comes Out on the Short End
of the Election Stick?

Everything goes along swimmingly until election day approaches,
when the possibility of losing starts to give you indigestion. So what
happens if a candidate or proposition loses? Is that the end of the
police union as you know it?

Probably not, since in many police unions the membership isn't keeping a box score with political winners and losers. Politics is still beneath many police officers; and they think that if you want to mess around with politicians, then you need to wear rubber gloves.

A loss will mean more to a union membership that has never endorsed or been involved in a referendum campaign before, and wasn't entirely sold on the idea in the first place. In one Mountain State, a union board of directors endorsed a mayoral candidate without consulting the membership, and when their candidate lost in one of the truly surprising upsets in American politics, the membership voted them out.

The big mistake that the board of directors made was bypassing the members, but even then their jobs might have been saved if they had endorsed a number of council candidates too, and done better in those races. Then they could use statistics to show a certain percentage winning record in council candidate endorsements (Remember the Benjamin Disraeli quote from the Preface: *There are three kinds of lies: lies, damned lies, and statistics.*).

Now you know why incumbents get all the endorsements! Still, if the police union educates the membership about the risks of endorsing or proceeding with a referendum, and that even a loss can send a message, the chances of weathering defeat are greatly increased.

The Worst Kind of Loss – the Benefit, Rights, or Working Condition Issue

But what if you happen to lose an election that is much closer to home, say for improving pay, increasing staffing levels, or gaining civil service rights. Now that's a fish of an entirely different color. Here the results have a direct bearing on the police union. The message that members often take home from this kind of defeat is that not only have they lost the issue, but that the public is a bunch of ungrateful pissants; and that there won't be a whole lot of warning tickets given out any time soon.

For police union leadership, this kind of reaction means that morale for the foreseeable future is shot. In one union in the Southwest, the loss of a civil service election meant that turnout for political events dropped from 180 volunteers to put up yard signs to 2 volunteers in the next council race. Attendance at the regular union meeting plummeted, and you could cut the depression at the police department with a knife.

How do you avoid this postelection despondency? The easiest way of course is to not tackle this kind of election in the first place, but then you'll never be in control of your fate. A better way is to explain to the membership before they enter the election fray is that they can lose; and if that should happen, the members should view the setback the same way the Corleones did in *The Godfather*: "Nothing personal – it's just business."

If the police union leaders have done a good job of handicapping the election and explaining that there might be a loss, the letdown won't be so severe. If your issue came very close to a victory, it may be almost as good as a win, since the city may be eager to compromise and avoid a loss in the future.

If you got your clocked cleaned in the election, the leadership didn't do its job! You embarked on an election you couldn't win, and the membership has a right to be angry.

What Happens After the Police Union Loses A Single-Issue Referendum?

What do you do after you've lost one of those life or death election campaigns over a benefit, rights or working condition issue? The first thing is to explain to the membership what the union intends to do to regain some political power. The members' fear of their group becoming irrelevant will often paralyze them – they go into a kind of collective fetal position.

Also, analyze the election results and decide what kind of argument or organization made the difference. If the Homeowner's Association beat you, then explain to its members the downside of having a crippled police department. If it's the Chamber of Commerce, set out to neutralize the group by having your union join and start attending all meetings. Then you can get into the inner workings of the Chamber and try to hijack the controls of the organization. If you can't do that, then you will at least become real people to the Chamber leaders, and not a faceless lump of police officers who just want more tax dollars.

This kind of community missionary work is extremely slow, and the results often are difficult to measure. But it has the virtue of paying off in the here and now, rather than after you're dead!

Finally, if you can't convince the membership to do anything, and they just want to hide under a rock after a loss, then tell them they're a bunch of weenies! Explain to these rough and tough officers that if they had acted this way the first time they got roughed up or lost a street fight, they wouldn't be cops now, they'd be hairdressers.

Getting beat is a part of life. Winning is getting up after you've been knocked down and trying again.

Chapter 32

NIGHTSTICKS, LIES AND VIDEOTAPES: WHEN THE BLAST IS AT GROUND ZERO, WHAT EVERY UNION LEADER NEEDS TO KNOW

Police unions will sometimes face a high profile incident such as a controversial shooting or allegation of excessive force. It is important to understand how to respond to this kind of situation if the rights and interests of the members(s) involved are at stake. Following are eight important rules to follow when faced with a high profile incident involving a member(s).

Rule Number One – Do Not Defend the Indefensible

With many patrol cars equipped with video cameras, eyewitnesses using the video on their cell phones, businesses with surveillance cameras, and the media on the scene instantly or filming from a helicopter, many high profile incidents are recorded for the entire world to be the judge of an officer's actions. Within minutes of a high speed chase or a SWAT shooting, the video is not only playing in the mainstream media, it is up on You Tube and similar web sites. Even worse are the screw-ups of officers acting badly off duty that are video-recorded and placed on the Internet by their friends or enemies.

Shortly after a high profile incident involving a member or members, the union leadership will be contacted for a quote or reaction. The first question will be, "Have you seen the video, and if not, would you like to see it?" The second question is, "Does the union condone such conduct by officers?" The union cannot defend actions by members that are indefensible to the general public and common sense. The union leader's response should be to step to the side of an overheated media's blast since the media is simply churning the controversy to get elected officials and management to go into melt down and respond, and to record anti-police groups screaming for heads to roll.

If the union stands directly in the blast and tries to stop it, the blast will overwhelm the union and discredit the union's real role in such a high profile incident. The union's role should be to reduce the media's prejudicing the public against the officer or officers, educate the public about police tactics, and defend the officer or officers right to a fair and impartial administrative, civil or criminal process.

Rule Number Two – Redirect the Message

If the media blast is too powerful to stop, it can be redirected with a little assistance from the union. The union should look to see if management or elected officials are overreacting and have jumped to conclusions about the "guilt" of the officer or officers. This is almost a certainty since the media is demanding a reaction from the head of the agency or the highest elected official. Elected officials and management seem to want to reaffirm to the media and public that the department is not out of control and the immediate response is usually that some officer will be disciplined or terminated.

As we all know, what the media and public see on tape is not always conclusive; and there is always a back story that led up to the incident and events happening outside the camera's view or obstructed from view. The media and public do not understand police training and believe that officers can shoot a pistol from an offender's hand or manhandle a drug-crazed addict without assistance from other officers.

The union needs to single out the overreacting elected official or management person and demand that they cease inciting the public when all of the facts are not in yet. Recent high profile incidents have witnessed elected officials and management stating the officer or officers would be terminated while CID and IAD are still at the scene or taking statements. The union's attack on the offending officials will start a war of words between the parties and distract the media. The focus will shift slightly and allow the union to redirect the media focus to the offending official's "convicting" the officers without knowing all of the facts.

Rule Number Three – Wrap Yourself in the Flag

If the high profile incident is really bad and there is no logical explanation for the officer's actions that the union can give to the media and public, the union should wrap itself in the flag. Simply put, the union states it does not know any more than the media or public and has no comment on the actual incident, but the union trusts the judicial system to sort out the facts and make a fair and equitable decision.

Union leaders can tell the media that honest and decent citizens of the community will serve on the grand jury or a later civil or criminal jury, and the accused officer or officers will get their day in court. The union must clearly state the union is not defending or condoning the officer or officers' alleged actions, but the union is defending their right to a defense.

The union may consider going on the offensive at this point. Television and/or radio advertising can be aired to defend the justice system and condemn elected officials or management for prejudicing the public against the officer or officers. Demand that the chief stand up for officers when they are right. Everyone has a choice to submit to arrest. If they resist arrest, they put into motion a series of reactions by the police that may lead to their injury or death. If the incident has racial overtones, make the message that the debate is about criminals and not race.

Rule Number Four – Remind the Public Who the Real Bad Guys Are in the Case, and Pray There Are Some

A high profile incident will mostly likely occur when someone starts acting badly or breaking the law and the police are called into action. If the incident involves a carload of preachers, revisit Rule Number Three. Since criminals fleeing in stolen cars, drug addicts stoned out of their mind, and drunks resisting arrest are the average high profile incident, the union needs to speak out about who the alleged victim really is. We all know that the media's first response is to get a comment from the grieving mother or family member of the alleged victim. Even when a bank robber is shot and killed by the police, the media report some woman screaming, "Why did they have to kill my baby? The police could have just wounded him."

If the alleged victim has a criminal record, the union needs to get the public record on this person and tell the media and public. While all people regardless of prior convictions deserve to be treated professionally, the media wants to paint the victim as defenseless and the police as thugs even when the person is a criminal resisting arrest and placing the life of the officer at risk.

Rule Number Five – Educate the Public About the Hazards of the Job

Murderers, rapists, robbers, burglars and thieves are the daily clientele of the police, and these thugs make decisions that cause the police to use their training and experience to get control of the situation. Everyone in our society knows more about police work than the police themselves. They have all seen *CSI* (name the city) and scores of police dramas on television and at the movies. *Walker, Texas Ranger*, is about a Texas Ranger who is a karate expert as are all law enforcement officers, and they can whip any criminal regardless of size and disarm any criminal with a well-directed shot to their gun hand. How dangerous can it be?

After a critical incident, the union needs to invite the media to ride along with officers, visit the training academy, and participate in the firearms training program in order to get first hand experience in the real world of policing. It is a good practice for the union to think about doing this year-round and not just after a critical incident. Educating the public and media about police training and tactics helps them understand why the police make certain decisions.

Rule Number Six – Time Heals All Wounds

If at all possible, the union should consider delaying any administrative hearing until after all civil and criminal matters are concluded. Time heals all wounds and the attention of the media and public wanes very quickly in our instant news and instant gratification society. Did anyone spend time watching the O. J. Simpson civil trail or the second Menendez brothers' criminal trial?

The longer a high profile incident is off the front page, the easier it is to resolve the case. While officers will oftentimes want an immediate resolution to the incident and to tell their story, it may or may not be in their best interest to expedite the process. Administrative discipline, civil actions and even criminal cases are highly politicized, and the officials in charging of prosecuting these cases sometime feel more media and public pressure immediately after an incident than a year or so later. The more controversial the incident, the more time is your friend.

Rule Number Seven – Public Trust is the Key

If police officers and the agency have a high public favorability approval rating, the easier it is to have the public trust the actions of officers in a critical incident. If the public has a low approval rating of its officers, there is a tendency by the public to believe the media reports that the officer probably was wrong in his or her actions.

Unions can do a lot to increase the approval rating of officers with the public, and in some cases the media, by being active in the community and building coalitions with community groups. Oftentimes community activists and business leaders will step forward and defend police officers in controversial cases. If community leaders come to the defense of their officers, it may lessen the likelihood the officers will face criminal charges, especially if the prosecutor has an elected boss, and it may sway management away from severe disciplinary action.

Rule Number Eight – You Cannot Control the Actions of Your Members 24/7

The only sin is not expecting anything to happen that would be characterized by the media as controversial. Law enforcement officers carry weapons that kill citizens and arrest people who do not want to go to jail. They are on the front-lines and their decisions are often instantaneous and may cause serious injury or death, or result in their own serious injury or death.

Every incident brings with it heavy media coverage, a guaranteed civil suit, a possible criminal investigation, and maybe disciplinary action. It is not a matter of if, but when the crap will hit the fan. Be prepared to handle just about any on-duty or off-duty incident that you can conceive of, and some you cannot conceive of. That is why your members elected you the union president.

Chapter 33

NO-CONFIDENCE VOTES: WHAT EVERY BOMB THROWER NEEDS TO KNOW BEFORE YOU LIGHT THE FUSE

A "No-Confidence Vote" on the chief [fill in the blank with sheriff, city manager, mayor, etc.] has been around for decades. Lately, unions have tried to disguise the no-confidence vote as a "membership," "morale," or "leadership" survey, but the principle is all the same — the union's members want regime change. The goal of the union's leadership should be broader and include using a confrontation tactic to readjust relationships in order to communicate the concerns of the union.

No matter what you call the no-confidence vote, it is the most controversial action that can be taken by a union because it is divisive internally and has an almost 100 percent chance of backlash from the person being targeted, elected officials, the media and possibly the public. And virtually no chief has ever been removed based solely on the officers voting to seek his removal.

It begs the question that if knowing that no-confidence votes are an explosive tactic, then why do unions almost always seem to want to conduct a no-confidence vote when they are unhappy? One answer is that when the members are unhappy they want to do what they perceive as an easy and uncomplicated "show of hands" that they blame the chief for their pain. The members seldom understand that the "show of hands" that they are unhappy with the chief is a public confrontation with their boss. The chief will have lost face with his bosses and the public when his own officers attack his leadership abilities.

Elected officials and the media will defend the chief in almost every circumstance.

The second question is why do unions screw up no-confidence votes so often? Union leaders and members overestimate the impact of a no-confidence vote and underestimate the backlash. They also get carried away with emotions, especially at a membership meeting, and the anger gets redirected to what they perceive as their only option. Little thought is given to what will happen after they throw the bomb. Very seldom do union leaders understand the purpose of a no-confidence vote, how to conduct one properly, and how to leverage a no-confidence vote as a part of an overall union strategy.

Developing a Long-Term Strategy

The long-term strategy of all unions should be to improve the living and working conditions of officers, which will then allow the employer to recruit the best applicants available and retain existing officers. While the chief may be a pain in the ass, he is not the sole reason for the problems in the department. If the union gets rid of this chief, another one who may or may not be better will be appointed. The devil you know may be better than the devil you do not know. Many unions regret ousting a chief they are having trouble working with and getting a new chief they cannot work with at all.

The union leadership needs to ask whether they can repair the communication problems with the existing chief. Perhaps building lines of communication, cooperation, respect and trust will allow the union the opportunity to solve problems within the agency. If the union believes it cannot convince the chief to work with the union on problem-solving, then the union should evaluate whether a no-confidence vote should be a part of its overall strategy.

Remember that a no confidence vote is just one salvo in a battle and not a nuclear blast that wins the war. Conducting a no-confidence vote without evaluating its impact on the department, union, and community is like not mobilizing the military or having a battle plan and then firing one missile at North Korea and being surprised that they fired back.

If the union leadership has decided that conducting a no-confidence vote should be a part of its long-term strategy, there are a series of steps the union needs to consider.

Poll the Members

Voting to conduct a no-confidence vote at a general meeting is a recipe for disaster. First, not all of the members can attend unless the union is very small and the members on duty can also attend the meeting. Second, many members will not feel free to express their opinions in an emotionally charged meeting. If the union also represents supervisors, the supervisors may feel that expressing their opinion in front of non-supervisors is disloyalty to the chief or a career-ending move. And third, the union's leaders may be surprised how weak and divided the membership really is about the chief. Not everyone will hate the chief.

The union needs to retain an academician to conduct a poll of the membership. In right-to-work states where some officers may not belong to the union, the union should decide whether to include all officers and not just union members to get a broader poll result. Local universities and colleges have professors who can design and conduct the poll to get the most accurate picture. It is money well spent for one simple reason. The chief and employer's first response will be the vote was a result of union leaders pressuring members at a meeting, or the questions were biased and cannot be accurately verified.

If the union wants to maximize media coverage of the no-confidence vote, the union should issue a press release that the members voted to conduct a no-confidence vote (or morale study or leadership survey), and the union has retained an independent professor to design and conduct the poll. After the poll results are tabulated, the union can appear before elected officials and have the professor explain how the poll was conducted and its conclusions. Next the union can drive the message with paid radio, television, newspaper or direct mail.

A sample membership survey can be found in Appendix 3. This sample can be modified to fit the circumstances and issues of your agency and membership.

Poll the Public

The union may be surprised about how the public feels about the chief. In fact, in many communities the general public may not be able to pick the chief out of a line-up. There is no way to know if the union's belief that the chief is incompetent resonates with the public without a valid public opinion poll. The union should retain a professional pollster who can accurately poll the public on the issues the union has identified. The cost of a public opinion poll can be controlled by reducing the size of the poll and the number of questions.

Never forget the cardinal rule of analyzing the public's opinion – **it is all about them!** The public only cares about the police, fire or other public safety employees if it **directly** affects their lives. All media releases and the poll should be about the external concerns of the union. Too few officers mean delayed responses to calls for assistance; high turnover of officers means wasted tax dollars on training officers; poor wages and benefits translates into an inability to recruit the best officers; mismanagement of resources has caused the crime rate to increase; etc. What has the chief done or not done to make the department inefficient or ineffective?

Never, ever, complain or whine about discipline, shift assignments or seniority. These are internal complaints, and while they may be important to the officers, the public could care less about them. If you make internal complaints the basis for the no-confidence vote, the backlash will be more severe and long lasting.

Spin Control

Get ready for spin control. If you fire a shot at someone, expect a shot back. It is always surprising that unions are caught off guard when the spin starts, and they are flipped upside down and beaten to a pulp by the media. The four most common spins are:

1. If the chief is a minority, the union is a racist.
2. If the chief is a female, the union is sexist.
3. If the chief is from outside the department, the union is defending the status quo and resisting change.
4. All chiefs will argue, the union is trying to handpick a chief they can control.

To control spin control, stay on message. If the union has conducted a valid membership poll and public opinion poll, the union knows two things: (1) the officers who work for the chief believe he is incompetent and needs to be replaced for the stated **external** reasons; and

(2) the public does not believe the department is as efficient or effective as it should be and a new chief may be needed.

Avoid being defensive and changing the public message. The facts are the facts. The chief has either mismanaged the resources of the department and it has impacted the delivery of services to the public; or he/she has not. Whether the chief is a minority, female, outsider, or insider is not relevant to the public debate. Do not take the bait and debate the spin – your campaign will go downhill fast.

There Will Be Backlash So Get Ready For It

Almost 100 percent of all chiefs who have faced no confidence votes have gotten the public support of elected officials, the city manager, and the media, even if the chief is later terminated. The media and elected officials will attack the union's motives. The general attack is that the union is protecting corrupt cops, refusing to be community oriented, resisting change and modernization, and in general opposed to being managed by the chief.

Again, it is surprising how many unions are caught off guard when the backlash starts. What did the union expect? That the chief would resign, the city manager or mayor would fire the chief, and the media would praise the union for pointing out how incompetent the chief is.

The next backlash is that officers may break ranks and publicly support the chief. That is why an internal poll of the members is so important. It may identify groups of officers who do not think the chief needs to be ousted or ridiculed. If the chief is a minority or female, it is common for minority and/or female officers to support the chief, especially if the chief has made inroads on issues of diversity inside the department. Another potential source of division is supervisors and minority unions (those unions representing less than a majority of the officers). The union needs to anticipate these divisions and work in advance to educate these constituencies as to the reasons for the no-confidence vote.

Be Prepared For a Long Struggle

There is **NO** one knockout punch in a campaign. The number one reason unions fail is that they do not have staying power! No-confidence votes are just a part of a long-term strategy to force change or at the minimum get the lines of communication unclogged. A confrontation tactic like a no-confidence vote is just a means to gain, or regain, respect and get everyone back on a level playing field. A smart chief will survive a no-confidence vote and recognize the need to communicate with the union and seek avenues of mutual concern.

Part VI

AMERICAN POLICING AT A CROSSROADS: ARE POLICE UNIONS TAKING ON THE CHALLENGE OR IMPEDING CHANGE?

Chapter 34

SOME INTRODUCTORY COMMENTS

Except for the United States, most countries use the term *police* for all civilian or domestic law enforcement. In the United States, the terminology is more confusing to a person unfamiliar with our criminal justice system. In the decentralized U.S. system, we have municipal police officers, county police officers, county sheriff's deputies, county constables, state police, state and county highway patrol, state troopers, and special agents at every level of government. In order to simplify the terms used in this part of the book, the term *police, police officer, police department* or *law enforcement agency* will include municipal, county, special district, state or federal law enforcement officers and agencies. The term *police chief* will include police chiefs, sheriffs, constables, or the head of a law enforcement agency.

The term *union* is the common denominator in the name of most labor organizations worldwide. There is no one common denominator when it comes to organizational names or affiliations for police labor organizations in the United States and most other countries. One theory is that since labor unions are identified by the general public and media as representing blue collar workers, police labor organizations overwhelmingly use the term *association, federation* or *lodge* instead of *union* in an effort to be identified more closely with professional organizations such as those representing doctors and lawyers. A reason for this reluctance to use the term *union* is rooted in their belief that police work is a profession and not a blue collar job or a craft. Since the most common international term to describe a labor organization is *union*, the term *police union* will be inclusive of all police and law enforcement labor organizations regardless of their name, agency or organizational affiliation as it has throughout this book.

As we enter into the twenty-first century where there is a global questioning about democracy and equality, it makes sense to question whether police unions are willing to mobilize and promote the ideals of justice and effectiveness when policing communities. The evidence so far indicates that the answer is a resounding **NO**. The reasons for this are complex, as are the solutions.

Chapter 35 examines the fragmented local, state and national police labor movement and the lack of a unified voice from police unions on issues including those pertaining to the democratization and improvement of policing in the United States. There is at present no coordinated strategy or networking by the various local, state or national police unions. This is somewhat worrying given that police unions have a major impact on the implementation or the rejection of new police policies and practices, especially at the local government level. The loudest and most unified voice coming from the various police unions is that they all oppose any control by the general public over police policies and practices through civilian review boards.

Chapter 36 will provide some insight into dilemmas created in the United States where the criminal justice system is decentralized. Yet simultaneous with this decentralized system, American policing is also changing from a civilian "community" police model to a more "national" militaristic police model. In addition, the cost of policing is increasing and agencies have had to examine the value of non-sworn civilians and private contractors doing jobs that were traditionally done by sworn police officers. Technology has displaced police jobs with the introduction of red light, speed and surveillance cameras. These changes, coupled with decentralization, greatly reduce the cooperation and interactions among police officers, police unions and law enforcement agencies at each level of government, and thus reduce the opportunities for change or reform. The rivalry between law enforcement agencies for funding, status and control at the local, state and federal level is well-known and creates an atmosphere of distrust and a lack of cooperation.

Chapter 37 reviews the federal legislation being pursued by national police unions and the impact on law enforcement officers caused by the lack of uniform national labor laws. Other than the Fair Labor Standards Act, the federal government has not adopted a national collective bargaining law, a Police Officers' Bill of Rights, or any uniform policies pertaining to wages, benefits, pensions, or working conditions. Despite this unfriendly terrain, there is no real networking between the various national police unions. Inter-union rivalries have hamstrung the national police unions and prevented the unions from achieving a greater success on labor legislation at the federal level. The national police unions have similar political agendas and compete to get a seat at the table with the political party in power.

Chapter 38 will identify the central challenge facing American police management and police labor unions – how to create a forum to develop a shared vision of the police profession; make recommendations to improve the effectiveness and efficiency of the police service nationwide; seek ways to balance the need for domestic policing and the new duties caused by international criminal activities; and outline how police agencies can get ahead of the curve on the global changes impacting the police profession and local communities.

Chapter 35

DISORGANIZED LABOR

Police Unions Collapse After 1919 Boston Police Strike

The late 1800s and early 1900s were a time of social unrest, political strife, and labor violence. After witnessing the economic gains made by trade unions, firefighters and other public workers, the American Federation of Labor (AFL) started getting requests for charters from local police benevolent associations who were clamoring to join organized labor.

The unionization of the police caused a firestorm of protest. Private corporations had traditionally called upon elected officials to use the police as strikebreakers. The use of police officers as strikebreakers caused bitter feelings toward police officers by trade union members and their leaders. Police chiefs saw the police service as an arm of the government like the military, and the chiefs did not want police officers forming unions and alliances with political, labor, and social activists. Politicians and police chiefs saw trade labor unions as a threat to the national security and felt they needed the police force to be independent of organized labor.

However, wages, benefits and working conditions for police officers were dismal and harsh, even for that period. After Boston firefighters formed a union and threatened a strike, the city increased wages and improved working conditions somewhat for firefighters and police officers. In 1919, the Boston Police Social Club requested recognition by the new police commissioner. The police commissioner refused to recognize the union.

The policemen appealed to the AFL for a charter and were accepted. When the union requested bargaining rights, the commissioner terminated the appointments of 19 union leaders. On September 9, 1919, a four-day strike started with 1,117 of the city's 1,544 policemen walking off the job. Widespread looting, hundreds of injuries, and 7 deaths occurred before the National Guard restored order. All the striking policemen were fired and never rehired.

The distrust and hatred of the police as strikebreakers caused the AFL unions to balk at calling a general strike to support the Boston policemen. It was a defining moment for the AFL and the fledgling police labor movement. The decisions made during this strike forever changed the police labor movement. Police unionism practically ceased to exist until the 1960s when police organizations started becoming more militant.

In 1969, fifty years after the Boston police strike, the American Federation of Labor-Congress of Industrial Organizations (AFL-CIO) received a request to charter a national police union. The AFL-CIO rejected the request because the same old hard feelings against the police still lingered. It was not until 1979 that the AFL-CIO chartered the International Union of Police Associations (IUPA) as a national police union. What caused the change of heart by organized labor towards police officers? The AFL and CIO peaked in membership when they merged in 1955, and without the competition between the two unions, the AFL-CIO's membership began a decline that exists to this day. By 1979 the AFL-CIO could not ignore the vast numbers of potential new police union members and put finances ahead of old grievances.

The Police Labor Movement After 1979

The police labor movement is a maze of different union affiliations. One would need a playbook to determine which associations, lodges and unions are affiliated with which state or national police unions. In addition, many police unions have dual affiliations. For example, the International Brotherhood of Police Officers (IBPO) is a part of the Service Employees International Union (SEIU) and has also affiliated with the National Association of Police Organizations (NAPO) for federal legislative purposes.

There seems to be some confusion about what *unionization, collective bargaining* and *meet and confer* means in American police labor relations. There is a false assumption that the police force is unionized only if the officers have collective bargaining rights with a binding impasse procedure and the officers belong to a national union affiliated with the AFL-CIO, or its recent splinter organization, Change to Win Coalition (CTW). In reality, when police officers form a local association, lodge or union for the purposes of improving their wages, benefits and conditions of employment, with or without the ability to collectively bargain or meet and confer with the public employer, the officers are unionized. There is no substantive difference between the police unions affiliated with organized labor (AFL-CIO or CTW) and the independent lodges and police associations. The terms *collective bargaining* and *meet and confer* are basically interchangeable terms in the United States and have no relationship to whether the officers have an impasse procedure or not.

The police labor movement is divided into two camps – the independent police labor organizations and the police labor organizations affiliated with organized labor through the AFL-CIO or CTW. Approximately 80–85 percent of all police labor organizations would be classified as independent and have no affiliation with organized labor. There are no accurate reports on how many of the 800,000 sworn officers are members of a police union. The best estimate would be 75–80 percent which would rank police officers with firefighters as having the highest unionization rates in the U.S. As stated earlier, it is often confusing because a local police union may have an AFL-CIO or CTW charter and also be affiliated with an independent labor group. Fundamentally, all local police unions are independent bodies with very similar constitutions, governance structures, ideologies, missions and strategies regardless of national affiliations.

The Fraternal Order of Police was the only national police organization to survive the 1919 Boston police strike. FOP was founded in Pittsburgh in 1915 as a social, benevolent and fraternal organization. While FOP has evolved since the 1960s into a labor organization, the FOP constitution still prohibits its lodges from being affiliated with organized labor. FOP reports a membership of 324,000, and it is unquestionably the nation's largest police labor organization. FOP has built its membership by appealing to police officers on two levels - the fraternal nature of policing as an extended family and brotherhood, combined with supporting primarily conservative political candidates. To emphasize their conservative political leanings, FOP's advertisements in *American Police Beat* newspaper show their National President seated next to President George W. Bush. There is a question about how many of the reported members are actually retired officers. FOP reports that they have a State Lodge in all 50 states. Some states have a separate fraternal state lodge and a FOP Labor Council that handles labor relations for the lodges.

The second largest national police organization is the National Association of Police Organizations (NAPO), which reports 238,000 members in 2,000 local police associations. NAPO, which is a federation of labor unions and not a labor union per se, is composed primarily of independent police unions who did not want to be affiliated with FOP. Since NAPO is not a labor union, FOP lodges can join without violating the National FOP Constitution that prohibits affiliations with organized labor, and police unions affiliated with organized labor can join NAPO without violating the prohibition against dual unionism in their constitution.

The remaining 15–20 percent of unionized police officers are members of associations and unions affiliated with organized labor through either the AFL-CIO or CTW. The AFL-CIO and CTW are umbrella federations of 57 unions with a reported membership of 13 million members. No records are kept on how many police officers are represented, but the best estimate on the number of police officers in organized labor is probably between 100,000 to 150,000. The International Union of Police Associations (IUPA) is the only national police union chartered by either the AFL-CIO or CTW. IUPA reports a membership of 100,000.

It would seem that just about every national union affiliated with either the AFL-CIO or CTW has police officers as members. The American Federation of State, County and Municipal Employees (AFSCME) reports to have about 10–15,000 police members. The International Brotherhood of Police Officers (IBPO) reports 10,000 members. IBPO is a division of the National Association of Government Employees which is a sector of the Service Employees International Union (SEIU). SEIU has police locals outside of IBPO. The International Brotherhood of Teamsters reports to have 20,000 police members. The Communications Workers of America has created a sector called the National Coalition of Public Safety Officers (NCPSO) for the national union's reported 25,000 police and corrections officers.

Some other examples of AFL-CIO and CTW unions with affiliated police unions include: Paper, Allied-Industrial, Chemical and Energy Workers' International Union; Marine Engineers' Beneficial Association; United Steelworkers' Union of America; United Automobile Workers Union; United Food and Commercial Workers' International Union; Operating Engineers International Union; American Federation of Government Employees; and International Longshoremen's Association.

It is immediately evident the number of police officers alleged to be members of unions exceeds the actual number of police officers in the U.S. There are two primary reasons. First, dual unionism is a common and accepted practice. In the private sector it is a violation of the union constitution to belong to more than one union with the same jurisdiction. To join another competing union is ground for expulsion from the union. Police officers in the same agency can, and do, belong to more than one union. The overlapping memberships allow national unions to each rightfully claim the same member.

Second, on the national, state and regional level membership inflation is not only common, but also accepted. All unions, but especially national police unions, puff up their membership numbers without the least bit of guilt. The national police unions all include retired members to make their membership numbers appear to be higher than they are. All police union membership figures must be viewed with some skepticism. More accurate membership numbers are only found when the union is representing a designated department where the authorized strength is publicly and officially known.

The Competitive Nature of the Police Labor Movement

The organizing and unionization environment of the police has always been turbulent, hostile, volatile, and disruptive; and there is today disturbing absence of cooperation between police unions at the national, state and local level. It has become even worse in the twenty-first century. Every state except Hawaii has multiple police organizations competing for members within each law enforcement agency. But even in Hawaii, the police officers that are represented in one bargaining unit by the State of Hawaii Organization of Police Officers (SHOPO) affiliated for a short time with the AFSCME (AFL-CIO) before disaffiliating and returning to independent status.

Switching national unions or returning to independent status is common. There is very little long-term loyalty among American police unions, either to the local, state or national union. Unions poaching other unions for members, disaffiliations, reaffiliations, decertifications, and splinter groups within a law enforcement agency are the rule and not the exception. For example, the independent San Francisco Police Officers Association affiliated with IUPA (AFL-CIO), disaffiliated and returned to independent status, and now is affiliated with SEIU (CTW). The Police Association of New Orleans (PANO) affiliated with the Teamsters Union, but after the disastrous 1979 police strike, disaffiliated and affiliated with SEIU (CTW). PANO later disaffiliated from SEIU and is now affiliated with the independent NAPO. Worchester, Massachusetts, police voted to disaffiliate from IBPO (SEIU, CTW) after a 30-year affiliation and affiliate with the New England PBA (IUPA, AFL-CIO).

More Fragmentation: Different Ranks, Different Unions, Multiple Affiliations

In the private sector in the U.S., federal law excludes supervisors from the right to form a union and collectively bargain. While some state laws exclude police supervisors from collective bargaining, there are generally non-supervisors and supervisors in joint or separate police unions in the public sector.

In many police agencies different unions represent the rank and file officers and supervisors. Oftentimes these local unions have different state and national affiliations. For example, the Association for Los Angeles Deputy Sheriffs represents rank and file deputy sheriffs and is affiliated with Marine Engineers Benevolent Association (MEBA, AFL-CIO). The Los Angeles County Professional Peace Officers Association represents sergeants and lieutenants and was affiliated with IUPA (AFL-CIO) and now with the independent FOP. New York City Police Department patrol officers are members of the Patrolmen's Benevolent Association (PBA). Detectives, sergeants, lieutenants and captains all have their own separate unions and bargaining rights.

Even in law enforcement agencies with one bargaining agent, other police unions exist with members from the same agency, which would be dual unionism in the private sector. In some agencies, one union is the bargaining agent and the second union is perceived as the fraternal organization. For example, the Los Angeles Police Protective League is affiliated with NAPO but has an FOP lodge with elected leaders representing its members on state and national labor issues on behalf of FOP. The Omaha Police Union (IUPA affiliated) and Seattle Police Officers Guild (Independent) have advertisements for the local FOP lodge in their union newspapers.

This dual unionism is not always as compatible as it would appear in Los Angeles, Omaha and Seattle. The minority union which may appear as benign or fraternal to the majority union can be a vehicle for dissident members to use to unseat the bargaining agent. Even where the members have ousted one union, that union may continue to exist and wait in the shadows for the majority union to make a mistake. Even if the minority union never achieves majority status again, the minority union strives to trip up the majority union's leaders, in particular during contract negotiations. Nashville police decertified the FOP and affiliated with the Teamsters Law Enforcement League (TLEL, CTW). Being decertified as the bargaining agent has not stopped the FOP lodge from remaining active and continuing to seek another certification vote. Police management, the media, and elected officials like to see a divided membership.

Union hopping and dual unionism by members creates an unhealthy atmosphere for police union leaders who fear that one misstep in dealing with the employer or management will result in dissident officers starting a drive to oust the union, not just the union president. The competition among the various police unions and the poaching of each other's membership does more damage to the stability of the local union than management could ever do. One need only look at the achievements of the Australian and Canadian police unions to recognize that in the United States the police unions and police officers themselves are to blame for the chaos and lack of a national collective bargaining bill.

What Does the Future Hold for Police Unity in the U.S.?

NAPO, FOP and IUPA have at various times participated in various conferences of the International Council of Police Representative Associations (ICPRA), formerly known as the International Law Enforcement Council (ILEC). ICPRA was formed by the Canadian Professional Police Association to bring together every even-numbered year the leaders of national police unions from democratic nations to discuss the future of the police profession.

The U.S. national police unions need to seek a forum similar to ICPRA to allow for a free and open debate about the role of police unions in shaping the future of policing and the police profession. A national police union forum should seek to adopt a set of principle agreements similar to the international ones adopted by ICPRA. The U.S. national police unions need to seek closer ties to the budding police union movement in less industrialized countries and offer to assist them in improving their wages, benefits, and conditions of employment.

A civil war cannot end without someone defeating the other side or the parties agreeing to reunite. Poaching at the state and local level breeds animosity and creates a national union leadership afraid to even communicate with another national police union. All of the national police unions have decentralized governance structures and are without any power or authority to force change on state and local affiliated bodies. This strife and turmoil will continue unless one or more of the national unions can set aside personal ego and historic grievances to unite one or more of the competing unions into a federation. The AFL and CIO decided that the financial and emotional cost of the fighting over workers was self-defeating and merged as the AFL-CIO in 1955. There is no substantive difference in services on the national level between FOP, NAPO, IUPA, IBPO, TLEL and NCPSO. They all profess to be focused on federal legislation and assistance to their state and local affiliates.

So why has there not been an effort at merging the national police unions into one powerful police labor union? Sergeant Harold Melnik, who was the president of the Sergeant's Benevolent Association of the New York City Police Department, has tried to answer this question. He shared his observations at the National Symposium on Police Labor Relations sponsored by the Police Foundation in 1974:

> There is no single individual who has openly come forth with the ability, acceptability and platform to rally all or most police organizations for merger into a national police union. . . . It can be said that while the police association leaders of the major cities recognize the awesome power that could be obtained through a national body properly led, a fear of assimilation with a loss of identity still exists in the minds of many of these leaders. Until the day comes when police officers readily identify themselves as a part of labor, only local and statewide groups will suffice and prosper.

Chapter 36

THE AMERICAN POLICING MODEL

Decentralized, Disorganized and Disconnected

The United States is a country founded by immigrants. These immigrants were often fearful of the military and national police forces in their homelands. This fear of a centralized national police force led elected officials in the U.S. to oppose the creation of a national police force or allowing the military to act as a domestic police force. Federal law enforcement officers represent only about 12 percent of 836,787 sworn law enforcement officers in about 18,000 law enforcement agencies in the U.S. Virtually every political jurisdiction in the U.S. has at least one law enforcement agency, and the vast majority of law enforcement agencies have less than ten officers.

There is no unified command structure for these 800,000 law enforcement officers and no shared communications between the 18,000 law enforcement agencies. No common mission, strategy or philosophy is in place or proposed by the federal government or advocated by police unions. There does not appear to be a significant level of trust between federal, state and local law enforcement agencies. This lack of trust was clearly demonstrated by the color-coded terrorist alerts issued by the Department of Homeland Security that gave local and state law enforcement agencies no greater information than was given to the general public and media. The public and law enforcement agencies quickly lost confidence in the alerts and little media attention is given to the color-coded alerts today.

The ability to implement change in American law enforcement agencies is complicated because so many different law enforcement agencies with concurrent and overlapping jurisdictions exist. It is impossible for the average citizen or visitor to differentiate between the multitudes of law enforcement agencies in a community. Many states, counties and municipalities have law enforcement agencies within the same jurisdiction that are not a part of the primary law enforcement agency. These states, counties and municipalities have separate law enforcement agencies with separate command structures to deal with the airport, parks, building code enforcement, fire marshals, school district, sanitation, corrections, courts, lifeguards, water authority, lakes, public housing, health department and virtually every conceivable state, county and municipal department.

This model makes the U.S. different from countries that have a more centralized policing system. For example, Ireland, Northern Ireland, South Africa and Scotland each have a single national police force. While there is a separate transport police and some island police forces in England and Wales, 43 police forces have been consolidated into one national bargaining unit for constables below the rank of superintendent. Australia has only 9 law enforcement agencies – six states and two territories and one Federal Police organization. Canada has a national police force that the federal government contracts to eight of the ten provinces to provide provincial police services, the three northern territories and 200 individual municipalities. There are three provincial services and only 200 municipal and 17 regional police forces in all of Canada.

The federal government in America has taken a step toward consolidating many of its law enforcement agencies. Congress created the Department of Homeland Security. However, many federal non-law enforcement agencies still maintain their own uniformed police forces. For example Congress, Supreme Court, State Department, FBI, Secret Service, Library of Congress, Parks Service, Interior Department, Labor Department, Veterans Administration, Government Printing Office and virtually all federal agencies maintain and control a uniformed police force.

In May 2003, The International Association of Chiefs of Police (IACP) conducted a study entitled "Consolidating Police Services: An IACP Planning Approach." The study reviewed the pros and cons of consolidating law enforcement services. Despite some consolidation of law enforcement services since the 1950s, very few of the 18,000 law enforcement agencies are seriously considering consolidating services.

The Impact of Global Events on Domestic Policing in the U.S.

There are many challenges to policing in the twenty-first century. Maintaining law and order on the domestic front oftentimes means a balancing test between the need for societal security and the desire for individual freedom and rights. Prior to September 11, 2001, it appeared to be the general consensus of politicians and the public that the policies and practices of law enforcement agencies should balance the desire for individual freedom and rights at least as importantly as the need for societal security. But this seems to be changing with the threat of terror dominating security concerns in the U.S., and indeed worldwide.

The move away from localized and community-oriented policing is most evident in the recent scaling down of the Community Oriented Police Services (COPS) program. President Bill Clinton created the COPS Program at the U.S. Department of Justice in 1994 to create 100,000 new police positions and issued millions of dollars in federal grants to state and local police agencies to hire more officers and use those officers to improve community policing at the grassroots level. The COPS program expired in 2000 but has been extended year to year by Congress. In 2005, the President and Congress have virtually depleted funding for the COPS program and shifted that money to training and equipping state and local police for a battle against terrorists.

The global crisis created by international terrorism has caused the majority of federal law enforcement agencies to shift their focus to combating terrorism both domestically and abroad. With the support of President Bush, Congress created the Department of Homeland Security – the most comprehensive reorganization of the federal government in a half-century. The Department of Homeland Security consolidates 22 agencies and 180,000 employees, unifying once-fragmented federal functions in a single agency dedicated to protecting America from terrorism. A comprehensive national strategy for Homeland Security was developed, focused on six key areas: intelligence and warning; border and transportation security; domestic counterterrorism; protecting critical infrastructure; defending against catastrophic threats; and emergency preparedness and response.

President Bush also won overwhelming support for the USA Patriot Act, a law that the administration believes gives intelligence and law enforcement officials important new tools to fight terrorists. This legislation is viewed by others as evidence of the shift away from individual freedoms and more toward societal security.

The federal government then shifted traditionally domestic law enforcement tasks that were being handled by federal law enforcement agencies and the military to state and local police forces. The overwhelming majority of American law enforcement agencies – federal, state and local – were not prepared for the shift in policies and practices to realistically handle international terrorism on a domestic and international level. A report published by The International Association of Chiefs of Police (IACP) stated that the nation's homeland security strategy is "handicapped by a fundamental flaw – it was developed without sufficiently seeking or incorporating the advice, expertise or consent of public safety organizations at the state, tribal, or local level." The IACP report also criticized the Bush administration for cutting grants to local police forces that has hampered state, local and county police in their day-to-day work from meeting with community groups.

The Price of Policing a Community

In addition to the rising costs of police wages and benefits, police agencies also face rising costs to recruit, train, and equip police officers. Elected officials and police management are being forced to evaluate what traditional police jobs can be sufficiently undertaken by civilian employees, private contractors and technology.

California Governor Arnold Schwarzenegger has pledged to privatize, reduce, and even eliminate pension benefits for state employees despite ongoing public disapproval from public employee and police unions. Governors in Massachusetts, Rhode Island, Alaska and Illinois are all reviewing the high costs to the taxpayers to maintain public employee pension systems.

Public policing is now under threat in this country. How to balance the cost of each police officer and define what constitutes police work is the critical question impacting all police agencies. American anti-unionism is driving down wages for all workers at the same time that the cost of putting a fully trained and equipped police officer on the street is soaring. And the police unions, in advocating for higher wages, may unintentionally have made the future of public police officers more insecure. Despite the problems and risks caused by poorly trained private security employees, police authorities and employers are likely to look for cheaper avenues to policing than the highly unionized public police employees.

Given the nationwide quest for cost-cutting in the public sector, it is hardly surprising that the number of civilian non-sworn employees of police agencies has been rising. In many agencies former police jobs are now done by civilian employees – background investigations of applicants, crime scene investigations, evidence technicians, property rooms, parking violations, non-emergency calls, building security, court security, prisoner transport, and detention.

This development has not occurred without a fight from police unions. Two recent examples illustrate the battle over the civilianization of police agencies. In Chicago, the police union won an arbitration overturning a city ordinance that allowed civilian employees to work traffic details formerly handled by uniformed officers. In Pennsylvania, the Governor and the State Troopers Association have clashed over whether to hire 270 more troopers or replace troopers in the central dispatch center with civilian employees. In another case, the union for San Diego police officers was approached to consider allowing the city to rehire retired police officers on a part-time basis for supervisor and non-supervisor positions to fill vacancies. If this had occurred, the police union would not be able to negotiate for these retired members and the jobs would be lost to active members. The city already has 1,000 mostly retired citizens in the Volunteers in Policing (VIP) program. The city furnishes vehicles and police radios to citizen volunteers to call in suspicious persons and report crimes.

Technology has also dramatically changed the police environment, and its ongoing incorporation into police agencies has led to the displacement of police officers. Speed and red light cameras generate tremendous amounts of revenue for governments without the cost of a police officer. Surveillance cameras in high crime areas have allowed police agencies to reduce the number of officers needed to patrol these areas.

The privatization of policing in the U.S. continues to grow. At present the estimated number of private security guards exceeds 4 million – four times the number of police officers. The debate over private contracting of police work is not whether police jobs will be displaced by private contractors, but how many police jobs will be lost. While the privatization of prisons has been the most public issue, private contractors are seeking to bid on just about every aspect of policing, including patrolling the streets. This issue is not peculiar to the U.S. – it the policing landscape throughout the world.

Where are police unions in reference to these major changes to the profession? With few exceptions, police unions have fought tooth and nail against civilianization, privatization and technology. It is much like the trench warfare in World War I. Despite the introduction of machine guns, tanks and aircraft, the leaders on both sides refused to change their tactics and fought back and forth over a few feet of ground. Technology had changed the landscape and no amount of insistence on the traditional methods could overcome these changes to the environment.

Police unions are losing ground to civilianization, privatization, and technology and the police union leaders know it intellectually. However, it seems that most leaders want to delay the inevitable until they leave office.

The Uniqueness of Political U.S. Policing

The police forces in Canada, Australia, New Zealand, and the United Kingdom are unionized, but are generally restrained or prohibited from being involved in election campaigns of individual candidates or political parties. Police unions in these countries have opted to focus on using public platforms and the media to shape public debate on policing issues such as the allocation of police resources for fighting crime and staffing levels. While in each of these countries there have been times when police unionists have openly endorsed particular political candidates and parties, this is the exception rather than the norm, and is frowned upon by the public and by politicians.

By contrast, the overwhelming majority of American police unions are politically active in the campaigns of those persons elected to control the police themselves. The direct involvement of American police unions in the political campaigns of the elected officials who control them is diametrically opposite to the national political views of most democratic countries. The vast majority of American police unions have a distinct political advantage over appointed police chiefs and law enforcement agency heads in openly campaigning for individual political candidates.

Traditionally, appointed police chiefs cannot endorse candidates for political office, work in political campaigns or make political contributions. This distinct demarcation between a police chief and politicians has started to fade. Appointed police chiefs are starting to appear more and more in the political *photo ops* of their elected bosses. Any time the U.S. President, the governor of a state, or a city mayor conducts a press conference involving crime or police-related issues, one can expect to see the police chief and uniformed officers standing as a backdrop for the press conference.

What separates the police union from the police chief in the world of politics is that the police union has the ability to endorse a candidate and work in the candidate's political campaign. But the greatest advantage for the police union is its ability to contribute money to the candidate. In many parts of the U.S., the police union's Political Action Committee (PAC) is the largest campaign contributor to a candidate. Despite protests from the editorial boards of newspapers about the perceived political power of many police unions, candidates for public office continue to seek the endorsement and resources of the police union. The real political power of the police union is its ability to deal directly with the elected officials, the media, and the public, and to bypass the police chief and government administrators. The ability of the police union to make a political end run frustrates police chiefs and government administrators wanting to change or reform police polices and practices.

As a result, police unions have become major players in the "Court of Public Opinion." The political power game in the U.S. revolves around money. The police union brings money to the game, but more importantly it brings the name and reputation of the police (not the police union) to the candidate. This power game is institutionalized into the American political culture and police unions can either play the game or have the game played for them – but it will be played regardless. With few exceptions, police unions for the most part have not taken this political power and used it to improve the efficiency and effectiveness of the department; to promote social reforms of the profession; or to seek bringing community activists into the decision-making of the police force. Having political power and then using it for the greater good of the profession and community does not seem to be happening among U.S. police union leaders.

Chapter 37

DECENTRALIZED LABOR LAWS

Incoherent Labor Laws

After decades of strikes and labor violence, the U.S. Congress passed the *National Labor Relations Act (NLRA)* in the thirties to extend the right to form a union and collectively bargain to certain private sector employees. The National Labor Relations Board (NLRB) was created to enforce this right and prohibited employers from committing unfair labor practices that might discourage organizing or prevent workers from negotiating a union contract. In reality, the NLRB has failed to protect employees who try to unionize as witnessed by the steady decline of private sector unionization. Union membership as a percent of the total workforce is about 12 percent. Union density in the private sector is about 7.6 percent and is about 36.4 percent of public sector. Today, just one in ten workers in the private sector is in a union, down from one in three a half-century ago.

The failed Boston police strike in 1919 led to the subsequent passage of draconian anti-union laws for police officers that basically ended police unionization until the 1960s. While private sector workers were fighting for protections to unionize and collectively bargain, police officers were not organized, and their union rights fell to the wayside.

Today, the police labor relations system in the U.S. is very complex. Congress has not seen the need to extend any federal protections and rights to state and local police officers. The U.S. is one of the few highly industrialized democratic countries that do not have uniform national labor laws for police officers. The decentralized American police model allows each state to determine its own labor laws and policies as regards the police. If a given state does not regulate police labor relations, the local government is free to adopt its own policies and practices. To date, about 39 states have some form of collective bargaining for public employees; however, a few states prohibit police officers from having bargaining rights. Twenty-two states have enacted right-to-work provisions that prohibit union membership being mandatory and prohibit unions from charging non-members a fee for the costs of bargaining. Some of the Southern states prohibit public employees and police officers from being recognized as a labor union and collectively bargaining.

The one substantive federal law impacting police officers is the *Fair Labor Standards Act*, which was passed by Congress and originally did not cover public employees. In 1985, the U.S. Supreme Court in a 5–4 vote extended the *FLSA* to cover all public employees. *FLSA* requires all employers to pay covered employees who are not otherwise exempt at least the federal minimum wage and to pay additional "overtime" compensation after 40 hours of work in one week. The U.S. Department of Labor promulgated the rules and regulations and decided to set special overtime standards for police officers and firefighters separate from non-uniform public employees. The law does allow officers covered by a collective bargaining contract to supersede *FLSA* provisions if the contract creates a better benefit.

Where Are the Police Unions on Federal Legislation?

There is no question that collectively American police unions on the local, state and national levels are major players in the political game and significantly contribute to both the success and failure of change and reform in the police profession. Police unions have been successful in raising professional standards, increasing wages and benefits, and improving the overall living conditions of officers, but this change has been city-by-city and state-by-state, and not a product of any coordinated federal legislative strategy by the national police unions. But the wins that have been achieved by the police unions are limited due to the fragmented and competitive nature of the police union movement in the U.S.

There is no national strategy around issues such as professionalism, reform, or any comprehensive approach to respond to the changes taking place in policing more generally. This is not to say that there is a total lack of a shared vision in the police union movement. An examination of the web sites of the independent FOP and NAPO, the AFL-CIO affiliated IUPA, and CTW affiliated Teamsters and IBPO reveal that all have similar postings for the same federal legislation. All national police unions support a federal collective bargaining bill that had been a moot issue with President Bush and a Republican-controlled Congress opposed to it. With the shift to a Democratic-controlled Congress, the U.S. House of Representatives in 2007 has passed H.R. 980, the "Public Employee-Public Employer Cooperation Act," to grant all public employees the right to collectively bargain. The bill failed to get out of a Senate hearing in late 2007.

Politically, strategic alliances have been forged between the various police union groupings. The 2004 national elections had the FOP – the nation's largest national police union – endorsing President George W. Bush for reelection based upon his signing of the "Right to Carry Bill" and for not excluding police supervisors from the protections of the *FLSA*. NAPO with 238,000 members endorsed Democrat John Kerry, but many of its affiliated local and state police unions broke ranks and endorsed President Bush. The dissenting NAPO affiliated police unions used the same arguments as the FOP as a reason for a police labor union to endorse President Bush. Ignored in these endorsements was the President's decision to merge 180,000 federal law enforcement officers into the Department of Homeland Security and abrogate their collective bargaining contracts and civil service rights, and the gutting of the COPS program that had put thousands of new police officers on the street.

Chapter 38

THE GREATEST CHALLENGE FACING
AMERICAN POLICING

Forging Shared Common Visions Between Unions and
Management

To date, the national police unions have campaigned individually, but rarely have had the foresight to campaign jointly, for expanding police officer labor rights via the U.S. Congress. Any quest for national bills governing the labor rights of police workers would, however, be contested by police management organizations despite the real contribution that collective bargaining arrangements have had for the morale and professionalization of police officers.

Even around seemingly shared policies, unions and police management have trodden separate paths. To some extent, this divergence is due to the exclusion of police unions from major decision-making forums. For example, in 1979 the International Association of Chiefs of Police, National Organization of Black Law Enforcement Executives, National Sheriff's Association, and Police Executive Research Forum established the Commission on Accreditation for Law Enforcement Agencies (CALEA) as an independent accrediting authority. The Commission has 21 members: 11 members are law enforcement practitioners and the remaining ten are selected from the public and private sector. None of the commission members is a rank and file police officer or a police union leader. Accreditation of a law enforcement agency is voluntary, time-consuming, and expensive. Many police unions do not support the accreditation program because they do not see any benefit to the rank and file officers. CALEA does not have any rank and file education program directed at police officers or police unions to gain their input or endorsement.

However, attaining national rights to collective bargaining would not necessarily impact directly on the union's positive contribution to police reform and democratization. First, local agreements and agency accreditation would only generate change in one community at a time and would not address the larger racial and social problems dividing the police and some members of the community. Second, collective bargaining agreements and national accreditation do not address such issues as decentralized police services, candidate recruitment, lateral movement of officers, and diversity in hiring and promoting minorities and women. And third, the unequal distribution of wealth that oftentimes determines the quality of policing in a community is not addressed by a local collective bargaining agreement or agency accreditation.

There is no current forum for national police unions and national police management organizations to pursue the development of a shared vision of the police profession. A review of the agendas of the national police unions and national police management organizations reveals that none of these groups routinely invites the other side to address issues of mutual concern. In fact, it would appear that neither side sees **any** issues of mutual concern. To make matters worse, national police unions do not come together to form a network with the capacity to lobby and effect changes. As a result, there is no police union network capacity to network with national police management organizations. In an age of networked communication and action, the policing profession in the U.S. has been left far behind.

The Absence of a Uniform National Professional Police Standard Framework

The U.S. has almost one million people employed as sworn police officers and police support personnel and no uniform national professional police standards. The standard of conduct, recruitment, training, policies and practices of 90 percent of all law enforcement officers is left to each state and local government.

The quality of policing in each community varies nationwide, greatly depending upon whether the state has mandatory training standards, the capacity of local government to provide competitive wages and benefits to attract qualified applicants and retain veteran officers, and the local financial resources available to fund a modern police agency. In virtually every metropolitan area, suburban police forces will be better staffed, equipped, and paid than the urban police force. Urban and suburban police agencies are generally better funded and trained than rural police forces. The majority of states that have a Peace Officer Standards and Training (POST) board issue only voluntary guidelines and have no ability to regulate individual police officers, training academies, or law enforcement agencies.

Three problems result from the lack of national uniform professional police standards. First, citizens, residents, and visitors to the U.S. have no basis for evaluating the conduct of police officers from one jurisdiction to the next. The effectiveness and efficiency of the police is largely dependent on the resources available in any given local community. Second, it is very difficult for police officers to move laterally to another agency at the city, state, or federal level. Union contracts, civil service laws, varying state training laws, multiple pension systems, and different promotional schemes are prohibitive in regard to professional police mobility.

Third, it is virtually impossible in a country with 18,000 separate and distinct law enforcement agencies to effectively change or reform the police profession without uniform national professional police standards by which law enforcement agencies and officers can be judged. Community activists and elected officials who desire change and reform have had to fight the battle at every local level. As a result, the world is changing much faster than the police profession; and there is not time to fight 18,000 separate battles to improve the quality of policing in the U.S.

One solution to this clutter of standards is the International Association of Directors of Law Enforcement Standards and Training (IADLEST). It is an international organization of training managers and executives dedicated to the improvement of public safety personnel. The mission of IADLEST is to research, develop, and share information, ideas, and innovations that assist states in establishing effective and defensible standards for employment and training law enforcement officers.

IADLEST has developed model minimum state standards to "set a floor" on officer professionalism. The Association has a reciprocity handbook with the employment criteria in all 50 states. IADLEST is not a government agency and does not have any authority to mandate professional police standards on a national basis. The Association is composed of standards and training managers and leaders; and none of their board members represent police unions or police management organizations.

If IADLEST could be federalized or an IADLEST-like federal agency could be created that would set mandatory national standards, the issue of inconsistent standards could likely be resolved. The opposition to such a model would be immense, but the benefits to the profession would be monumental.

A New Model – a National Police Labor-Management Council

What is required is the creation of a national police labor-management council. In order for this council to occur, national police management organizations and national police unions would need to initiate informal discussions with one another. This process could be facilitated by a panel of academicians who have links with police management, labor, and criminal justice reform. In coming together in a joint forum, the parties would have to agree that they have a vested interest in communication and the exchange of ideas with the ultimate goal of confronting the challenges presented to the policing profession locally, nationally, and globally.

It is hoped the parties would agree on a more structured national police labor-management council composed of representatives of police management and police unions at the federal, state and local levels of government. The council should also include academicians, researchers, criminal justice reformers, and community activists either on the board or in *ex-officio* positions. One option would be to gain the support for an American Police Labor-Management Council (APLMC) from the U.S. Congress in either legislation or funding to an existing federal agency such as the U.S. Department of Justice. Such a council could provide a forum for debate and a conduit for all of the stakeholders concerned about the changing police environment and profession.

The APLMC's primary agenda should be to seek to develop a shared vision of the police profession; make recommendations to improve the effectiveness and efficiency of the police service nationwide; seek ways to balance the need for domestic policing and the new duties caused by international criminal activities; and outline how police agencies can get ahead of the curve on the global changes impacting the police profession and local communities. The APLMC would be the **only** national voice of the police that is inclusive of police management and labor, which would make its recommendations to the U.S. Congress and the President more meaningful.

Eight Issues For a Police Labor-Management Council

There are eight issues that an American police labor-management council could focus on:

1. Uniform national police professional standards. There is a need for mandatory uniform standards of professional ethics, training, policies, and practices for every law enforcement agency and law enforcement officer in the U.S. The diversity in hiring standards, training, wages, and benefits causes some law enforcement officers to see other officers as less qualified.

2. Build a network for communicating. One task for the Council would be to establish centralized communications tools for rank and file officers, police union officials, police managers, community activists, and the media. Local, state and national police unions, national police management organizations, and law enforcement agencies all have web sites and internal forums, but there is no linkage between the web sites and forums. The Council could act as a conduit for bringing these diverse networks together such as bulletin boards for information exchange.

3. Lateral movement within the police profession. After the adoption, funding and implementation of a uniform professional standard for all law enforcement officers in the U.S., the Council should seek to develop avenues for lateral movement at all ranks. Federal legislation should be proposed to address pension portability, seniority, civil service rules, and collective bargaining contract conflicts. A business model could be adopted that allows for the free market enterprise system to work. A true professional has the ability to market their talents and skills to various employers. Law enforcement agencies would be able to compete for the most skilled and experienced officers. Officers could be identified and offered employment where their skills are most needed.

4. Defining the core components of public police work. The cost in wages, benefits, training, and equipment to put a police officer on the street is continuing to soar. Competition between agencies for the best candidates and police unions bargaining better contracts is driving the cost even higher. Both police management and labor have failed to take heed of the rapidly changing policing environment. Civilians, volunteers, retired officers, and private contractors have already begun to take over many of the roles traditionally done by sworn officers. A Council could advocate for the rights and integrity of the public police if they had a shared understanding of what the core roles and functions of the public police are. Related to defining core components would be a determination regarding the kinds of education, training, and supervision that the public police require.

5. Modernize police recruitment processes. Virtually every law enforcement agency in the U.S. is facing a problem recruiting qualified applicants. In most jurisdictions a person desiring to become a police officer must untangle a myriad of civil service rules and regulations and apply at each separate police agency. The business and military recruitment models need to be examined and adopted. Young people today use www.monsterjobs.com and other Internet search vehicles to post their resumes. A national law enforcement job data bank created and managed by the Council would assist candidates and agencies meeting each other's needs.

6. Diversify the police profession. If the Council wishes to promote community policing, what is required is a police agency that reflects the community. While every agency claims to be interested in hiring more minorities and women, very few agencies have made the changes necessary to make the police profession more appealing to minorities and women. Police unions have shortsightedly resisted changes and reforms to civil service and collective bargaining contracts that would make promotional schemes, seniority, special assignments, and leave provisions more minority and female friendly. The Council needs to conduct research and develop models that reflect modern work rules that would attract minorities and women to law enforcement. For example 1,600 recruits recently graduated from the New York City Police Department academy where more than half of the class were minorities. New Zealand police are actively recruiting gays and lesbians, females, and people from different ethnic backgrounds.

7. Bring community groups to the table. The lack of trust and respect for the police in many communities, especially by minorities, gays, and poor people, cannot be overcome if these stakeholders do not have a seat at the table. The police world (both management and labor) has an us versus them attitude. Police officers believe that no outsider can really understand how hard it is to be a police officer in a democratic society. Police officers see themselves caught in a continuing no-win situation of being called racist by minorities regardless of the facts, second-guessed by police management who are afraid to support officers even when they are right, abandoned by politicians when the media circus begins and used by the media to increase ratings. The circle the wagons approach by U.S. police unions has only caused more anger and resentment towards police officers. The Council should encourage a free and open debate about how communities and social justice oriented organizations can be a part of the solution. Police unions need to accept the profession warts and all and acknowledge that there is a need for change and reform on a constant basis.

8. Advocate for an international role for U.S. police officers and police unions. Police forces in Australia, Canada, New Zealand, and many other countries see international police service as way to provide less advantaged countries with much needed training and guidance in developing a professional police service. These police officers return after their foreign assignments with experiences and knowledge that cannot be gained from working only in their home countries. Because the U.S. does not have one federal law enforcement agency like the Australian Federal Police to act as a conduit for federal and state officers to serve on international police missions, the U.S. contracts with private companies to recruit former U.S. police officers to serve in these assignments. State and local police comprise 90 percent of U.S. police forces, and unless they retire or resign, the opportunity to serve on an international police force is not available. State and local police officers of all ranks are losing out on this experience and knowledge, and in turn U.S. police are not exposed to global police networks. The Council should advocate for the Department of Homeland Security to provide officers for international police duties, and not just hot spots like Iraq, Afghanistan, and Kosovo; and to allow state and local police officers to serve and return without penalty to their hometown agencies. Using active federal, state and local police officers instead of for-profit corporate security guards would accomplish several goals – enhance the image of U.S. police officers internationally; expand the global police networks to include rank and file police officers; and U.S. police representatives would be accountable to the public and not the shareholders of a private corporation.

Conclusion

Despite the decentralization, fragmentation and disorganized nature of American police agencies and police unions, the fundamentals are in place for progress to be possible. Elected officials, police management, and police unions have started to recognize the changing nature of police work, global forces impacting on domestic policing, the need for new costing arrangements for policing, and the need for qualified professional police officers. Each group is aware of the detrimental effect of a failure to network and communicate effectively.

While the police unions have been very successful in winning improved conditions of service for the police, this success has proven to be a double-edged sword. The high cost of policing has forced the general public, media, elected officials, and police management to reconsider what constitutes public police work and what jobs are better done with a cheaper non-police substitute; and has resulted in increasing civilianization and privatization of policing.

At present, police management and labor in the U.S. seem to be operating in parallel universes that occasionally cooperate or collide. Networking is not taking place either between police agencies or between police union representatives. This situation has resulted in a lack of a shared vision among policing professionals and representative bodies. Police unions are not networking with each other, much less with community organizations and police management. What is required, given the competitive arena of police agencies and unions, is a safe haven where all of the stakeholders in the police profession can gather and exchange information and ideas, and develop common strategies. But to date, none of the national police unions or national police management organizations has made any effort to host symposiums on the future of the police profession and to include the other organizations.

Those that represent the police profession need to think more nationally and globally. They need to think critically about the shifts that are taking place in policing and what policing arrangements would benefit both communities and police officers. Police unions (and management) should think beyond their own narrow self-interest and engage more meaningfully with minority and community organizations. The future of the policing profession needs to be reviewed with some recognition that not all police work needs to be done by a sworn police officer.

Police unions and management need to keep their membership abreast of the changes that are taking place in the policing environment. This communication will allow police organizations to move ahead with police reform with the support of individual police officers. A knowledgeable social base will promote the effectiveness of the unions and police management to directly shape the debate and the shifts that are already underway in policing.

Sadly, police unions in the United States have until now focused only on achieving economic gains for their members; and they have expressed little or no interest in the advocacy for justice and effectiveness of policing communities. The big question is: Will police unions take on the challenge or throw up roadblocks to the evolving policies and practices of the police?

Part VII
UNITED STATES CASE STUDIES

Chapter 39

INTRODUCTORY REMARKS

In our first book, the case studies were used to illustrate important principles that had been discussed in various chapters. This book offers new case studies for the same purpose. The case studies are broken into two parts: issues in the United States and international issues.

For the U.S. segment, each of the co-authors has written a case study. Ron DeLord looks at the national recruitment crisis that affects virtually every law enforcement agency in the country, and offers solutions to the problem. Michael Shannon discusses a 2005 campaign he was involved in with the Police Officers Federation of Minneapolis against the Mayor. John Burpo talks about a nasty 2005 bargaining confrontation that took place between the police union and City Manager in Bullhead City, Arizona. Jim Spearing outlines a battle between the Coastal Florida PBA and Flagler County State's Attorney over alleged brutality in the jail, a battle that is continuing as this book goes to press.

An additional contributor to the U.S. case studies is Ted Hunt, past president of the Los Angeles Police Protective League and who is now enjoying a pleasant retirement in Costa Rica. He makes us rethink many of the assumptions we all make about the structure of policing in this country.

There are three international case studies as well, a feature that was not included in the first book. Greg O'Connor discusses unionism and policing in New Zealand. Police union leaders in this country should pay particular attention to Mr. O'Connor's cautionary tale about how constricted thinking could cost jobs and union members in their respective agencies and unions. Professors Monique Marks and Jenny Fleming examine the spread of police unionism around the world. Finally, Mark Burgess offers the reader a glimpse of policing and unionism in Australia.

One other comment is in order about the case studies. In our first book, we enjoyed taking shots at Time Warner and Ice-T in a case study about the infamous 1992 fight that we instigated over the *Cop Killer* song. It has come to our attention that the prestigious Harvard School of Business devotes some time to that affair and to how corporations should **not** behave when faced with a crisis. Who knew that we would make it all the way back to those stuffy halls of ivy in Boston!

Chapter 40

THE IMPACT OF THE NATIONAL POLICE RECRUITING CRISIS ON POLICE MANAGEMENT AND POLICE UNIONS

Ron DeLord

The Situation – The National Recruiting Crisis is Creating a Bidding War For a Dwindling Resource

Newspapers nationwide are reporting shortages of police applicants in the United States. It was recently reported that 80 percent of the nation's law enforcement agencies had vacancies they could not fill. In Texas alone, Houston needs 1,200 officers, Dallas 800 officers, and San Antonio 500 officers. In California, the City of San Jose signed a new contract with the police union to pay their experienced officers more than $100,000 a year and a 90 percent pension after 30 years.

The demand far outstrips the pool of applicants who are clean-cut, have no criminal record, are willing to do dangerous work, are physically fit, have at least a high school education and some college hours, have the ability to work with people in highly stressful situations, and will commit to the job for 20–30 years. Corporate America desires the same people, and they have more flexibility in who they can hire than do law enforcement agencies. Many law enforcement agencies hire only 5 percent to 10 percent of all applicants. Finding one in every ten applicants acceptable makes the recruiting crisis even harder to overcome.

Recruitment cannibalism has emerged as law enforcement agencies have started bidding wars in aggressively raiding other agencies for their sworn officers. The Houston Police Department lured 53 deputies from the sheriff's department to apply for a $12,000 higher salary, $7,000 signing bonus and a modified 12-week academy. San Diego is offering a $5,000 signing bonus to experienced officers to join their department. Baltimore police are going to Puerto Rico to recruit the low paid Spanish-speaking officers in that commonwealth. Scottsdale, Arizona, an affluent suburb of Phoenix, is recruiting in Boston in an effort to lure its officers to a higher paid job with better weather and a lower cost of living.

Departments have hired major public relations and marketing firms to create advertising campaigns in their state and across the nation designed to appeal to younger applicants. Las Vegas police have an advertising campaign targeted at 18 to 25-year-olds using cartoons. Austin, Texas police have started a media blitz using banners around the city, radio ads, and signs with "Buckle up with a New Career" in parked police cars.

The effects of the rising cost of policing create a Catch-22. If agencies lower their hiring standards to fill empty academy classes, the long-term effect will be more officer misconduct, more media attacks on officers and the agency, and lessened public respect for the police. A lessened public respect for the police causes law enforcement to lose its legitimacy. If law enforcement agencies continue to raise wages and benefits to compete for the declining number of applicants, it causes another problem.

The corollary to rising wages and benefits to hire, train and retain sworn officers is that the agency must seek cost-saving measures in other areas. Agencies are reconsidering "what is police work?" The new definition of police work is translating into a lower percentage of sworn officers per agency through privatization, civilianization, technology, reduced health insurance for active and retired officers, and eliminating defined benefits for new hires. Today, the percentage of non-sworn employees in an agency exceeds 30 percent nationally and is growing. The number of sworn officers may be growing in many agencies due to population growth, but the percentage of sworn officers in the agency is shrinking.

The Problem – Police Agencies are Selling a Product Few Young People Are Buying

The total compensation in wages and benefits for sworn officers may be comparable or better than that in the private sector, but agencies cannot make the sell to younger applicants. Recently, Jason Abend, Executive Director of the National Law Enforcement Recruiters Association, was quoted in the newspaper as saying, "Several factors have combined to leave police departments hard-pressed to fill their ranks. They include mass retirements by the baby boomer generation, a strong economy providing better-paying jobs in the private sector, and a military that is bulked up and repeatedly extending the service commitment of soldiers who might otherwise become police officers."

More significant is the fact that agencies have been slow to recognize the changing demographics occurring in society; in particular, the generational differences between baby boomers, Generation X, and now Generation Y applicants. Agencies have compounded their recruiting problems by adopting aggressive advertising and recruiting models that are primarily targeted at raiding other agencies, and do not resonate with Generation Y applicants.

The real underlying problem is that law enforcement agencies are selling a product few young people are buying. As former Texas Agriculture Commissioner Jim Hightower commented, "You can put lipstick and a dress on a pig, but it is still a pig." Except for a few television glamorized jobs like the FBI and DEA, the truth is that 99 percent of all police work is stressful, potentially dangerous, boring for long periods of time, underappreciated, overlyregulated, micro-managed, seniority driven, bureaucratic, heavily disciplined, 24/7 shift work, little time off from work, premature death, and high rates of alcoholism, divorce and suicide. And more importantly, operational police work is not always viewed by the media and public as the best professional job choice by young people with a college education.

Agencies must face reality and admit it is not a seller's market. Those days are gone, perhaps forever. To require applicants to negotiate the maze of often antiquated civil service rules and regulations, collective bargaining agreements, locate information about the test dates, try to figure out comparative salaries and benefits, and wait months for physicals, background investigations, interviews and academy classes, just aggravates the disadvantage police recruiters already have competing against private sector employers. Agencies need to mimic the business models that have developed a user-friendly web site, have easy access to information about comparative salaries and benefits, expedite applicant processing, and in general, have an attitude that the applicant has a choice of jobs. The bottom line – agencies must sell themselves to the applicant, not vice versa.

It is a buyer's market for the "me generation" accustomed to instant communication and information. Their lives are not work-centered, and they want more from a job than the promise of a 30-year pension at the end of the rainbow. The higher starting salaries will get their attention, but to close the deal to join the police department, they will need to feel that they will be included in decision-making, be recognized for their achievements, have flexible work schedules, and work for an agency with high moral values. The recruitment of Generation Y into policing will call for not just a new strategy by agencies, but a shift in the police culture to place more value on quality of life and working conditions.

Law enforcement agencies still have some major hurdles even if the agency improves its processing and modernizes its practices and policies. Policing is still a quasi-military operation that is 88 percent male and predominately white. The lack of a diverse work force and flexible life style choices put police agencies at a distinct disadvantage when competing with the military and major employers, especially for the very shallow pool of women and minorities who might be interested in a law enforcement career.

One example ignored by law enforcement agencies is that the education profession has recognized the value in having its female teachers who have given birth to return at some point to the job. Law enforcement agencies treat pregnancy as a disease and rarely grant extended leaves to female officers who desire to be stay-at-home mothers. This inflexibility prevents qualified and skilled female officers from returning to the agency when their children reach school age.

The Question – Why Have Police Unions Not Been Invited, Encouraged or Challenged to Provide Solutions to the Recruiting Crisis?

Recent studies, reports, and media articles about the national police recruiting crisis fail to mention police unions as being a part of any study, having any responsibility for the problems associated with recruitment, or participating in any forums on the subject. Elected officials, police management, and the media like to use police unions as the whipping boy for the lack of progress on police reforms. It is true that police unions, who have for the most part been self-centered and elitist in their quest for higher wages and benefits, have not elected to participate in social reform. It is also true that elected officials, police management, and the media have not viewed police unions as equal partners.

The answer to why police unions have been ignored is simple – there is a general lack of trust, respect, cooperation and communication between police management and police unions. Old habits are hard to break. The parties have been adversarial for so long they cannot fathom operating as equal partners to solve fundamental problems within the profession. The parties are more comfortable rearranging deck chairs on the Titanic.

Police unions are the elephant in the room when it comes to the recruiting crisis in particular, and reform in general. Police unions cannot be ignored if the problem is to be solved. Ego, pride, habits, traditions, and feuds need to be set aside by all parties. The truth is that police unions are powerful political forces in every community, and there is no end run around them. If police unions are invited, encouraged, and challenged to step up to the plate and assume responsibility for making the reforms necessary to attract and retain qualified officers, then police management must see the unions as equal partners and not just a sounding board for management ideas.

The competition for applicants has driven up wages and benefits, and some police union leaders see this competition as manna from heaven. Police union leaders with vision know this is a shortsighted view. They know that they must educate their members to the fact that this crisis is also a problem for their members. First, the impact of spiraling wages and benefits is depleting the number of sworn officers as a percentage of the agency. Second, there is growing media attention to the widening gap between the wages, pensions, and health insurance benefits in the private and public sector. Perhaps if officers understood the long-term impact of this crisis, they would support their leaders in seeking joint partnerships with management to work toward some solutions.

References

Air Force recruiters stake out new territory in GSD&M ads. *Austin American States-man*, September 14, 2006.

Baltimore Recruiters Draw Large Crowds in Puerto. *The Baltimore Sun*, July 7, 2006.

Bureau of Justice Statistics, Local Police Departments 2000. Law Enforcement Management and Administrative Statistics, Washington, D.C.: U.S. Department of Justice, Office of Justice Programs, 2003.

Cities Face Troubles in Hiring Cops. *San Antonio Express News*, June 28, 2006.

Dallas Police Struggle to Recruit Officers. *Dallas Morning News*, February 4, 2006.

Federal Bureau of Investigation, Uniform Crime Report, "Crime in the United States, Law Enforcement," Washington, D.C.: U.S. Department of Justice, 2004.

HPD, Union Agree on Incentives for Seasoned Officers. *Houston Chronicle*, February 13, 2006.

International Association of Chiefs of Police, Police Leadership in the 21st Century, *Recommendations from the President's First Leadership Conference*, Washington, D.C.: International Association of Chiefs of Police, 1999.

Law Enforcement Wants You: Austin police department and other Texas law enforcement agencies desperately looking for recruits. *Austin American-Statesman*, August 14, 2006.

Lee, Richard, Generation X Police Officers: What makes managing them different? *Officer.Com*, January 9, 2006.

Los Angeles Police Under the Gun to Recruit: Fierce competition from other departments is making it tough for the agency to meet its hiring goals. *Los Angeles Times*, July 2, 2006.

Mitchell, Janet, President's Message, *Victoria Police Association Journal*, May 2006.

Police Enhance Recruiting Efforts: Attrition has HPD trying to lure officers from across Texas. *Houston Chronicle*, January 17, 2006.

Police Recruiting Takes Page from Comic Books. *Las Vegas Review Journal*, April 28, 2006.

The Rand Corporation, Occasional Paper, Infrastructure, Safety and Environment, Police Personnel Challenges After September 11: Anticipating Expanded Duties and a Changing Labor Pool, Arlington, V.A.: The Rand Corporation, 2005.

To Fill Jobs, HPD Finds a Bonanza in County: Lured by more pay and better benefits, 53 Harris deputies have applied. *Houston Chronicle*, February 2, 2006.

Chapter 41

HOW A COALITION OF POLICE OFFICERS AND CITIZENS TOOK ON THE MAYOR OF MINNEAPOLIS AND WON

MICHAEL R. SHANNON

"My name is Barbara Howard and I believe I'm the only witness to testify before this committee who has a contract out on her life." That dramatic statement was the beginning of four hours of testimony before the Minneapolis City Council's Truth in Taxation Committee that set the agenda for budget discussions and put public safety at the top of the council's priority list.

What's more, it was a dramatic turnaround from the political environment of only a week before.

At that time, in early November, 2006 Mayor R. T. Rybak was working hard to pass a budget plan that cut eight police officers from the department's on–the–street strength of 637 officers. This would have resulted in the fewest number of officers in the last 25 years, down from a high of 938 officers in 1997 to only 770.

My client in this fight was the Police Officer's Federation of Minneapolis (POFM) and it was obvious that in the very few weeks before the budget vote in December the Federation would need reinforcements to win.

In fact we would have to employ all three of the "C's" of successful public information campaigns if we were to have a hope of winning. Those "C's" are:

1. Context
2. Coalition
3. Confrontation

Our first efforts were to build the coalition for the confrontation. Barbara Howard, quoted above, is the owner of a beauty shop in a part of the city plagued by drug dealers and disorder. Her frequent 911 calls and attempts to clean up the neighborhood had earned threats on her life and rumors of a contract to kill her.

Howard became the first member of the coalition and she was followed by homeowners, a pastor, businessmen and women, a mental health professional, community activists, and a fraud investigator for a major downtown business.

We found these volunteers by contacting officers whose primary assignment involved some type of community policing. These officers knew the individuals in crime–plagued neighborhoods, and they made the first contact with potential witnesses before POFM board members closed the deal.

These individuals agreed to be witnesses at the city council's budget hearing and to appear at news conferences during the fight. They also worked to recruit friends and family to swell the ranks of citizens who wanted more, not fewer police officers.

Once a witness agreed to testify, we conducted individual interviews. During these interviews, we explored the background of their individual crime problems and what they thought of the mayor's proposal for additional cuts to the department.

Remarks or testimony was then written for each individual based on the information gained from the interview. Their story provided the context for the talking points delivered at the hearing. Giving a witness suggested talking points before the hearing also served to keep them on message and insure that the important points were delivered within the time frame allotted each person. A witness who was particularly nervous could simply read the testimony, rather than speak extemporaneously.

Those witnesses became the basis of the coalition. The context was provided by the city across the river – St. Paul, Minnesota.

Context is where facts or issues are put in perspective for citizens and those not intimately acquainted with the details of the controversy. In the abstract 637 police officers might sound like a lot to the average citizen who thinks one officer is too many when he's getting a ticket.

But when you add context, pointing out that 637 is fewer officers than were on the job on 9/11, and that during the time when Minneapolis was cutting police officers, St. Paul was adding officers, then the facts start to have an impact.

Minneapolis has fewer officers today than on 9/11? People were first amazed and then many were angry. Particularly those who had experienced Minneapolis' increase in crime firsthand.

Now 637 is no longer just a number – it's an indication of decline, an explanation for the increase in crime and an indictment of the mayor's priorities. The addition of Saint Paul, and its increase in officers, shows that a mayor who puts a premium on public safety will find a way to keep the police force intact.

Yet all too often facts are not put in context for the public and as a result legitimate issues are defeated by half–truths and spin. In the case of Minneapolis, the mayor based his case on the cut in funds provided to the city by the state of Minnesota and expiration of federal funding for the so–called "Clinton cops." His contention was that with the cut in funding he was forced to cut the police budget; and furthermore, he was forced to cut the budgets of all city departments by 10 percent to make up for the shortfall.

In the abstract this makes sense. In context it is lunacy. St. Paul suffered from the same budget cuts, yet enlightened leadership in the Twin City was adding police officers. Instead of budget cutting by decimation, the St. Paul mayor cut the fat and pumped up the muscle.

As POFM President John Delmonico commented to the media, when your income is cut by 10 percent you don't tell the bank the mortgage payment will be 10 percent lighter this month. You cut what you spend on non–essentials so you can continue to pay for the essentials.

It's not the role of the POFM to set police policy in the city and my advice to union leadership is usually to stay out of staffing arguments. In this instance the Federation felt it had to step in when elected leadership wasn't leading and overworked officers on the street were feeling the brunt of citizen dissatisfaction with public safety. Under those circumstances, manpower became a working conditions issue and a legitimate concern of union leadership.

At the same time a police union asking for more police offices can seem self–serving to the tax–paying public, hence the need for the coalition. But in coalitions, bigger is always better and we had the added benefit of reinforcements from the invisible coalition: poll results. The POFM had recently done an opinion poll that showed the majority of voters overwhelmingly wanted more police officers.

Now it became a question of timing. Typically you want to start a public opinion campaign as early as possible, since it takes time to re-cruit a coalition and create a sense or urgency among the public. Four to six months of preparation, planning and execution is preferable.

That was a luxury we did not have. In fact, we had only two frenet-ic weeks before the budget vote. The first week was spent building the coalition, doing research and preparing for the budget hearing. From the date of the hearing until the vote was only eight days.

Normally I would have a news conference a week before the hear-ing to reveal the results of the poll demanding more police officers, possibly concluding with a walk to city hall to deliver the poll to the mayor and each of the council members. With us on the walk would have been as many other members of the coalition as we could recruit.

Then on the morning of the budget hearing we would have anoth-er news conference featuring two or three of our most dramatic wit-nesses to give the media a teaser of their testimony. Then the rest of the week would be devoted to building pressure and the final "C:" confrontation.

This arrangement gives us two opportunities for news coverage and more time for the issue to penetrate into the mind of the general pub-lic. It also gives us more time to organize.

Unfortunately, we could not try to maximize our news impact. The morning of the hearing we held the news conference with the poll results. Since polls are just numbers and not visual, we had large color graphs made for the broadcast media with copies on CD for print media. During this news conference we made no mention of the wit-nesses we had scheduled for the hearing that afternoon.

Why no mention of the witnesses? Since I've stressed how crucial they are to the success of our effort, why hide the witnesses under a bushel now? Simple, news coverage dynamics dictate what we present in any one news opportunity. You never want to give the media a choice of topics to cover at a news conference.

If you give the media two newsworthy events during a news conference you cut your chances of getting the coverage you want in half. This is because a broadcast reporter will only have limited amount of time to devote to coverage of your event, so he is typically not going to cover two subjects. Instead, the reporter will pick the topic that appears to be the most newsworthy and cover that. Topic, ignoring whatever else transpired at your event.

If we had presented both the witnesses and the poll information, we would have been doing what is called **stepping on your message**. The most important fact to our campaign was the poll result which showed overwhelming citywide support for more officers, but if you give the media a choice between covering the numbers contained in a poll and a living, breathing human being with a story; the human will beat the numbers every time. Reporters can interview people – and our witnesses were very dramatic – but you can't interview an opinion poll and writing the story requires reading. All of which is more trouble than shoving a microphone in someone's face. So our poll would have been ignored.

It was important the council members know the results of the survey, (we thoughtfully provided them with a copy of the graphs in their council mailbox that morning) but even more important was that the council realizes the media and the public at large is aware of the survey.

Besides, we already knew the hearing would be covered that afternoon, so our witnesses would not be ignored. With that morning news conference we began the confrontation process. The Federation received extensive broadcast coverage of the survey results and the next day the newspaper featured our budget hearing witnesses, which meant we were off to a good start.

Wednesday of that week we had another news conference to play a radio spot that began that morning comparing crime rates between Minneapolis and St. Paul (again, I would have preferred to wait a week for the commercial and devote all news coverage to the ad, rather than have two news conferences in the same five–day period, but we didn't have that option).

The radio commercial we played for the assembled media began:

Minneapolis and St. Paul are the twin cities, but when it comes to violent crime – they're not so equal.

In Minneapolis we have an almost one-third greater chance of being a victim. FBI statistics reveal 11.95 violent crimes per thousand residents, compared to St. Paul's 7.62.

So what's the difference between the two cities – other than your chances of staying alive?

The spot closed by urging citizens to call their council member and demand they add more police officers. This tactic is living dangerously. The corollary to Pavlov's Dogs is when the bell rings, there better be some dinner. If the public doesn't call when you ask them to, the political powers–that–be assume you are a paper tiger and your campaign collapses. The leadership of the Federation assured me calls would be no problem.

Once again we had good turnout for the news conference, but even better – the salesman at radio station WCCO called that morning and said that after the spot ran callers swamped the station's switchboard asking for the mayor's phone number.

Why listeners called the radio station for the number instead of city hall remains a mystery, but we were very happy with the response. One of the more interesting calls that morning was from Mayor Randy Kelly of St. Paul who thanked the radio station for all the kind words regarding safety in his city.

To keep the momentum on our side, the president of the POFM, John Delmonico, appeared on radio and TV talk shows throughout the week. He talked about the poll, the lack of officers, the new cuts in manpower and the crime situation. Each appearance reinforced our message and either reminded voters about or introduced voters to the issue.

What he did not talk about was how to pay for the officers. That's the job of the elected officials, not the job of the cops. If the mayor and the council can't find a way to pay for public safety, then they need to find a career that doesn't require such tough decisions. What we did suggest was they call the Mayor of Saint Paul, Randy Kelly, for advice since he does not seem to have a problem keeping and hiring police officers.

The public campaign was generating so much notice that Gov. Tim Pawlenty sent Mayor R. T. Rybak a letter advising him on how he could free up money to hire more officers. It was a letter that Rybak ignored.

The final effort came on Monday, December 13, when the council voted on the budget. Coalition members were again on hand for a news conference prior to the vote and they packed the council chambers.

The result of all the POFM's hard work was a complete victory. The council meeting was dominated by our public safety agenda, and a revised Council budget that did not cut a single police officer. In fact, in an about-face the council pledged to find ways to add officers in the coming year.

There were three elements that were crucial to the Federation's success in this campaign.

1. The issue of public safety and police officers was very important to the majority of voters in the city.
2. The POFM had the financial resources to take the issue to the public in a very visible manner.
3. The leadership of the Federation, President John Delmonico, Treasurer Lyall Delaney and the rest of the board of directors were active, motivated and extremely hard-working.

Chapter 42

THE CASE OF THE ARIZONA CITY MANAGER WHO JUST HAD TO HAVE HIS OWN WAY: THE 2005 BULLHEAD CITY POLICE CONTRACT DISPUTE

JOHN BURPO

One of the authors has an amusing expression that has application to many circumstances: "You can't make chicken salad out of chicken ____." For example, you could use it to describe a police union leader who is dim-witted, inarticulate, and insensitive to members, politicians, and the community – thankfully none of our readers! The following case study, however, is a great example of a police union that did make chicken salad when the "____" around them was so deep that there looked to be no way out.

Bullhead City, Arizona is located in northwestern Arizona, right across the Colorado River from Laughlin, Nevada, a place that some have described as a mini-Las Vegas (make that "mini, mini, mini"). Bullhead City has a population of almost 40,000, mainly Caucasian, but like most Arizona cities, also a growing Hispanic community. Laughlin, with its one long street of casinos and restaurants, is the primary source of jobs for Bullhead residents.

The Bullhead City police officers and their association – the Bullhead City Police Officers Association (BHCPOA) gained meet and confer rights in the late 1990s. In 2005, the BHCPOA had 56 members and represented police officers but not supervisors. While there are some differences between meet and confer and collective bargaining that labor law theorists can legitimately argue about, the dynamics are the same for both processes. If the union is powerful, it will achieve its goals; if it is weak, it won't.

The President of the BHCPOA at the time was Jerry Duvall, an energetic and committed leader of his union. Jerry was a transplant from Wisconsin and an avid Green Bay Packers fan. During bargaining preparations and then during the tough campaign that followed, Jerry, other BHCPOA leaders and I spent many a night in a small guest house behind Jerry's main home that was decked out with every conceivable Packer paraphernalia, and where the ghosts of Bart Starr, Paul Hornung, and Max McGee loomed large.

The BHCPOA Enters 2005 Negotiations Upside Down on the Power Curve, and Things Go Downhill from There

Jerry Duvall was the first to admit that his organization was not well positioned for negotiations at the start of 2005. The union had no friends on City Council and had not worked at developing friends in the community. City Manager Frank Abeyta ran municipal operations with an iron fist: the City Council appeared extremely compliant to the Manager's direction, and employees had virtually no voice in City policies. The BHCPOA was the only employee group to have representational rights in the City, and the City had consistently made "take it or leave" offers to the BHCPOA.

When the City Manager hired a professional negotiator from New Mexico to represent the City's interests, BHCPOA's state-wide affiliate AZCOPS called me to assist in negotiations. Our first meeting in February did not bode well for a positive outcome. The City's negotiator proposed onerous ground rules that barred the union from talking to the City Council, the public, the media and even our own members up through and including the advisory arbitration impasse procedure. This particular ground rule had been imposed by the City Manager in previous negotiations; and the BHCPOA bargaining committee and I agreed that this ground rule stifled the union's flexibility to have a dialogue with our members, the Council, and the public about negotiation issues.

The progress of negotiations continued to stall at the second meeting as the City continued to press for this condition, even in spite of our pointing out that the meet and confer ordinance and agreement both made ground rules voluntary. When the City's negotiator proposed mediation to resolve the dispute over ground rules during the second bargaining session, it was clear to our side that if the City was going to try and impose ground rules that we couldn't agree on, then the rest of issues under negotiations would meet a similar fate.

In my 30+ years of negotiating agreements for law enforcement officers, I have negotiated agreements for police unions as large as 2,000 employees and as small as 20. The Bullhead City bargaining was the only time that I have ever had a serious argument over ground rules. It seemed absolutely silly that the City would hold so firmly to an issue that meant so little, but the City's position was suggestive of a larger principle at stake – the question of whether the BHCPOA would continue to willingly accept imposed settlements. If your union is ever going to have a relatively equal relationship with the City in negotiations, then the answer to this question is clearly no.

We therefore rejected the City's proposal for mediation. I advised the City's negotiator that we were going to discontinue negotiations, have a conversation with the public, and that something bad was going to happen. When I tell the employer's representatives that something bad is going to happen, I already have a pretty good idea of what the "bad" is going to be. Apparently, the City's negotiator either wasn't listening or thought that I was bluffing, because he cavalierly dismissed my remarks.

The BHCPOA and AZCOPS Go Into High Gear with a Major Assault on the City Manager

We realized around the time of our first meeting with the City that we would need some ammunition in the event that a fight developed. There had been some rumors floating around town that City Manager Frank Abeyta had purchased some property from a real estate developer who was also a member of the City Planning and Zoning Commission. At the same time as our second meeting with the City, one of our BHCPOA leaders and AZCOPS attorney Martin Bihn were in the middle of researching this rumor.

It turns out that over the preceding year, the City Manager had purchased four different parcels of property worth almost $400,000 that were either directly or indirectly related to the real estate developer. Now I don't know whether Mr. Abeyta had some extra money on hand that he just wanted to invest, or whether he and the developer had a truly arms length business arrangement; and I don't really care. But I do know that the chief administrative official of a municipality should not be doing business with a developer who will be coming before the City for requests on zoning and tax abatements, and who is also on an important City Commission – it just doesn't look good.

Anyone who has read this far in the book knows that a union can't run a public campaign around bargaining ground rules. Who would really care about whether the union has the right during negotiations to talk with the Council, the public, or its own members? But the public does care about crime and the public does care about how elected and appointed officials conduct themselves. That is why the Bullhead City public campaign revolved around crime in the community and the City Manager's real estate purchases.

In April, 2005, AZCOPS President Jim Parks held a news conference in front of Bullhead City Hall surrounded by BHCPOA President Jerry Duvall and other officers. Parks talked about Abeyta's four property purchases tied to the real estate developer, and said that "it is highly unethical for a public official to do business with a real estate developer who asks for favors from the City, and who is also on a City Commission." Parks went on to say that "In all my years of serving the public as a police officer, I have never seen such as blatant conflict of interest between a public official's duty to serve the public without even the appearance of impropriety and the official's personal land speculation."

Parks then talked about how burglary crimes were up, calls for service and response times had increased, and staffing levels weren't even at authorized strength. He also pointed out that Abeyta was well compensated as City Manager and gave a run down of the Manager's significant salary and perks obtained through a public records request.

Parks then hit on the point that would become the centerpiece of the public campaign: "The City Manager needs to pay more attention to public safety problems in Bullhead City, and less attention to land speculation. Abeyta's desire to feather his own nest is one of the reasons why there are public safety problems in the City." He finished by asking that the City Council and County attorney conduct investigations into the land purchases.

The BHCPOA and AZCOPS Campaign Kicks into High Gear and the City Pushes Back

The press conference kicked off an intense public campaign. A dramatic minute-long radio ad produced by AZCOPS ran throughout the first week of the campaign, calling attention to crime problems in Bullhead City and the Manager's perceived interest in feathering his own nest rather than in dealing with these problems. If you have ever tried to buy radio time in a small community where a Sacred Cow is being attacked, expect some resistance. One of the local stations refused to run the ad, but fortunately another station in a neighboring community agreed to run it.

Simultaneously with the radio ads, BHCPOA members began block walks throughout the city, handing out leaflets outlining the issue and using talking points to discuss it with citizens. Phone calls and e-mails were organized among members, families, and friends to contact City Council members about the crime problem and the City Manager's land deals. In the block walks, phone calls, and e-mails, members and other participants were given talking points in order to stay on message. Research was also begun on an initiative to change the meet and confer ordinance to require pay comparability with five other Arizona cities – this research would have led to "Plan B" if our public campaign stalled.

City officials did not take kindly to the BHCPOA's and AZCOPS's efforts. The City Council called an emergency meeting and in a show of support for Abeyta, gave him a $10,000 raise. Council members, the local radio, and newspaper all roundly condemned both the BHCPOA and AZCOPS.

As a consequence of all this public pressure, several members quit the union because they felt that the union's tactics were heavy-handed. Jerry Duvall and the other union leaders became concerned whether they would be able to hold their organization together during this very tough fight against a formidable opponent. Even though I had prepared both the members at a meeting and the leaders on several occasions for the blast that would follow this course of action, they didn't realize how ugly it really was going to be.

Someone Blinks and a Compromise is Settled Upon

Any time that there is one of these pitched battles over an important issue, someone is going to blink first and open the door for a compromise. In this case, Frank Abeyta blinked, meeting with Jerry Duvall and telling him that the union's campaign had caused him great public embarrassment. He said that he would prefer that I never show my face again in Bullhead City, and that he would be willing to remove his professional negotiator from the process if I stayed away.

Jerry Duvall discussed the matter with me and I told him that the end is much more important than whether I showed up or not. He should declare victory, go back to the bargaining table, and make a deal with the City.

That is exactly what happened. BHCPOA and City representatives went back to the bargaining table; and no one seemed too concerned about ground rules at this point. The parties settled on a one-year agreement for an across-the-board 8 percent wage increase.

The Aftermath

One of the humorous incidents that took place toward the end of this campaign was that Frank Abeyta called the Tucson Chief of Police. He wanted to know whether Jim Parks was a full-time Tucson police officer (he was). Then he wanted to know what Parks' salary was. The Chief told Abeyta that he could make a public information request for the salary like anyone else.

Several months after this brouhaha had died down, Frank Abeyta resigned as City Manager. I have no idea whether he was forced out over this incident, wanted to spend more time with his family, or got the bug to become a full time real estate investor. No one in the city was willing to give the real reason. I do know that he was an administrator who was clearly accustomed to having his own way and that this campaign caught him totally off guard.

The Lessons Learned

Our readers have likely become so learned in the preceding sections and chapters that the lessons don't even have to be discussed. But just in case you are reading the book from back to front, here goes:

1. Use a message that is simple, relevant, and gets people's attention. Any message about the real issue – bargaining ground rules, would have had people scratching their heads in puzzlement. Instead, we used the tie in between crime problems and the City Manager's inattention to these problems because he was too busy buying land. **These are issues that the public cares about!**

2. Go outside the experience of the adversary. We definitely hit a home run on this Saul Alinsky principle. The City Manager and other officials were caught completely off guard by our campaign, both by the message and how we delivered the message.

3. Personalize the debate. No one understands a fight between the union and "the City" because "the City" is an abstract notion. The fight must be personalized – there must always be a "boogeyman" that is in the cross-hairs. In this instance, Frank Abeyta made an inviting target.

4. Cause the adversary enough pain to make him cry "uncle." You want to drive up the pain and discomfort level to the point that your adversary just wants it all to be over. Since you are feeling the pressure from your side as well, you have to get him there before you cry "uncle."

5. Never go outside the experience of your members. Another Alinsky principle, and I really blew this one! The BHCPOA leadership and members – all very wonderful officers, had never been in an ugly confrontation before. This campaign went well beyond the edge of their envelope and it took a year for the hard feelings to heal inside the union. Looking back though, I can't see any other option that would have compelled the City Manager to move.

6. You must overcome your desire to be liked. This principle was discussed in the chapter on leadership. Some time after this fight, a management negotiator who is a good professional colleague of mine told an audience at a public meeting in Arizona that what I had done in Bullhead City was "unprofessional." In the bottom of my heart, I know that a personal attack on Frank Abeyta is not something that "nice" people do; and maybe on Judgment Day, I will be called before my Maker and have some serious explaining to do. But while I am still in the Here and Now, then I am going to do what is right and best for the members, and will do whatever it takes to get the job done. That's what I did in Bullhead City, and I haven't lost one night's sleep over it.

Chapter 43

A STATE ATTORNEY'S ABUSE OF POWER ATTRACTS NATIONAL ATTENTION

Jim Spearing

This is a story about how adverse media coverage can try and convict your members long before they have a chance to defend themselves. It is also a tale of how labor leaders can fight back and turn events in their favor.

Since 2005, the Florida PBA had been locked in a desperate struggle to reveal the truth about the arrest and incarceration of Lisa Tanner, the daughter of Flagler County State Attorney John Tanner and to clear the name of the innocent officers involved. This battle grew to such intensity that the story reached national proportions.

Lisa Tanner was arrested by Flagler Beach Police (not her first rodeo) for disorderly intoxication and resisting arrest. She had to be carried to the patrol car. At the jail, she became abusive to corrections officers, clogged the cell toilet with her shoes, and urinated on the floor. At this point, corrections officers placed her in a restraint chair and, for their own protection, videotaped the incident. The tape was promptly turned in to management and subsequently released to the press.

The tape caused quite a furor and, taken out of context, looked bad for our guys. However, an initial investigation concluded no wrongdoing on the part of the corrections officers, and the case should have ended there. It didn't.

State Attorney John Tanner unleashed the full powers of his office to persecute the arresting officer and the corrections officers at the jail.

First, he launched his own investigation of the Flagler County Jail issuing "hip pocket" subpoenas and threatening to jail any officer who wouldn't knuckle under. He then jury-shopped his daughter's case to find a grand jury willing to indict the officers who restrained her.

State Attorney Tanner then turned on the arresting officer in an effort to destroy his law enforcement career. He even went so far as to send a letter to criminal defense lawyers vowing to not prosecute any case involving the arresting officer. Can you imagine a states attorney willing to troll the criminal community to reopen and dismiss cases as payback?

All these abuses resulted in Florida Governor Jeb Bush appointing a special prosecutor to review the entire mess and guess what . . . John Tanner became the center of the investigation. So what is a powerful states attorney to do? Why, spend over $200,000 in taxpayer money to suppress the results of the independent investigation.

We suppose it was inevitable that such shocking behavior would eventually attract the attention of the national media. Initially, the PBA was slow to respond to these outrages preferring to battle the issue in court. State Attorney Tanner seized the initiative by going on every talk show he could to vilify law enforcement.

The PBA finally struck back with everything it had: radio, full page ads and multiple press events. Their efforts resulted in widespread media attention and a more honest and truthful recounting of events related to the arrest and jailing of Lisa Tanner. As of this writing, State Attorney Tanner is on the defensive, circling his legal wagons at taxpayer expense.

Here are a couple of lessons for police labor leaders from this sad incident:

- Never let the lawyers run your campaign. Lawyers serve a vital purpose but they live in a world where there are rules, fairness, and due process. We live in a world of politics, perception and, when it comes to law enforcement officers, a presumption of guilt, not innocence.
- Never let a shot go unanswered. We allowed State Attorney Tanner and his daughter to seize the public stage and dominate the debate for an unconscionable period of time. We need to strike back instantly when our officers are under attack.

- Remind the public who the bad guys are and how difficult and dangerous law enforcement can be. Our campaign reminded folks on why Lisa Tanner was in the jail in the first place and the fact that prison is not Club Med . . . we don't put mints on your pillow. Had Lisa Tanner conducted herself with dignity by complying with law enforcement, she would not have been arrested and jailed.
- Stand up for your members. Perhaps the most sacred trust placed in PBA hands is the duty to fight to the bitter end, to defend the rights and honor of our members. They need to know we have their back.
- Keep the pressure on and never, ever give up. I'm certain John Tanner, in hindsight, rues the day he decided to tangle with PBA. His actions have resulted in disgrace and embarrassment for him politically and his family. We will continue the fight until our officers are exonerated and state attorneys across this state learn the lesson that there are consequences for abusing of their powers.

We'll keep you posted as further events unfold.

Chapter 44

FUTURE ISSUES: WHERE ARE WE GOING?

TED HUNT

The future of organizational management will be based on collaboration. Particularly the future of police organizations will be based on collaboration, which literally means to co-labor, to work together; that is, to cooperate. Community policing and problem-solving policing cannot work without it. Ultimately, the chief of police has the last word and is the responsible person (unless you go to court). Only a foolish chief will refuse to collaborate with stakeholders of which there are four principal groups:

1. The chief's boss (mayor or city council or city manager);
2. Special interest groups;
3. Taxpayers/voters; and
4. Police union.

Police unions have a voice in public policy because they are powerful. Unions fought their way to the table through politics and confrontation. Politicians and city administrators pay attention to you because they know if they don't, you can really hurt them up to an including dealing a death knell to their political careers. They know that when it comes to street combat the police union is usually one of the toughest dogs on the block. You may not always win a political fight, but when you fight the other guy comes out bloodied and bruised.

Being involved in creating public policy is critical for a police union. Have you ever been given a new policy directive and said to yourself, "What on earth are they thinking? This will never work." Many times the policymakers get input from politicians or special interest groups, and that is how they come up with ideas that won't work. The union is needed in the policy decision-making process to bring reality and practicality to the debate. If you have a seat at the table, you have input.

In addition, some poorly conceived policies, when carried out, lead to a catastrophe, a public image crisis and possible criminal action. The politicians and administrators will run for cover even though they developed the policies. They will start pointing fingers at the officers and the union that is left to defend the officers who simply were following the policies that the politicians and administrators made. It is called scapegoating.

As part of the policymaking process, you have to show them that your input has meaning and is valuable. We do that by elevating our thinking. There are serious issues on the horizon that police unions need to think about and seriously discuss in order to know which way you want to go. Unions can no longer afford to be reactive; they have to be proactive and collaborative.

You should look out for the best interests of your members, but you should also look out for the best interests of the communities you serve. Without a strong socioeconomic community your tax base shrinks along with the need for officers and the ability to pay a decent wage. Having a safe vibrant city is in your best interests. When the city has more in the city coffers, you can be paid more.

You also have to be involved in the fundamentals of organizational development such as establishing or reviewing the department's vision (*what is the future supposed to look like*), values (*what is important and what gets rewarded*) and mission (*why do you exist in the first place*). You have to be involved in setting policies, goals and objectives. Very few administrators have had recent field experience and many of them started to climb the ladder before they got enough experience. Your input and that of your members is needed.

Let's now take a look at some of the issues that you may face over the next five or ten years.

Conflicting Organizational Beliefs and Values

In many organizations the beliefs and values are in conflict, not only between internal factions but between what the organization says it desires and what it actually values and rewards. The most poignant example is the rhetoric which says patrol officers are the back bone of the department. That is what they say they value – the back bone of the Department. But the reality is patrol officers are treated poorly (not valued). They have the worst working conditions and are heavily scrutinized. This clear conflict between beliefs and values exists in almost every agency – conflict between what is espoused and the reality.

Administrators say that they practice community policing. Rank and file officers are the ultimate key to the success of community policing, but they are still subjugated to pre-Community Police Era management models and limiting old paradigms (Angell, 1976; Birzer, 1996; Meese, 1993). Officers are expected to do "community policing" but aren't empowered to be "community police officers" (Goldstein, 1990; Meese, 1993). Most police agencies remain locked into the system of hierarchy requiring rigid procedural compliance, which prevents officers from solving many of the problems in the communities that they serve (Birzer, 1996).

What passes for leadership today is based on a ninteenth century industrial management model where workers toiled on assembly lines and managers counted how many fenders they put on a car or how many tons of coal they shoveled. But knowledge- based service work, especially something as critical as community policing, cannot necessarily be measured that way.

Peace officers need to be rewarded for innovation, not punished for trying. Field practitioners must be treated "as mature men and women . . . more trust and confidence [must be placed] in them . . . [and] give them more responsibility and a greater stake in the outcome of their efforts" which will result in "greater sense of fulfillment and job satisfaction" (Goldstein, 1990, p. 28).

Finally, in most police agencies the support functions have become more valued and more rewarded than the primary function. As a result, people are drawn to the support functions because the salaries, benefits, and working conditions are better, and lead to increased prestige for the support personnel. Unions should work with management to resolve this fundamental problem. So many other things will work themselves out when the basic problems are resolved.

Questioning Fundamental Concepts

Complex decisions are being made about fundamental concepts of police organizations including questions about personnel – the people you represent. Personnel positions will continue to be challenged and you will have to justify them. For example:

- Do detectives have to be sworn?
- Do helicopter pilots have to be sworn?
- Do chiefs have to be sworn?
- Is there a need for a chief of police or would it be better to elect the leaders such as a dean of a university?
- Should policies, procedures and programs be established by an elected board of practitioners and then implemented by administrators?
- Should errant behavior be subject to jury by peers?

These kinds of questions only scratch the surface of issues that our profession is wrestling with. Consider the following issues as well:

1. Reserve Officers: Scabs or Assets? Reserve officers are legally authorized peace officers who work without pay. Many full-time officers look down on the reservists and others believe that reservists are "scabs" filling positions that would otherwise be for regular officers. But some cash-strapped cities depend on the free labor to ensure public safety. Should unions work to eliminate reserves? Should they control the hours, shifts and assignments that reserves work? Should unions fully integrate reserves into the association?

2. Tiered Authority Status. Some believe that policing has begun to price itself out of the market; and that is why there is significant growth in civilization, private security agencies and private prisons. The Los Angeles Sheriff's Department has established two tiers of sworn deputies. Jail deputies receive modified training that allows them to be peace officers but prior to assuming a patrol assignment they must return to the Academy for additional training. Should there be multiple tiers, and if so, how many? What will the differences be in pay, benefits, and officer's rights?

3. Tiered Functional Status. Police agencies are increasingly more specialized, which creates "elite units" who receive special perks and bonuses, sometimes deserved and sometimes not. What is measured is what is made; in other words, rewards go to that which is valued. How are officers evaluated and rewarded? Do measurement systems measure what matters?

4. Private Police – Railway Police. The history of policing in the U.S. and Canada is deeply rooted in the railway police, which are in fact private police departments. When railways dominated the transportation of goods and people (1940s), there were approximately 9,000 railroad police officers, today there are approximately 2,300 in North America (Norfolk Southern). They are "authorized to enforce the laws of any jurisdiction in which the rail carrier owns property" (U.S. Congress c.). In many states including California, railroad police are authorized to enforce all of state laws (California Penal Code sections 833.e.1 and 833(2)).

5. Franchise Police. The San Francisco Patrol Special Police (SFPSP) date back to 1847 and are a separately chartered police agency with franchise patrol areas. SFPSP are supervised by the San Francisco Police Department (SFPD) and subject to the policies and procedures of the Police Commission. They wear SFPD uniforms, carry firearms and use the SFPD radio system. They have fulfilled the basic requirements of Peace Officers Standards and Training. One would be hard-pressed to distinguish this private police force from SFPD. A similar private police organization exists in Cincinnati, Ohio.

6. Security Companies. In the 1960s police officers outnumbered security guards nearly two to one. But as the 1960s came to an end the expansion of public policing subsided and private guard services "exploded" (Forst, 2000; Sklansky, 2006). By "2003, there were approximately one million security guards (including airport screeners) employed in the United States – compared to 650,000 U.S. police officers" (Parfomak, 2004).

7. Contract Police. The security giant Wakenhut and others have tried to secure contracts to police city streets but "The major barriers to police privatization include tradition and attitudes, concern about control and accountability, union opposition, [and] legal restrictions . . ." (Fixler & Poole, 1988). In 2007, one of the world's largest "international security contractor[s] [announced it] would like to hire, train and deploy 1,000 private agents to temporarily augment the Border Patrol's mission along the Mexican border" (McLemore, 2007). Should policing only be supplied by government? Is it immoral to make a profit based on police activity – how many citations you write or how many arrests you make?

8. Part Time Officers. The use of part-time employees is common-place in the United Kingdom. The Police Federation of England and Wales has published a pamphlet that explains how part-time police officers are paid (POLFEDb). Police unions in the U.S. must consider what the U.K. has already addressed. Should there be part-time employees and if so, how should they be compensated; specifically salary, annual leave, additional hours, overtime (POLFEDb) and pensions (POLFEDc).

9. Job Sharing and Per Diem. Job sharing is a program where two people fill one job, each as a permanent part-time employee. They split up the hours, pay, benefits, including holidays and vacation days based on how many hours they each work. Per Diem means "by the day." Getting paid by the day for one shift of work is very common in nursing. It allows a nurse the opportunity to earn a competitive salary but work only when and where he/she wants. It maximizes flexibility for the employee and employer. If per diem were instituted at police agencies, the department could grow and shrink based on the need for officers. Unions have to ask: what are the pros and cons to having these types of employees working for your department? How would they affect your other members? How would they affect your association? How could they affect public safety?

10. Automation. You drive through a yellow traffic signal and suddenly you see a brilliant strobe light. You're on Candid Camera. You have just been caught by an automated traffic officer. There are also automated speed traps. Are they a boon to traffic safety or simply an immoral attempt by cities to generate revenue? How are your members affected by these machines? How do they affect your association? How could they affect public safety?

Conclusion

As policing continues to transform, police unions will have more of an opportunity to be a full partner in a collaborative effort to guide and direct the department. Unions must move from a **REACTIVE** model to a **PROACTIVE** posture. We all need to elevate our thinking and to continue the quest of lifetime learning.

You are elected to lead. Administrators are appointed to leadership positions. The department is just as much yours as it is theirs. No one has a monopoly on good ideas. Your input is just as important. You have the right and obligation to your members to lead and to help guide your department. You need to kill policies that could hurt your members and the safety of the public, and support policies that help your members and the safety of the public.

Through collaborative leadership we can work together to find solutions to the problems that plague the officers, the department and the safety of the people we swore an oath to serve.

References

Aldcroft, D. H. (1970). The inter-war economy: Britain, 1919–1939. New York: Columbia University Press.

Angell, E. (1976) Organizing police for the future: An update of the democratic Model. *Criminal Justice Review, 1*: 35–51.

Bea, K., D. Teasley, and C. Doyle. *Crime Control Act of 1994 Selected Highlights of H.R.3355 As Passed.* [Washington, D.C.]: Congressional Research Service, Library of Congress, 1994.

Benson, B. L. (1998). *To serve and protect: Privatization and community in criminal justice.* New York: New York University Press.

Birzer, M. L. (1996). Police Supervision in the 21st Century. *FBI Bulletin*, p. 6.

Butterfield, R., C. Edwards, and J. Woodall. "The new public management and managerial roles: The case of the police sergeant," *British Journal of Management*, vol. 16 issue 4, December 2005, p. 329–341.

California. (2007) California Penal Code 2007 (California Penal Code), Eagan, MN: Thompson West Publishing.

Cannon, Lou. (1997) *Official negligence: How Rodney King and the riots change Los Angeles and the LAPD.* New York: Random House.

Commons, D. Among the lessons he personally taught me over the years.

Dobrin, Adam. (2006). Professional and community oriented policing: The Mayberry Model, *Journal of Criminal Justice and Popular Culture, 13* (1), p. 19-28.

Daleiden, J. R. (2006) A clumsy dance: The political economy of American police and policing. *Policing, 29*(4), 602–624. Retrieved August 24, 2007, from Criminal Justice Periodicals database. (Document ID: 1160880681).

Fixler, P. E. Jr., and R. W. Poole, Jr. Can Police Services Be Privatized? Annals of the American Academy of Political and Social Science, Vol. 498, The Private Security Industry: Issues and Trends (July 1988), p. 108–118.

Forst, Brian. The privatization and civilianization of policing. Boundary Changes in Criminal Justice Organizations, vol. 2. National Institute of Justice, U.S. Department of Justice, NCJ 182409, July 2000.

Goldstein, H. (1990). *Problem-oriented policing.* New York: McGraw-Hill.

Hartmann, F. X., ed. Debating the Evolution of American Policing: An Edited Transcript to Accompany The Evolving Strategy of Policing. Perspectives on Policing, No 5., National Institute of Justice, U.S. Department of Justice, and the Program in Criminal Justice Policy and Management, John F. Kennedy School of

Government, Harvard University, November 1988.

Internet Data Base Incorporated, a subsidiary of Amazon.com [on-line] available from: http://www.imdb.com/title/tt0062539/plotsummary

Kelling, G. L., and M. H. Moore. The Evolving Strategy of Policing. Perspectives on Policing, No 4., National Institute of Justice, U.S. Department of Justice, and the Program in Criminal Justice Policy and Management, John F. Kennedy School of Government, Harvard University, November 1988.

Levin, M. B. (1971). *Political hysteria in America: The democratic capacity for repression.* New York: Basic Books, pg. 29.

McLemore, D., Private contractor may help Border Patrol: DynCorp wants to hire temporary agents, but officials say they don't need the help. *The Dallas Morning News,* September 6, 2007.

Meese, E. III. Community Policing and the Police Officers. Perspectives on Policing, No 15., National Institute of Justice, U.S. Department of Justice, and the Program in Criminal Justice Policy and Management, John F. Kennedy School of Government, Harvard University, January 1993.

Moyer, D., & E. Alvarez. (2001). *Just the facts, Ma'am: The authorized biography of Jack Webb, The Creator of Dragnet.* Santa Ana, CA: Seven Locks.

Monkkonen, E. H. History of urban police, in *Modern Policing,* vol. 16., eds. M. Tonry and N. Morris, 547–580. Chicago: University of Chicago Press, 1992.

Norfolk Southern Police Department, History of the Railway Police, [on-line] available from http://nspolice.com/history0.htm

O'Connor, T. A brief guide to police history [on-line] available from: http://faculty.ncwc.edu/TOCONNOR/205/205lect04.htm

Parfomak, P. W. *Guarding America: Security guards and U.S. critical infrastructure protection.* CRS Report for Congress (Congressional Research Service - The Library of Congress), November 12, 2004, [on-line] available from http://www.fas.org/sgp/crs/RL32670.pdf

PAV: *History of the Police Association of Vistoria, AU* [on-line] avialable from: http://www.tpass.com.au/About_Us/History.html

POLFEDa: *History of the Police Federation of England and Wales* [on-line] available from: http://www.polfed.org/default_history.asp

POLFEDb: Police Federation of England and Wales. "*Part-Time Remuneration Advice.*" (Pamphlet) undated, circa 2006.

POLFEDc: Police Federation of England and Wales. JOB CIRCULAR NO: 34/2007, PART-TIME OFFICERS AND PENSIONABLE PAY, 11 June 2007.

Rugh, J. L. (1992). *Labor relations, World War II, Before, during and after: The autobiography of a one-eyed Jack: A close look at labor history during war and peace, 1937–1971.* San Gabriel, CA: J.L. Rugh.

Russell, F. (1975). *A city in terror: Calvin Coolidge and the 1919 Boston police strike.* Boston: Beacon Press.

Schrag, Z. Moses. Nineteen Nineteen: The Boston Police Strike in the Context of American Labor (A.B. thesis, Harvard University, 1992).

Sklansky, D. A. (2006). Private police and democracy. *The American Criminal Law Review,* Winter 2006; 43, 1; Criminal Justice Periodicals, p. 89–105.

U.S. Congress a. House. Violent Crime Control and Law Enforcement Act of 1994. 103rd Cong., 2nd sess. H.R.3355, (Enrolled as Agreed to or Passed by Both House and Senate), Public Law No: 103-322.

U.S. Congress b. Congressional Record: Daily Digest - Tuesday, September 13, 1994.

U.S. Congress c. Senate. Crime Control Act of 1990. 101st Cong., 2nd sess. S. 3266, (Enrolled a Agreed to or Passed by Both House and Senate), Public Law No: 101-647.

U.S. Department of Justice. 1997. "Police Integrity: Public Service with Honor," NCJ 1638111, National Institute of Justice, Officer of Community Oriented Policing Services.

Watts, E. J. 1981. St Louis Police recruits in the twentieth century." *Criminology 19*: p. 77–113.

Part VIII

INTERNATIONAL CASE STUDIES

Chapter 45

POLICE UNIONS AND THE REFORM AGENDA

GREGORY O' CONNOR

The first few decades of the twenty-first century are poised to take on historical significance for the police representative union movement throughout the Western world. Police forces around the world are changing radically. Governments are increasingly unwilling or unable to meet growing community demands for police services through reliance on a force comprised solely of traditional sworn generalist police constables. More targeted, specialized and often less expensive workforces are being introduced alongside police officers to meet some of the service demands.

The evolution is occurring at an increasing rate. Civilianization of support roles with little or no public contact has been followed by non-police staff moving into public safety and "reassurance policing" roles. Assuming – as current experience suggests we must – that this evolution cannot be prevented, there are two possible outcomes for police unions. One is relatively less coverage within a growing, but increasingly fragmented workforce, and correspondingly less industrial influence. The other possible outcome is increasing influence, through increased coverage of a more diverse occupational membership.

The Demand Gap

The police reform agenda is driven largely by the growing gap between public demands, and government ability or willingness to meet these demands through buying more traditional police services.

As a side note, the inability or unwillingness of governments to commit the necessary public funds to this single area of public spending is not limited to policing. Public demands for services are growing across the board: communities demand better and more expensive health care, education, infrastructure, and the costs of providing these services are increasing at rates that public revenue cannot match.

Governments are being forced to look for cheaper solutions across the whole range of public services. The supposed ability of the market to deliver efficiencies means policymakers quickly turn consideration to deregulation and private sector involvement in service delivery. Combined with falling unemployment, and tighter and more competitive labor markets, labor-intensive areas of public spending such as police services inevitably find themselves in the sights for reform.

The challenge police unions face is how to ensure that they are able to engage in, influence and protect their members' interests through the reform agenda. Success will mean the potentially disastrous outcomes are avoided, and union influence is maintained or strengthened. Failure means a future of irrelevance.

The Changing Face of Policing

The days of policing being the exclusive domain of sworn police constables are numbered. In fact, in most jurisdictions they're arguably already gone. In the United Kingdom, since the introduction of Police Community Support Officers (PCSOs) in 2002 the evolution is beyond argument. Yet, to many in the police union movement, this observation remains highly controversial and fiercely debated.

Police have a unique relationship with society, both constitutionally and socially. Unlike public servants, who serve administrative government, a police officer's responsibilities are to the law, order and public safety: protecting and serving the public and, in doing so, exercising the coercive powers of the State.

The relationship and balance that makes for effective policing is difficult to define in legislative or academic terms. For that reason policing has traditionally been viewed as a craft, where technical skills learned in academies or police colleges are supplemented by learning on the job, mentoring, and induction into the police culture by experienced officers who, in turn, learned the same way from their predecessors.

The instinct of sworn police, including those who control police unions, is to want to protect this unique craft of policing. Policing, to them, cannot just be distilled down to a skill set learnable by any average jobseeker. To an officer who has become part of the police culture and tradition, and learn the craft, "police" is what they are – not what they do.

Responding to Change

The evolution of policing through civilianization runs counter to this instinct. So to does the accompanying evolution in thinking to focus on concepts of "service." "Customer service focus," "service-oriented policing," "public service satisfaction," and even the change in organization names in some jurisdictions from "Police Force" to "Police Service" are all symptomatic of an underlying shift in thinking that does not sit comfortably with the craft-based conception of policing.

Thinking about policing as "service delivery" almost immediately decouples policing from the traditional sworn constable empowered to exercise coercive force to keep the peace. New and existing roles within or alongside police forces are able to be defined by the specific skill sets necessary to deliver a specific service to an organizationally acceptable standard. The skills identified as being required to deliver that service are not always the wide range of competencies demanded of the traditional sworn constable. So civilian staff can be recruited to fill those roles, be trained only in the minimum required set of skills, and be paid accordingly.

Police administrations usually argue that civilianization frees up real police officers to do real police work. They argue that people do not – or should not have to – go through police academies just because they have an ambition to be a dispatcher, jailer, crime scene analyst or police photographer. The argument is usually accompanied by evidence that sworn police numbers are also rising, making it difficult for opponents to argue there has been a fundamental shift away from the central importance of sworn police constables.

Nevertheless, police unions often respond to civilianization of traditional police roles by fighting with every ounce of industrial muscle they can muster. This response could destroy police unions in the long term. An historical analogy illustrates the point. In New Zealand, as elsewhere, coal was the economy's principle fuel until the middle of the last century. The coal miners' union effectively controlled fuel supply, and consequently grew to become a very powerful labor organization that was used to getting its own way.

When the government began to tentatively follow the international move away from steam and towards new diesel-electric locomotives for the railways, the union saw this as a threat to one of their most powerful levers of influence – transport – and launched strike action to fight the move.

The action backfired. The government increased its order for diesel locomotives, and the union lost its influence first over transport, and then rapidly over the rest of the economy. Now, the nation's once most powerful union no longer exists.

The miners failed to appreciate that they were not in the coal mining industry: they were in the power industry. They falsely believed that because they controlled all the coal, they held a monopoly. They tried to abuse a power they mistook for a supply monopoly, and as a result they were marginalized and became irrelevant.

Police need to learn from that experience. Police are not in the police industry. They are part of a much wider industry, which could be described in neutral terms as the "personal safety and security industry." This is the same industry prison officers, security guards, alarm monitoring companies, locksmiths, and many others also work in. It's an industry with many more service suppliers than just police. Consumer demand in this industry is driven almost solely by perceptions of insecurity, to the point where it could almost be termed the "fear of crime" industry.

The "Fear of Crime" Industry

This is not to say that police, or any of the others working in this industry, are nothing more than cynics fuelling public fear of crime for their own ends. On the contrary, crime is real, devastates the lives of innocent victims, and demands a response. But it is inescapable that the perceived value of the services offered by security providers including police is driven by the relative public fear of crime.

Policing was not always this way. Prior to the major societal changes brought about during the 1960s, 70s and 80s which saw huge increases in drug use, unemployment, crime, and the consequent sharp decline of inner-city quality-of-life, policing was a relatively benign profession.

Examination of shift occurrence books in stations or precincts prior to the 1960s shows police were not particularly busy, and what did occupy them was not often overly serious. Patrol and beat policing was the norm, with incident attendance sporadic.

At that time, it might actually have made sense to talk about the "police industry." There was relatively little public fear of crime, and consequently few private providers of services responding to public demand.

But that's almost the opposite of policing in the twenty-first century. Public demand for safety and security services has increased dramatically over the past few decades, hand-in-hand with crime and, more importantly, increasing fear of crime. The role of increasingly sensationalized crime reporting in this increasing fear of crime, even where real crime is dropping, has been well-documented.[1]

Publicly-funded traditional police services have not been sufficient to satisfy all of this demand. This market gap has encouraged growth of a significant private security sector over the past few decades. It has also placed continuous public pressure on elected local and national governments to invest ever more in public security services. And these are no longer only traditional police.

The public and private resources available to buy reassurance against crime are finite. Governments, national and local, are increasingly looking for new and creative solutions to deliver more reassurance "bang" for the taxpayer's buck. Responses include greater use of (civilian-monitored) surveillance cameras in inner city areas; city-funded security patrols; city-supported volunteer "eyes and ears" patrols; civilianization of police support roles; and, in the case of the United Kingdom, a second-tier police force of PCSOs.

It is little wonder, then, that police administrations faced with these realities across Western jurisdictions have increasingly adopted a "service" focus. This is the industrial landscape in which police are now operating. From the union perspective, the interests of members must now be represented and safeguarded in a competitive market. Police

---

1. See, for example, *Fear of Crime*, John Howard Society of Alberta (1999) and citations contained; and reported studies by the Criminological Research Institute of Lower Saxony (KFN) in 2004, the US Center for Media and Public Affairs in 1998, and numerous other studies and surveys in a range of Western jurisdictions.

do not hold a monopoly supply position; and any union that makes the mistake of believing it does hold such a position is likely to go the same way as the coal miners' union.

Industrial Strength in a Competitive Market

The foundation of union strength lies in its breadth of industrial coverage. In a competitive market, and assuming sufficient alignment of interests, logic dictates that police unions should be aiming to represent the greatest possible percentage of the workforce. Bluntly put, the more of the industry unions represent, the more influence they can command, and – provided the influence is used effectively – the better off the union and its members will be.

There's more than one way to control the largest percentage of a workforce. The traditional police union approach, as discussed above, is to fight the entry of "competitors." These tactics might meet with short-term success, but the social and economic drivers of reform are too fundamental. Unions might appear to win the big, high profile confrontations but eventually suffer death by a thousand cuts.

The other response is to actively seek to broaden industrial coverage beyond sworn police constables.

The New Zealand Police Association is unusual compared with police unions in most other jurisdictions in that it represents not only sworn officers, but also non-sworn police staff. This puts the Association in a strong position within the reform environment. A paradigm shift has already been made that allows the union to see new civilian police staff not as competitors, but as potential members – adding to, rather than diluting the union's strength.

This breadth does not unduly compromise the specific interests of sworn staff. In fact, it is critical to safeguarding those interests in the long term.

Influencing the Reform Agenda

Public policy thought and legislation are beginning to catch up with a reform agenda that has largely been driven by political pragmatism. The United Kingdom passed legislation creating second-tier police in 2002. Debate on legislative reform in Australia is well underway. In New Zealand, the 1958 Police Act is now being replaced with a new statute that envisages a "unified workforce model" empowering the commissioner to employ a broad of specialized staff with such powers as are necessary to perform a given role.

Police unions need to be engaged in and influencing the reform agenda if the most disastrous possible consequences – perhaps including entrenched two-tier policing; paring back of sworn police roles, powers and pay, redefining of sworn policing as emergency response only – are to be avoided. Effective long-term influence requires constructive and responsible engagement. Industrial belligerence, in a reform environment, is at best risky and at worst potentially fatal – as the coal miners found out.

Using Industrial Leverage For Long-Term Influence

Police unions exist, fundamentally, to negotiate pay and conditions with governments – usually indirectly, through police administrations, but the bottom line is that governments hold the treasury purse strings.

The same fear of crime phenomenon that is driving the demand gap also determines the value of security services. A union that controls a significant proportion of the service providers has industrial leverage relative to the level of fear of crime.

Governments rely on popular support for their longevity; and law and order is an electoral winner and loser. In New Zealand, monthly surveys run by research company UMR Insight track the "most important public issues." Law and order is rarely outside the top three, and is often the uppermost concern of the 700 or so citizens polled despite New Zealand having comparatively low levels of serious crime by most objective measures.

Law and order is almost unique as a public issue, in that emotional charge and moral judgment set the agenda. Public debate on criminal justice issues is usually conducted in very stark, simplistic terms of right or wrong, wrapped up in emotions of anger and outrage.

Emotion is the most powerful influence on human decision-making, whether the decision is on what brand of running shoes to buy, or what government to elect. Emotional issues like law and order have the power to shift voters in big numbers.

Public policy considerations – costs, benefits, trade-offs – very rarely enter into the public consciousness when it comes to law and order. News media plays a huge part in this. Irrationality in the law and order debate is not only legitimized by media reportage, it is encouraged and celebrated.

The problem for governments is that people expect "the system" to reflect their own emotional charge and moral judgment. "The system" is seen to have failed when it doesn't, and public anger is directed at those they see as responsible: ultimately, the government.

The temptation for many police unions in this environment is to wind the law and order debate up, in the expectation that the government will have to invest more in police to allay public fears. Such tactics might win battles, but they will lose the war.

A union that overplays the tactic of fuelling public fear forfeits its claim to be involved in and taken seriously in the police reform policy debate. It becomes too easy for policymakers to marginalize unions as predictable, narrowly self-interested and lacking in any ability to make any worthwhile contribution to debate.

The objective of the New Zealand Police Association in its media and public engagement is to be the credible, balanced voice on law and order issues. The Association represents its members views and interests on policing, but also acts as a credible and informed commentator on broader law and order issues. The Association believes that public, media, and political credibility is in its members' long-term interests.

There is an obvious tension in adopting the long-term view. Union leaders, like governments, depend on popular support for longevity in their positions. For most members, a union is only as good as its last pay round and some members might believe better outcomes could be won in any given year by adopting more combative tactics.

Yet the long-term game must be played, if police reform is to avoid its worst excesses. Becoming a credible, constructive contributor to the debate achieves this end in two ways. First, media and the public respond to law and order issues by immediately asking: "What do police think?" Associations that establish a track record of well-researched, well-considered, coherent and credible commentary stand in stark contrast to police administrations that are increasingly running scared from any media profile at all in the highly-politicized law and order debate.

Policymakers have no pragmatic option but to allow such credible associations inside the policymaking tent. Failure to do so risks unwelcome and unnecessary policy confrontation through the media, an outcome that serves nobody's long-term interests.

Second, the more an association builds a reputation of credibility and constructive engagement, the more politicians are compelled to court the association's support. The value of the voice within the debate increases, and so the damage that would be done to politicians through outright confrontation increases. In contrast, unions that "cry wolf" regularly toughen political hides, eventually exhaust public sympathy, and diminish their political leverage.

Reform Outcomes

Police unions, then, are facing a global trend of policing reform. This trend is being driven by underlying social and economic factors, which are resulting in a public demand for safety and security services that governments cannot or will not meet through traditional sworn police services alone.

If this trend cannot be resisted in the long term, then unions need to make a strategic decision as to how they best maintain their influence and safeguard the interests of their members (including sworn police officers) across the long term.

Limiting industrial representation to sworn police officers, and fighting to protect the position of these officers as the monopoly providers of policing services, is doomed to fail. "Non-police" are encroaching more and more on traditional roles of public safety and security every day, through civilianization, private security in public spaces, and second-tier policing.

Such a strategy relies on industrial belligerence, threats and political confrontation. Some battles may be won. But the outcome of such a strategy must eventually be relatively less coverage within a growing but increasingly fragmented workforce. This means correspondingly less industrial influence and less ability to represent and protect the interests of members.

The other strategic approach is to build credibility and reputation, and apply that to engaging in and influencing the reform agenda. By doing so, the interests of sworn members can be safeguarded, and the worst potential outcomes of reform have a better chance of being avoided. At the same time, actively seeking to broaden coverage to incorporate civilian staff means increasing influence, through increased workforce coverage even though the membership is more diverse.

Increasing the value of the union's voice as well as its coverage, despite reform, puts the union in the best possible position to protect its members' interests in the future – whether by engagement, or, in a worst-case scenario, by confrontation.

Chapter 46

EXCEPTION TO THE RULE: THE SPREAD OF THE POLICE UNION MOVEMENT ACROSS THE WORLD

Monique Marks and Jenny Fleming

It is widely recognized that the trade union movement is in decline internationally. Membership levels are declining and questions are being raised about the capacity for the trade union movement to use its once considerable influence to assist in shaping economic and social policy. A number of reasons have been offered for this decline. They include anti-union legislation and policy; a deregulated labor market; the decline of the manufacturing sector in many countries where the union movement was strongest; and the casualization of the workforce generally and the trade union movement itself that in many cases has failed to address these new circumstances either through their business plans or general recruitment strategies. Despite these circumstances, police unions (where they exist) have maintained very high membership rates and there are clear indications that the police trade union movement is likely to expand.

In this chapter, we talk about the growth and the increasing cohesiveness of the global police union movement. We begin by making some observations about why the police union movement remains strong in a world where trade unions are struggling to survive. We then turn to the emergence of an international police union network constituted mainly by police union bodies from western democratic countries. Lastly, we look at what we believe are important challenges confronting the police union movement, challenges that must be met if they are to maintain their strength and extend their influence and networks.

Why is the Police Union Movement Different From Other Unions?

In many parts of the world police are actively campaigning for their rights as citizens and as workers. In places like the United States and Canada, police unions have produced Bills of Rights for police officers. In countries that are in transition or are defined as less developed, such as Argentina, police view themselves as both workers and as professionals. They know that they have little control over their work process and that they sell their labor power to the state for what in these countries is often a very poor wage.

Police officers in the less developed parts of the world or in countries that have recently democratized are now demanding labor rights. This is particularly evident in parts of Southern Africa, but also in Eastern European countries. In these parts of the world, police unionism and collective bargaining are now on the agenda of police organizations for the first time. Where possible, these developments have been encouraged and supported by "strong" police unions. These unions have played an active role in assisting "weaker" police employee representative organizations to formalize collective labor institutions and processes.

Public police have traditionally been drawn from working class backgrounds, many from families with strong traditions of unions in the mine and railway industries. This has changed over time for many reasons. In the "developed" world, many of those traditional and large scale industries have gone into decline or all but disappeared and with these changes has gone the workers' identity as a part of a readily identifiable "industry grouping." This has resulted in the loss of the "common bond" and has constrained unions' ability to build and organize from that fertile pool. Additionally, police recruits in established democracies are now expected to pursue tertiary education in some form, while in developing countries this is not the case.

However, in both cases the active construction by police unions of the public police as a distinct and separate group of workers has led or maintained this greater propensity for the police to organize collectively. In established democracies such as Canada and the United

States of America, police now talk about their rights to be treated as equal citizens with access to the same labor rights as other employees. It is only very recently, for example, that the Royal Canadian Mounted Police have been awarded the right to collective bargaining. In developing countries working class identities add an additional impetus to the call for labor rights. What then is different about police employees and why do their unions manage to sustain their membership and their influence?

Police employees are unique because they remain a captured audience for the union movement. Their work remains highly labor intensive and despite the incursion of neo-liberal policy frameworks and the rising momentum of private security organizations, there is ongoing pressure from the public and from the police to resist the privatization of policing. While there is a rapid growth of private security across the world (particularly in places like South Africa, Australia and the United States), there has also been a steady increase in the number of police that are employed.

Second, police unions have become a prominent feature of the modern police agency. They are important "insider" groups within the police and are influential in determining a range of organizational policies and planning processes. They also have a strong voice (often a conservative one) in the determination of criminal justice policy and administration. Police unions are remarkably successful in achieving workplace benefits for their members and play a significant role in protecting the legal interests of their members. Police officers know that to secure and increase these benefits, police union membership and support is important. Therefore, it is not surprising that police unions in Australia, New Zealand, United Kingdom and even South Africa enjoy membership levels of almost 100 percent.

A third reason for the continuing relevance of police unionism, particularly in countries where police have not traditionally been organized, is because of the considerable influence of the formal and informal police union network. These networks have already, and will most likely continue to, provide emerging police unions with technical support, advice, and in some cases financial resources. The member organizations of these networks have their own individual histories, organizational structures, and ways of operating. The diversity of experience and knowledge that leaders of these unions bring together and to new groupings is a powerful resource for police unions across the world to draw upon in developing more effective labor-management processes and institutions in their own jurisdictions.

Police Union Networks: The Case of the ICPRA

In recent years, police unions from across the world have come together, forming a strong international network with the real potential – from the bottom up – to influence how police officers experience their working lives and to shape what policing as an enterprise might look like in the future. We will focus here on what we see as the most significant of these police union networks, the International Council of Police Representative Associations (ICPRA).

This network was established by the Canadian Police Association in 1996. Initially the network called itself the International Law Enforcement Council (ILEC). ILEC's network comprised of police unions from Western Europe, Australasia and North America. Members would meet biannually to discuss and debate a range of topical issues. The police union movement is very diverse and certainly there are significant differences between the various organizations. However, despite the differences, the unions/associations in each country confront very similar issues. These issues include concerns about recruitment and/or retention, the growing influence of second tier policing, the practice of offshore police deployment, and the future of policing generally and what this might mean for the police workplace of the future. Those in attendance were usually executive members of national trade police unions, a real coming together of the most seasoned and well-resourced police unionists in the world.

In 2004, the network established a general secretariat. Two years later, network members renamed the organization to the International Council of Police Representative Associations (ICPRA). ICPRA members include some of the most established and powerful police unions in the world including the Police Federation of Australia, the New Zealand Police Association, the Police Federation of England and Wales, the National Association of Police Organizations, Fraternal Order of Police, Scottish Police Federation, Danish Police Union, British Transport Police Federation, Police Federation of Northern Ireland, Garda Representative Association and the Canadian Police Association.

ICPRA's overarching goal is for police unions from across the world to share information, to support fledging police unions in all parts of the world, and to discuss issues of mutual concern to police unions from a range of countries. By doing this, the ICPRA hopes to provide the international police union movement with a collective voice for influencing policing futures. The ICPRA's assistance vis-à-vis Swaziland is a case in point.

The ICPRA has offered advice and support to the nascent police union in Swaziland. The President of ICPRA sent a letter to the Minister of police in Swaziland and to the Swaziland Police Chief explaining the benefits to police organizations and to police members that derive from awarding police officers basic labor rights. The letter received a significant amount of public attention and news of the letter was reported in the national newspaper, the *Swazi Times*. Members of ICPRA, namely, the Scottish Police Federation, the New Zealand Police Association, and the Police Federation of Australia have provided financial aid to the new union. This financial aid has been used to furnish new offices and to help pay for their legal defense. The Dutch Police Union, which is not a member of the ICPRA, is assisting the Swaziland Police Union by contributing to their office rental payments and through technical support.

The ICPRA and EUROCOP (the industry federation for the police in Europe), through their member organizations, now provide emerging police unions with technical support, advice, and even financial resources. The member organizations with their own individual histories, organizational structures and ways of operating, provide emergent unions with a range of different models for organizing and bargaining. Both organizations are committed to advancing police officers' labor rights. At the time of this case study, EUROCOP is focusing its efforts to improve the collective and individual rights of Portuguese police.

Looking Beyond the Glory

What we have presented is the "bright side" of police unionism globally. But there are also "dark sides" which include both real obstacles that exist for police achieving basic labor rights as well as some real weaknesses within the police union movement at present. We will look briefly at the existing obstacles and then turn our focus to the problems and future challenges.

1. Obstacles to police unionism and police labor rights attainment. In many developing countries and new democracies, police unionism remains threatening in the eyes of police authorities. Police managers and employers worry that if police have the right to unionize and to collectively bargain, they could choose to engage in strike action. Yet the reality is that police unions across the world have been reluctant to strike (although many of these countries had a wave of strikes in the early part of the twentieth century and are now prohibited from doing so by legislation), and most police unions have not argued for the right to withdraw their labor. Police unionists from the United States, Australia, and the United Kingdom argue that the right to withdraw police labor will have negative consequences because the communities that the police serve are most harmed by strike activity; and those outside the law are the ones who are likely to benefit from such action.

In the absence of the right to strike, police unions across the world have called for the institutionalization of dispute resolution and arbitration processes. In most countries legislation constrains the boundaries of police industrial action. Grievance procedures, tribunals and conciliation and arbitration avenues are all designed to prevent "aggressive industrial bargainers." Police unions have been actively involved in shaping and promoting these alternative institutions and processes with positive results in terms of labor peace and social dialogue. They have also developed and implemented a range of industrial strategies that circumvent the strike action and antagonistic labor/management interactions. We could also add that in democratic countries, police unions invariably have the support of the community, which frequently gives them a lot more scope in bargaining power and industrial activity.

Police managers in countries such as some of the eastern European countries, some jurisdictions in the United States, and most of Africa are cautious of extending collective bargaining rights to their members because they believe, (as most police managers do) that rank-and-file engagement in collective bargaining and co-determining processes will undermine management prerogative. The unions lay emphasis on workplace issues – pay and service conditions – and also training, diversity management, disciplinary systems, and professionalism issues which impact directly on how effectively police can do the job that is expected of them. The resource and disciplinary ramifications of these agendas can be confronting to managers.

Management and employer anxieties mean that police in places like Swaziland have a long and difficult road ahead of them. They will have to "prove" that the benefits of extending labor rights to the police outweigh the perceived costs. The interventions from police unionists in places where police labor rights are firmly entrenched will probably be very helpful to fledging police unions. The recent court decision to extend collective bargaining rights to the Royal Canadian Mounted Police has crystallized the arguments for police labor rights and may well prove to be an important precedent.

2. Deficits within the police union movement. The fact that the police union movement is strong in many western democracies does not mean that police unionists from this part of the world can rest on their laurels. The greatest weakness of the police unions is that they have tended to become narrowly focused on workplace improvement and status enhancement issues. This has meant that some unions have failed to address broader changes that are taking place in the policing landscape and pursuing conventional "tried and tested" approaches to issues that may require new ways of thinking. For example, the unions have not reconsidered their diehard calls for increased numbers and higher pay in the light of new governance arrangements and fiscal constraints. Police union responses are, for this reason, sometimes viewed as predictable, conservative, reactive, and unimaginative.

Police unions also have a tendency, like other trade unions, to be highly bureaucratized. Rank-and-file union members within these oligarchic organizations are controlled by a tiny minority of police union leaders. The result is that the democratic aspirations of trade union structures are potentially problematic. While police unions have high membership rates, police union leaders (particularly those who do not want to return to active police service) have become "entrenched" within these organizations, some being reelected for more than three terms of office. This situation has meant that they effectively do what they think their membership would want them to do to ensure that they remain in office. This type of thinking has often been at the expense of actively engaging their membership in new ways of thinking about both old and new problems.

So, for example, perhaps arguing for more public police officers is not the best way to solve localized crime police problems. Perhaps encouraging non-police groupings, like community constables or other civil society groupings, to find localized solutions and engage in (non-core) policing activities may be more effective than getting more uniformed officers on the streets. Perhaps police unions should spend more of their energies in participating in networks involving both state and non-state actors whose purpose is to make communities safer. Expanding the unions' knowledge base in the context of policing and ways of "doing business" would be a positive step forward for the police union movement.

Many police organizations in the U.S., U.K. and increasingly in Australia are beginning to draw on research in their own management deliberations, and are beginning to work with universities and private consultants to explore new ways of policing and focusing on evidence-based research that might inform their policy and practice. Given this, it would be pertinent for police unions to contemplate focused research agendas of their own; in the first instance, perhaps to explore internally just exactly what the membership feels about some of the "big issues" but perhaps more importantly to engage more fully in contemporary debates about where policing is going.

Police unions and associations alike have carved their place at the decision-making table in most western democracies. They are in a position to contribute constructively to these debates – doing their own research (which some of them are actually doing) will enhance that position. We believe that if unions don't do this in the long term, they will limit their capacity to engage in, and shape the ever-changing field of policing. As a result, the voices of police employees in confronting the professional challenges ahead will be less distinctive than would be the case if the police unions expanded their organizational schemes, embraced the value of research, and incorporated its findings into its debates, and if necessary its confrontations, with management and governments.

Networks like ICPRA and EUROCOP have demonstrated a real commitment to assisting fellow police officers in countries that lack a liberalized police labor relations framework to secure labor rights and build representative employee organizations. But their efforts are limited by the looseness of their own network arrangements. The ICPRA, for example, does not have a mechanism for coordinating and harnessing the resources of their member organizations. They do not have a "research" fund or agenda. There is no pooling of funds that would allow one of the office bearers to travel to Swaziland to directly assist the new union with capacity building or with developing a legal defense case. The network is heavily reliant on the goodwill and resource capacity of its individual member organizations in reaching out to police officers who are trying to organize collectively in countries that are outside the traditional fold of those who founded these networks. It might be time for these police union networks to consider formalizing and of bringing "weaker actors" on-board.

Conclusion

The police union movement is unique within the global trade union movement. Police unions retain high membership levels, and the police union network is growing in strength despite a general decline in trade unionism internationally in most other sectors. Regional and international networks of police unions are growing in strength and influence. Even in countries characterized by extremely authoritarian governments, police officers are now using the language of rights and citizenship and are determined to have their collective voices heard. While in Southern Africa at present the only country that awards police the right to unionize and to bargain collectively is South Africa, there are voices elsewhere challenging current police regulations and labor legislation. These efforts are likely to be supported and even advanced by organizations like Police and Prisons Civil Rights Union in South Africa and international networks like the ICPRA.

Resistance to the extension of labor rights to the police is likely to continue. But what needs to be borne in mind is that, despite government apprehensions and senior police management attitudes towards police unions, where they do exist and are strong, the sky has not fallen and chaos has not ensued. If international police union experience is anything to go by, management and employer fears about the strike imperative of police unions and the erosion of managerial prerogative seems unwarranted.

Through collective representation and access to collective bargaining, police unions have added considerably to the fabric of police organizations. Through collective representation, police officers have been able to engage significantly in co-determination processes and participate in decision-making forums; often contributing significantly to improvements within the organization and the bolstering of rank-and-file morale.

The presence of police unions may in fact facilitate smoother processes and decision-making within police organizations, given shared professionalism agendas and a climate of social dialogue. Police are more likely to be receptive to management initiatives if they have reason to believe that the department will not treat them in an arbitrary fashion. Police managers and employers across the globe would be well-advised to review their oppositional stance and to consider them as mediums for positive change and as partners in building the more responsive and effective policing agencies.

However, arguably the ability of the police unions to retain their strength and influence is dependent on their pushing the boundaries of their narrow industrial focus. What is required is a shift away from reactive unionism to a proactive unionism that has as its starting point a concern with linking up improved police working conditions to public service delivery and community safety. Police union networks need to build their capacity to directly assist police officers with attaining labor rights in countries that are democratizing – a strong research base will facilitate this. This is where the police union industry is most likely to grow in years to come. It is also in those parts of the world discussed in this chapter that debates (and interventions) about police rights and improved policing are most urgent. Police unionists have a wealth of knowledge about the inner workings of police organizations, the possibilities of change, and the importance of networking arrangements which needs to be shared with policing scholars and police managers.

Further Reading

Marks, M., and Fleming, J. (2007). Police as workers: Police labour rights in Southern Africa and beyond. *SA Crime Quarterly*, No. 19, March, 13–18.

Burgess, M., Fleming, J., and Marks, M. (2006). Thinking critically about police unions in Australia: Internal democracy and external responsiveness. *Police Practice and Research: an International Journal*, Vol. 7 (5) December, 391–409.

Marks, M., and Fleming, J. (2006). The right to unionise, the right to bargain and the right to democratic policing. *The Annals of the American Academy of Political and Social Science, Special Issue*, Vol. 605 (1) May, 178–199.

Marks, M., and Fleming, J. (2006). The untold story: The regulation of police labour rights and the quest for police democratisation. *Police Practice and Research: An International Journal*, Vol. 7 (4) September, 309–322.

Fleming, J. Marks, M., and Wood, J. (2006). Standing on the inside looking out: The significance of police unions in networks of police governance. *Australian and New Zealand Journal of Criminology*, April, 71–89.

Fleming, J., and Marks, M. (2004). Reformers or resisters? The state of police unionism in Australia. *Employment Relations Record*, Vol 4 (1).

Chapter 47

PROFESSIONAL REGISTRATION FOR AUSTRALIA'S POLICE

MARK BURGESS

Introduction

For nearly two decades police associations and unions across Australia, through the Police Federation of Australia and New Zealand and more lately its successor the Police Federation of Australia (PFA), have supported the following strategy for the professional development of policing:

1. The development of National Common Core Competencies;
2. The development of a National Core Training Curriculum based on national competencies;
3. The alignment of all police training courses and qualifications, allowing for police inter-jurisdictional recognition;
4. The recognition by education institutions of common police qualifications allowing for accreditation and transfer across Australasia;
5. The regulation and validation of police training by the police industry itself through the Australasian Police Professional Standards Council (APPSC);
6. An Australian lateral and cross-jurisdiction entry system;
7. A Professional Police Registration Board;
8. A Professional Police "Certificate to Practice."

The PFA has argued that police enlistment standards should be based on Australasian standards, determined from time to time by the

APPSC, which is recognised by the PFA and the New Zealand Police Association (NZPA) as both are members.

A primary goal of the PFA is the pursuit of enhanced police professionalism through education and training in a strategy embracing professional practice standards for basic training, complemented by ongoing professional development through the higher education (university) sector.

As both the PFA and NZPA support inter-jurisdictional mobility within the Australasian Police Industry involving police who are recruited from police forces throughout Australia and New Zealand, we believe that such a process will assist mobility.

Why a Police Registration Scheme?

In support of our argument for police professional registration, the PFA believes that police are a central element of a democratic society. Indeed, a democratic society requires a police force that is subject to the rule of law, can intervene in the life of citizens only under limited and carefully controlled circumstances, and is publicly accountable.

Peel's Principles of Policing tabled in a Bill in the British Parliament in 1829 expressed the idea that police are not merely tools of government but rather are the people's police, an idea that underpins the theory of constabulary independence. This is reaffirmed when it is readily accepted that police in democratic societies should not be subject to interference and direction by the executive government.

Uniquely, police are empowered to legally use force, to engage in summary punishment, to use covert surveillance, to stop, search and arrest citizens, and to deprive citizens of their liberty in accordance with the law and judicial processes.

Given the potential for abuse of such powers, police face numerous external and internal controls. Externally, controls range from Court scrutiny of police behavior and processes, to parliamentary law-making and ongoing oversight, executive government control and policy-setting, and various police oversight bodies, commissions of inquiry, auditors and ombudsmen. Internally, police systems and integrity controls also operate, together with selection, training, defined procedures, policy guidelines, and supervision arrangements.

The office of constable confers a particular and unique discretion on the police officer in the use of his or her powers. This discretion is what distinguishes police from other public employees and makes their exercise of authority unique. The basis for the principle of individual discretion lies with Enever v R (1906) 3 CLR 969, which established:

> . . . that a constable, whether his powers were established at common law or by statute, holds the office of constable and his powers are exercised personally and not as a matter of delegation. He bears an original authority and responsibility.

Discretion is a central and important feature of every decision made by a police officer to charge a person. Police must consider issues such as fairness, justice, accountability, consistency and wider community interests and expectations when deciding whether or not to prefer a charge. By virtue of their office all police officers are expected to be accountable for such decisions. The decisions should not display arbitrary and inexplicable differences in the way that different people are treated. Upon making a decision the officer must then ensure both consistency and compliance with statutes and prosecutorial policies.

Entities such as Commissions of Inquiry, Crime Commissions, Ombudsmen, Coroners, Directors of Public Prosecutions, and Police Internal Affairs Units are mandated to test the discretion of an officer when complaints regarding the officer's conduct are raised.

For all of the above reasons, the exercise by police of their powers is a unique expression of the authority of the State and is appropriately conferred on an officer who is professional, highly trained, accountable, and subject to the oath of office and code of conduct that governs the use of the discretion given by the office of constable. The unique authority afforded police officers is sound reason for governments in the western world limiting police powers to sworn police officers.

However, in recent times in Australia the PFA has had to argue repeatedly against legislation proposing the extension of police-type powers to other government agencies and their personnel. It is vital that governments and parliaments resist any shortcuts that involve extending police powers to other officials, and avoid covering any deficiency in police numerical strength by giving others police powers.

This issue was considered recently at a hearing of the Australian Senate Legal and Constitutional Affairs Committee's Inquiry into the Crimes Legislation Amendment (National Investigation Powers and Witness Protection) Bill 2006. In January 2007 the Secretary General of the Law Council of Australia, in response to questions from the Committee about the PFA's submission to the Inquiry in respect to granting search warrant powers to non-sworn police personnel of the Australian Crime Commission (ACC), said:

> Our submission actually objects to granting persons powers that are ordinarily reserved to police officers. We do so in the context of a proposal to extend the grant of powers to civilian members of the ACC. . . . The justification provided seems to be that there is turnover in the police staff working for the ACC, which is apparently difficult to manage, so this is the proposed solution. We do not think that is a sufficiently good enough argument to warrant the arrangement.

Restricting such powers to sworn police officers in the professional police service is ultimately for the protection of the public. Ensuring national standards in policing, and ensuring that all sworn officers meet those national standards, gives governments and the community certainty that the policing service across Australia is consistent and acts in the community's best interest. Through a system of national police professional registration, the public can be assured that every police officer who exercises police powers has met the national standard.

A National Registration Scheme versus State Based Schemes

Australia is a federation of the Commonwealth and six states – Queensland, New South Wales, Victoria, Tasmania, South Australia, and Western Australia and two territories, Australian Capital Territory (ACT) and the Northern Territory. Each state and territory has its own independent police force administered by its government. The Australian Federal Police (AFP) is Australia's federal law enforcement agency. Policing the nation's capital, the ACT, is done by an arm of the AFP that has been contracted to provide a community policing service to the ACT government. The eight police forces range in size from New South Wales with over 15,000 officers, to the Northern Territory with just over 1,000, a total of approximately 50,000 officers. Whether Australia should have eight state-based registration arrangements, or a single national police registration scheme is a live issue.

The Health Workforce Example

At its April, 2007 meeting, the Council of Australian Governments (COAG) announced that it had agreed on arrangements for a new national system for the registration of health professionals and the accreditation of their training and education programs for implementation by July, 2008. The new scheme, COAG concluded, would deliver many benefits to the Australian community including health consumers. National standards in each profession would mean stronger safety guarantees for the community. Patients would know that wherever the health professional is from, they are registered against the same, high-quality national professional standards.

COAG agreed that the new scheme should support workforce responsiveness, flexibility, sustainability and innovation. National registration, they said, would also mean that doctors, nurses and other health professionals would be able to practise across State and Territory borders without having to re-register. This, it was suggested, would improve workforce mobility, allowing health practitioners to move easily to a new State, to serve elsewhere in times of emergency, or to provide locum services at various locations.

The new system will initially cover nine health professions: medical practitioners, nurses and midwives, pharmacists, physiotherapists, psychologists, osteopaths, chiropractors, optometrists and dentists (including dental hygienists, dental prosthetists and dental therapists).

Key features of the new arrangements include a continuing role for Health Ministers, a single, consolidated scheme, and a new national professional board for each of the nine professions. Each profession will develop standards for its profession for approval by Health Ministers. Individual registration and accreditation decisions will remain the responsibility of the professions.

Community representatives will play a key role in the new scheme and Health Ministers will be assisted by an independent Advisory Council that will provide transparent policy advice to Ministers. COAG has also agreed to further consider the membership of the Advisory Council.

The package of COAG health professional registration reform measures is largely supported by the Australian Medical Association (AMA) (Australia's peak doctors' Association) in their pre-election publication *Key Health Issues for the 2007 Federal Election* released on

September 6, 2007 where they raise the issue of National Registration and Accreditation. They point to the long-term problems associated with attempts to harmonize standards across States and Territories to allow portability of registration across borders with a minimum of red tape.

The AMA indicates that the last attempt to achieve portability of medical registration in 2003/04 failed because not all the States and Territories could agree on harmonising legislation. In relation to the COAG outcomes, the AMA has concerns about the Government having too much control over the profession, therefore they want to ensure that education and training is accredited by a medical council that is independent of Government.

The medical and broader health sector experience should be a lesson for us. Policing, like nursing for example, is a practice-based activity and would be amenable to the approach to registration used for the nursing profession.

The Case for National Police Registration

The PFA believes that we will not get consensus to form eight police registration boards based on jurisdictional boundaries, with harmonized standards and legislation. We argue that the only way effective police registration will be achieved for the benefit of all police officers and their communities is through the establishment of a National Board.

Policing is ideally placed to make the move directly to a national scheme, without having to first establish state and territory registration schemes. The National Police Registration Board we propose would have input from governments, but be independent of government. Applying Peel's Principles as the cornerstone of the profession, such a board must have community representation through available community leaders.

Many would question why we would seek registration when we only have eight (8) potential employers of police in Australia even though we have approximately 50,000 police.

While there might be an argument for such a scheme in the United States where there are in excess of 18,000 police forces, the argument goes that in Australia the bureaucracy and cost involved in registration would outweigh any advantages gained.

Historically in Australia professional registration in many professions has been state-based. With the exception of Victoria Police, which has commenced negotiating a professional registration scheme for that state through an industrial instrument, no other state has made formal moves towards registration of police.

The PFA believes that to wait for all jurisdictions to establish registration schemes in their own time, and then try to make them compatible and national, could take many years, if ever, to be achieved. However, moving directly to a national police registration scheme would mean that the wider community is assured that all sworn officers across Australia met and maintained the set minimum standards.

The PFA believes that police are one of the fundamental pillars of a free and safe democracy. Policing is a physically and morally dangerous occupation in which practitioners deal constantly with complex, and often ambiguous problems. Policing requires high levels of judgment, discretion, dispute resolution, problem solving, and physical and moral courage. Police exercise *original*, not delegated, authority and have considerable autonomous discretion. In other words, policing is an intellectually challenging and quintessentially professional task, yet it is not accorded the public recognition and status of a profession.

Police officer mobility between state and territory police forces, the Australian Federal Police and the Australian Crime Commission, is now such that a national police registration scheme is essential.

In the PFA's view a national registration scheme should be designed to:

1. improve the status of the police profession;
2. facilitate inter-jurisdictional mobility;
3. protect the police professional domain; and
4. provide and maintain, on the community's behalf, proper standards of policing practice and professional membership.

Key Functions of a National Police Registration Scheme

In June 2007 the PFA publicly released a document, *Law and Order in Australia: Policies for the Future*. In that document, formally presented to all federal political parties in the lead up to the 2007 Australian Federal Election, the PFA called on all parties to advance policing as a profession in Australia by committing to the development of a National Police Registration Scheme.

The key functions of that Registration Scheme, we argued, would be to:

1. develop education and training standards and accredit educational and training institutions;
2. maintain a register of those institutions and their programs that meet the standard;
3. establish a National Code of Police Ethics;
4. establish a National Police Code of Conduct;
5. be responsible for coordinating the police body of knowledge;
6. be responsible for defining the core business of policing; and
7. maintain a register of all Australian Police Officers who meet the requisite standards.

To achieve such an outcome will require the goodwill of all stakeholders. This issue is too important an issue for Australia's police officers and their communities to be left to politicians and police commissioners to determine. While police commissioners are part of the profession and are themselves constables of police, they are principally police employers. They are members of the profession, not its owners as is the case in any other profession. There is also established precedent that police commissioners are subordinate to elected governments and are directly accountable to Ministers.

Therefore, rather than leaving this matter to police commissioners, it is vital that the PFA, as the body elected to represent Australia's 50,000 police officers, takes command of this important issue and devises a scheme, in consultation with other stakeholders, that suits the needs of its members.

APPENDICES

Appendix 1

POLICE UNION POWER RATING

On a scholastic scale of 90-100 (A), 80-90 (B), 70-80 (C), and 60-70 (D); and below 60 (F), rate the status of your association on the following subjects:

1. **Leadership.** Do you believe that your union has leadership that is committed to the goals of the union; is honest, credible, and hard-working; has vision; and has the support of a majority of the membership?
2. **Membership.** Does your membership understand the goals of the union, and does at least 20% participate from time-to-time in the activities of the union?
3. **Money.** Does your union have sufficient financial resources to meet its current monthly obligations and reserves to deal with any major crises or confrontations (e.g.; lawsuit against your employer, public campaign over a contract dispute)?
4. **Political action program.** Does your union have a continuing political action program which includes a PAC, endorsement of candidates, and involvement of leaders and members in political campaigns?
5. **Publication.** Does your union have a regularly-produced publication that is distributed to members and political/community players; and effectively describes the goals and activities of the union?
6. **Image-building.** Does the union make a conscious effort to present its "non-union" side to the public through supporting community-based charities and other worthwhile programs?
7. **Coalition-building.** Does the union make a consistent effort to work with other community organizations and/or leaders on projects that benefit the union, the other groups (and/or leaders), or both organizations?
8. **Strategic planning.** Does the union have a consistent, long-term strategic plan that analyzes the community you work in, sets priorities, evaluates finances and resources, and reviews organizational structures?

HOW TO SCORE: Add up all eight numeric grades and divide by 8.

90-100 average: Your union should have one of the best contracts in the country. If you don't, get a better negotiator!

80-89 average: Your union is doing a lot of things right. Pay attention to a few more details of the "Ways to Build Power" and your future looks bright (and your membership will likely reelect you to another term, making your spouse ever so happy!)

70-79 average: Your union is doing just okay, but is teetering on the brink of disaster. The next contract negotiations will involve a tough fight with limited options, a poor to mediocre wage and benefit package, and a frustrated membership. A long weekend Board of Directors retreat to reinvent the union is definitely in order – leave the golf clubs at home!

60-69 average: The Big Bad Wolf is at the union's doorstep, ready to huff and puff, and blow your house down. Members aren't showing up at meetings – in fact, the leaders aren't even showing up at meetings. The only members with any enthusiasm left want to start a new union or affiliate with another group. Bring in a credible police labor relations expert who can give you some fresh, new ideas. Listen carefully and proceed quickly to Rebuild Mode.

Below 60: We don't want to offend anyone, but the words "brain-dead," "DOA," "turn-out-the-lights-the-party's-over," and "stick a fork in it" come immediately to mind. If this rating fits, throw one hell of a farewell party, kiss the union goodbye, and start all over again.

Appendix 2

POLICE UNION STRATEGIC PLANNING TEMPLATE

What is Strategic Planning?

A systematic method for setting policy in the union by:

• Analyzing key aspects of the world in which the union operates;
• Gaining clarity on the union's objectives;
• Assessing the money and other resources that the organization has to achieve its objectives; and
• Reviewing how well the union's existing methods of operations do in achieving objectives.

What Are the Major Components of Strategic Planning?

• Analyze the environment
• Set union priorities.
• Assess present union resource allocation.
• Evaluate to ability of present union organizational structures to achieve new priorities.

Analyzing the Environment

• Has the union analyzed the environment and determined "who's who" as an individual and organizational power broker in the community?
• Does the union have lists and contact information for these individuals and organizations?
• Does the union know "how to get things done" in your community?
• Does the union command respect as a "force to be reckoned with" in the community, or is it merely a "force to be placated" during budget deliberations?
• What is your message today? What will it be during the next negotiations?
• Can the union effectively communicate its message to the politicians and the power brokers in the community and have them act on your concerns?
• Can the union "make or break" a politician?

323

- How many elected officials will support the union if it means denying the money to another special interest?
- Has the union made coalitions with other powerful individuals and organizations who can influence the actions and decisions of the power brokers?
- Has the union offered to help other powerful individuals and organizations who have specific issues of concern to them?
- What is the union's image in the community? How can this image be improved?

Setting Priorities

- List the top five priorities that the union has set for the next three to five years
- If none have been set, what should be the top five priorities?
- Does the Board of clearly understand these priorities, and are the Board members committed to carrying out these priorities?
- Do the members clearly understand these priorities, and are the members committed to carrying out these priorities?
- Do any of these priorities "break new ground" in the way the union has been doing business over the past few years?
- Does the union reevaluate its priorities from time-to-time?

Assessing Finances and Resources

- What is the yearly income versus expenses of the union?
- What percentage of that income are dues versus other forms of income?
- What are the reserves of the union?
- What are our affiliations and how to we get more value from them?
- Has the union evaluated the membership to determine which civic or social organizations they belong to?
- Has the union obtained signed pledge cards from members committing a certain amount of money and or time in the case of a confrontation?
- Has the union examined its spending habits to determine whether its spending matches its stated priorities (i.e.; costs for board travel and entertainment versus expenditures for membership services?)

Evaluating Organizations Structures

- When was the last time the union reorganized its structure or amended its constitution?
- Is there a need to change it at this time?
- How many members are in the union?
- How many employees work for the group (include release time of leaders)? Do a brief job description of each employee.
- Make an organizational chart of the union.
- How many members serve on the bargaining team?

- How many committees does the union have? Is it too few or too many?
- How many members on average attend a meeting?
- Compare the union's priorities with the organizational structure and answer whether it is efficient or not.
- How can our membership communications processes be improved (e.g.; magazine, website, bulletin boards, other)?

Appendix 3

POLICE DEPARTMENT JOB SATISFACTION SURVEY*

Please answer each question by placing a checkmark in the box at right that most accurately reflects your views. Space is provided for you to make any additional comments. Please attach a separate page if additional space is needed.

Strongly Agree	Agree	Undecided	Disagree	Strongly Disagree	Not Applicable

1. I find my job satisfying.

☐ ☐ ☐ ☐ ☐ ☐

Additional Comments:

_____

_____

_____

_____

_____

2. There is a spirit of teamwork among my co-workers.

☐ ☐ ☐ ☐ ☐ ☐

Additional Comments:

_____

_____

_____

_____

_____

Strongly Agree	Agree	Undecided	Disagree	Strongly Disagree	Not Applicable

3. PD offers sufficient opportunities for career advancement.

☐ ☐ ☐ ☐ ☐ ☐

Additional Comments:

_____

_____

_____

_____

_____

4. I have confidence in the fairness of police administration.

☐ ☐ ☐ ☐ ☐ ☐

Additional Comments:

_____

_____

_____

_____

_____

5. My immediate supervisor is an effective leader.

☐ ☐ ☐ ☐ ☐ ☐

Additional Comments:

_____

_____

_____

_____

_____

6. Communications are good in my division.

☐ ☐ ☐ ☐ ☐ ☐

Additional Comments:

_____

_____

_____

_____

_____

Strongly Agree	Agree	Undecided	Disagree	Strongly Disagree	Not Applicable

7. The public's safety is more than adequately protected by the policies and procedures of police administration.

☐   ☐   ☐   ☐   ☐   ☐

Additional Comments:

_____

_____

_____

_____

_____

8. I have job security.

☐   ☐   ☐   ☐   ☐   ☐

Additional Comments:

_____

_____

_____

_____

_____

9. I understand what is expected of me for advancement within the department.

☐   ☐   ☐   ☐   ☐   ☐

Additional Comments:

_____

_____

_____

_____

_____

10. I feel free to discuss problems with my immediate supervisor.

☐   ☐   ☐   ☐   ☐   ☐

Additional Comments:

_____

_____

_____

_____

_____

Strongly Agree	Agree	Undecided	Disagree	Strongly Disagree	Not Applicable

11. There is little or no favoritism shown in my division.

☐ ☐ ☐ ☐ ☐ ☐

Additional Comments:

_____
_____
_____
_____
_____

12. If problems arise in my division, they are usually resolved quickly.

☐ ☐ ☐ ☐ ☐ ☐

Additional Comments:

_____
_____
_____
_____
_____

13. I am informed about what is happening within the department.

☐ ☐ ☐ ☐ ☐ ☐

Additional Comments:

_____
_____
_____
_____
_____

14. There are enough officers on my shift to quickly respond to each call for service.

☐ ☐ ☐ ☐ ☐ ☐

Additional Comments:

_____
_____
_____
_____
_____

Strongly Agree	Agree	Undecided	Disagree	Strongly Disagree	Not Applicable

15. I understand what is expected of me in my work.

☐   ☐   ☐   ☐   ☐   ☐

Additional Comments:

_____
_____
_____
_____
_____

16. MPD is a better place to work now than it was last year.

☐   ☐   ☐   ☐   ☐   ☐

Additional Comments:

_____
_____
_____
_____
_____

17. I feel I am making a contribution to the success of the police department.

☐   ☐   ☐   ☐   ☐   ☐

Additional Comments:

_____
_____
_____
_____
_____

18. The number of police officers on my shift allow time for me to use pro-active, self-initiating police tactics to protect the community.

☐   ☐   ☐   ☐   ☐   ☐

Additional Comments:

_____
_____
_____
_____
_____

Strongly Agree	**Agree**	**Undecided**	**Disagree**	**Strongly Disagree**	**Not Applicable**

19. Co-workers treat me with respect.

☐ ☐ ☐ ☐ ☐ ☐

Additional Comments:

_____

_____

_____

_____

_____

20. Police administration has genuine concern for the welfare of its employees.

☐ ☐ ☐ ☐ ☐ ☐

Additional Comments:

_____

_____

_____

_____

_____

21. My attitude toward my profession has improved during my employment at PD.

☐ ☐ ☐ ☐ ☐ ☐

Additional Comments:

_____

_____

_____

_____

_____

22. My attitude toward the police department has improved during my employment at PD.

☐ ☐ ☐ ☐ ☐ ☐

Additional Comments:

_____

_____

_____

_____

_____

Strongly Agree	Agree	Undecided	Disagree	Strongly Disagree	Not Applicable

23. I feel I have access to police administration.

☐   ☐   ☐   ☐   ☐   ☐

Additional Comments:

_____
_____
_____
_____
_____

24. I am satisfied with my present assignment.

☐   ☐   ☐   ☐   ☐   ☐

Additional Comments:

_____
_____
_____
_____
_____

25. I seldom feel stressed or stretched too thin because there are an adequate number of officers on my shift.

☐   ☐   ☐   ☐   ☐   ☐

Additional Comments:

_____
_____
_____
_____
_____

26. I have confidence in the leadership of the police department.

☐   ☐   ☐   ☐   ☐   ☐

Additional Comments:

_____
_____
_____
_____
_____

Strongly Agree	**Agree**	**Undecided**	**Disagree**	**Strongly Disagree**	**Not Applicable**

27. The PD is managed efficiently.

☐ ☐ ☐ ☐ ☐ ☐

Additional Comments:

_____
_____
_____
_____
_____

28. My immediate supervisor keeps me informed of policy changes.

☐ ☐ ☐ ☐ ☐ ☐

Additional Comments:

_____
_____
_____
_____
_____

29. I am satisfied with my opportunities for advancement.

☐ ☐ ☐ ☐ ☐ ☐

Additional Comments:

_____
_____
_____
_____
_____

30. I am satisfied with the current system of promotions.

☐ ☐ ☐ ☐ ☐ ☐

Additional Comments:

_____
_____
_____
_____
_____

Strongly Agree	Agree	Undecided	Disagree	Strongly Disagree	Not Applicable

31. I am satisfied with the department's disciplinary process.

☐   ☐   ☐   ☐   ☐   ☐

Additional Comments:

_____

_____

_____

_____

_____

32. I would be treated fairly if accused of wrongdoing.

☐   ☐   ☐   ☐   ☐   ☐

Additional Comments:

_____

_____

_____

_____

_____

33. I have confidence in the quality of Internal Affairs investigations.

☐   ☐   ☐   ☐   ☐   ☐

Additional Comments:

_____

_____

_____

_____

_____

34. If I were currently in charge of PD, I would feel the department is on the right track.

☐   ☐   ☐   ☐   ☐   ☐

Additional Comments:

_____

_____

_____

_____

_____

DEMOGRAPHIC DATA

Please circle the appropriate response.

35. My age is:

21-29
30-39
40-49
50-59
60 plus

36. My years of service are:

1-5
6-10
11-15
16-20
21-25
26-30
31 plus

37. My current assignment is:

Patrol
Services
CID

38. My current level of education is:

GED
High School
1 year of college
2 years of college
3 years of college
4 years of college
Bachelor's Degree
Bachelor's Degree +
Master's Degree

39. Marital Status:

Single
Married

*The authors want to thank Media & Political Strategies, Inc. for supplying this job satisfaction survey. For more information about how to draft and conduct a similar survey, you can contact the kind folks at this organization at HPO Box 1235a Liberty Hill, TX 78642 or call 512.515.7624.